Fodor's 89
Hong Kong

Fodor's Travel Publications, Inc.
New York and London

ISBN 0-679-01658-9

Fodor's Hong Kong

Editors: David Low, Jacqueline Russell
Area Editor: Robin Danhorn
Contributors: Shann Davies, Patricia Davis, Barry Girling, Saul Lockhart, Harry Rolnick, Donald Wise
Art Director: Fabrizio La Rocca
Cartographer: David Lindroth
Illustrator: Karl Tanner
Cover Photograph: Philip Jones Griffiths/Magnum Photo, Inc.

Design: Vignelli Associates

Special Sales

Contents

Foreword *v*

Highlights '89 *viii*

Fodor's Choice *ix*

Introduction *xvi*

1 Planning Your Trip *1*

Before You Go *2*

Visitor Information *2*
Guided Tours *2*
Package Deals for Independent Travelers *3*
Tips for British Travelers *3*
When to Go *4*
Festivals and Seasonal Events *5*
What to Pack *6*
Taking Money Abroad *7*
Getting Money from Home *7*
Currency *8*
What It Will Cost *8*
Passports and Visas *9*
Customs and Duties *10*
Traveling with Film *10*
Language *10*
Staying Healthy *11*
Insurance *11*
Renting Cars *12*
Student and Youth Travel *12*
Traveling with Children *13*
Hints for Disabled Travelers *13*
Hints for Older Travelers *14*
Further Reading *15*

Getting to Hong Kong *16*

From North America by Plane *16*
From North America by Ship *17*
From the United Kingdom by Plane *17*
From the United Kingdom by Ship *17*

2 Portraits of Hong Kong *19*

"Doing Business in Hong Kong," by Saul Lockhart *20*

"The Hong Kong Way of Life: Living with an Uncertain Future," by Donald Wise *34*

"Food and Drink in Hong Kong and Macau," by Barry Girling *43*

"A Shopper's Paradise," by Patricia Davis *49*

3 Essential Information *53*

Arriving and Departing *54*
Important Addresses and Numbers *54*
Staying in Touch *55*
Getting Around *56*
Guided Tours *59*

4 Exploring Hong Kong *61*

Orientation *62*
Hong Kong Island *63*
Kowloon *81*
New Territories *85*
The Outer Islands *87*
Major Sights and Attractions *90*
Museums and Libraries *93*
Parks *94*
Beaches *96*
Hong Kong for Free *99*
What to See and Do with Children *99*
Off the Beaten Track *100*

5 Shopping *102*

6 Sports and Fitness *123*

7 Dining *127*

8 Lodging *141*

9 The Arts and Nightlife *156*

10 Macau *167*

Index *207*

Maps

Hong Kong Territory *xii–xiii*
World Time Zones *xiv–xv*
Western and Central Districts *66–67*
Wanchai, Causeway Bay, Happy Valley, North Point *74–75*
The South Side of Hong Kong Island *78–79*
Kowloon *82*
Shopping *104–105*
Dining *130–131*
Lodging *144–145*
Macau *175*
Taipa and Coloane Islands *182*

Foreword

This is an exciting time for Fodor's, as it begins a three-year program to rewrite, reformat, and redesign all 140 of its guides. Here are just a few of the exciting new features:

★ Brand-new computer-generated maps locating all the top attractions, hotels, restaurants, and shops

★ A unique system of numbers and legends to help readers move effortlessly between text and maps

★ A new star rating system for hotels and restaurants

★ Restaurant reviews by major food critics around the world

★ Stamped, self-addressed postcards, bound into every guide, to give readers an opportunity to help evaluate hotels and restaurants

★ Complete page redesign for instant retrieval of information

★ FODOR'S CHOICE—Our favorite museums, beaches, cafes, romantic hideaways, festivals, and more

★ HIGHLIGHTS '89—An insider's look at the most important developments in tourism during the past year

★ TIME OUT—The best and most convenient lunch stops along the shopping and exploring routes

★ Exclusive background essays that create a powerful portrait of each destination

★ A mini-journal for travelers to keep track of their own itineraries and addresses

We wish to express our gratitude to the Hong Kong Tourist Association in New York and Hong Kong for their assistance in the preparation of this guidebook.

Although every care has been taken to assure the accuracy of the information in this guide, the passage of time will always bring change, and consequently, the publisher cannot accept responsibility for errors that may occur.

All prices and opening times quoted here are based on information available to us at press time. Hours and admission fees may change, however, and the prudent traveler will avoid inconvenience by calling ahead.

Fodor's wants to hear about your travel experiences, both pleasant and unpleasant. When a hotel or restaurant fails to live up to its billing, let us know and we will investigate the complaint and revise our entries where the facts warrant it.

Send your letters to the editors of Fodor's Travel Publications, 201 East 50th Street, New York, NY 10022, or 30–32 Bedford Square, London WC1B 3SG, England.

Highlights '89 and Fodor's Choice

Highlights '89

Visitors without advanced hotel reservations shouldn't have trouble finding a place to sleep in 1989 because almost all the international giants of the industry are completing new hotels. **Marriott** will open its second hotel; **Holiday Inn,** its third; **Ramada,** its second, an upmarket Ramada Renaissance; **Hyatt-Regency,** its second, a super-luxury Grand Hyatt; and **Conrad** (formerly Hilton International), its second. Local chains are building an equal number. Is there a glut in the offing? None is forecast. The territory, it seems, fills rooms as fast as it builds them.

Visitors should find their passage through **Kai Tak Airport** easier as the final improvements to the passenger terminal are completed. But there is not much anyone can do about the single runway, so traffic congestion, and no doubt the midnight to 6 AM curfew, will remain as the government plows ahead with its umpteenth study on whether it needs a new airport.

If you think you are tired of waiting in endless lines of vehicles to snake through the Cross-Harbor Tunnel, imagine how local residents feel. Some help may be available by the year end, if the second harbor tunnel is completed on time.

Hong Kong is well known for putting up and tearing down in record time, so if you decide to have a meal at the excellent **Landau's,** you will not find it in its familiar digs in Causeway Bay because the building's gone. The restaurant has moved to the Sun Hung Kai Centre, 30 Harbour Road, in Wanchai, on Hong Kong Island. Still on the subject of now-you-see-it, now-you-don't, **Sutherland House** in Central, whose basement has been home to the **Godown,** is also a hole in the ground. The Godown, famous for the past two decades for its great slabs of roast beef, Nepalese curries, jazz, late night music and dancing, and just plain good times, has moved to Admiralty Centre, Tower II. In its place? A new 150-suite (no "rooms," like the other hostelries in town) **Ritz-Carlton Hotel,** which aims to be the poshest joint around—quite a chore in a place that regularly scores three hotels on everybody's Top Ten list (The Mandarin, The Regent, and The Peninsula).

On the other side of the coin, in a new building just opened at 100 Peak Road—on the Peak, of course—you'll find the latest addition to the Jimmy's Kitchen chain—**JK's.**

Royalty watchers take note: the Prince and Princess of Wales are scheduled to open the spanking new **Hong Kong Convention & Exhibition Centre** in November.

On a sad note, swimmers should double-check before heading to a beach. More than a half-dozen, including some on the south side of Hong Kong Island, have been closed due to pollution. And Hong Kong's most popular beach, **Repulse Bay Beach** (also on the south side of the island) was declared "marginal" in 1988. The government is working hard and fast to solve the problems, but check with your hotel or the Hong Kong Tourist Association before heading for a day of fun in the sun.

Fodor's Choice

Special Moments

Hong Kong The view of Hong Kong and Kowloon when coming in by plane

The dazzling view of Hong Kong from the Peak

The harbor, night or day, for the soul of Hong Kong

The passing scene from the top deck of an island tram

Sung Dynasty Village, for a glimpse of ancient China

The colorful tableaux of legends and mythology at the Aw Boon Haw (Tiger Balm) Gardens

Macau Protestant Cemetery near Cameos Museum

Taste Treats

Hong Kong The wine list at Charlie's in Pui O, on Lantau Island

Dim sum lunch—anywhere

The taste of Peking duck skin and the smell of beggar's chicken

A marketstall Chinese breakfast of *congee* (rice porridge) at Kowloon Park Road/Haiphong Road, Kowloon

A Chinese dinner at a garish floating restaurant at Aberdeen Harbour

Macau African chicken at Henri's

The cottage loaf bread served before meals at Flamingo, at the Taipa Resort

Buffet dinner at Furama Hotel's revolving rooftop restaurant

Afternoon tea in the grand lobby of the Peninsula Hotel

A drink in the Regent Hotel's lobby bar, with panoramic views of the harbor

Museums

Hong Kong The Railway Museum at Tai Po

The Aw Boon Haw Villa jade collection

The photography collection at the Hong Kong Museum of History

Space-age shows at the Space Museum

Macau The Maritime Museum, one of Asia's finest

Excursions

Hong Kong The view of the coastline from the Ocean Park cable car

Crossing the harbor on the Star Ferry—second class, at water level

A tram ride all the way from Kennedy Town to North Point

A bus ride around the island to Repulse or Stanley bays

Macau Driving a mini-Moke

The double-decker bus ride over the bridge to Taipa Island

A pedicab ride for leisurely sightseeing

Special Events

Hong Kong Candlelight parades in honor of the mid-Autumn moon and at the Dragon Boat Festival in June

Bun Festival (May) on Cheung Chau Island

Horseracing at Happy Valley track

Macau World-class excitement at the Grand Prix

The Good Friday Passion Parade, the first weekend of Lent

Temples and Shrines

Hong Kong The Temple of 10,000 Buddhas, Shatin, with its gilded, mummified Holy Man

Po Lin Buddhist Monastery, on Lantau Island

Wong Tai Sin Temple for fortune-telling, racing tips, and cures

Macau A-Ma Temple, dedicated to the goddess of the sea

Dining

Hong Kong Chesa *(Very Expensive)*

Gaddi's *(Very Expensive)*

Au Trou Normand *(Expensive)*

Lai Ching Heen *(Expensive)*

Jumbo *(Moderate)*

Peking Garden *(Moderate)*

Rangoon *(Inexpensive)*

Macau A Galera *(Moderate)*

Lodging

Hong Kong Excelsior *(Very Expensive)*

Mandarin Oriental *(Very Expensive)*

The Peninsula *(Very Expensive)*

Holiday Inn Harbour View *(Expensive)*

Harbour *(Moderate)*

Imperial *(Moderate)*

Shamrock *(Inexpensive)*

Macau Hyatt Regency and Taipa Island Resort *(Expensive)*

Pousada de Sao Tiago *(Expensive)*

Nightlife

Hong Kong	Bar City in New World Centre, Kowloon
Macau	Crazy Paris Show at Lisboa Hotel

Street Markets

Hong Kong Jade Market, Kansu Street, Kowloon—the world's only jade market

Night Market at Temple Street, off Jordan Road, Kowloon

Bird Market on Hong Lok Street, near Mong Kok MTR station

"Poor Man's Nightclub" at the Macau Ferry Terminal, Central, 8 PM to midnight

Luen Wo Market, near Fanling in New Territories

Parks and Countryside Walks

Hong Kong Tai Lam Country Park, open country just minutes from Kowloon

Dragon's Back in Shek O Country Park

Lantau Island, Shek Pik to Tai O

Victoria Park, Causeway Bay, to watch early morning practitioners of t'ai chi ch'uan (shadow boxing)

Macau Camoes Gardens

For Free

Hong Kong A ride up the "glass bubble" elevator at Hopewell Centre to see the city lights at night

Any Chinese temple

Street markets and back lanes .

The smaller zoological and botanical gardens

For Children

Hong Kong Ocean Park, a huge marine park with dolphin shows and cable car rides

Peak Tram, for the thrill of the steep ascent

Space Museum, to feel what it is like to take a ride through space

Lai Chi Kok Amusement Park, for games, sideshows, and rides

Aw Boon Haw (Tiger Balm) Gardens

Sung Dynasty Village, to see the lion dance and fortune-tellers

Shopping for a new Walkman cassette player and blue jeans

Macau The games room at the Lisboa Hotel

Hong Kong Territory

0 — 2 miles
0 — 3 km

PEOPLES REPUBLIC OF CHINA

Deep Bay

Lo Wu

Lok Ma Chau

San Tin

Mai Po

Lau Fau Shan

Yuen Long

Ha Tsuen

Kam Tin
Walled
Village

*Tai Lamn Chung
Reservoir*

Tuen Mun

Shek Kok
Tsui

Tsuen Wan

*Tsing
Yi*

Chek Lap Kok

Peng Chau

V

Tung Chung

Mui Wo

Lantau Island

*Silver Mine
Bay*

Tai O

*Hei Ling
Chau*

Cheung
Sha

*Cheung Chau
Island*

*Shek Kwu
Chau*

Soko Islands

South China Sea

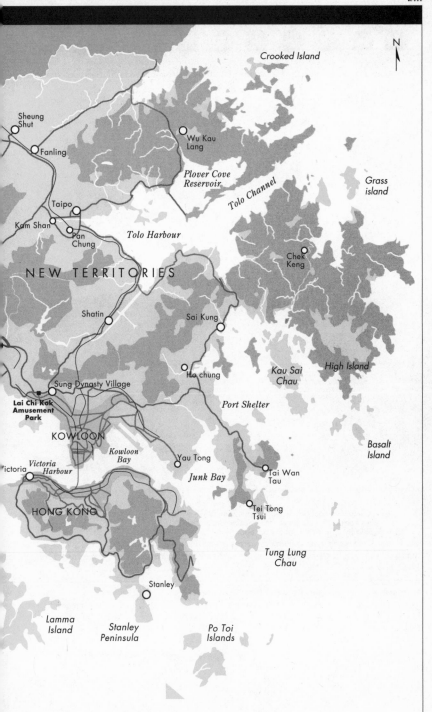

World Time Zones

MONDAY
SUNDAY

International Date Line

+12 +13

-9

-10

-3

-4

7

3

-11

-10

4

-7

7

-5

-4

5

-8

8

9

14 15

13

17 16

6

10

18

11

2

12

+11

22

19

+12

20

-5

-4

-3

1

23

21

-3

24

| +11 | +12 - | -11 | -10 | -9 | -8 | -7 | -6 | -5 | -4 | -3 | -2 |

Numbers below vertical bands relate each zone to Greenwich Mean Time (0 hrs.).
Local times frequently differ from these general indications,
as indicated by light-face numbers on map.

Auckland, **1**	Denver, **8**	New York City, **16**	Rio de Janeiro, **23**
Honolulu, **2**	Chicago, **9**	Washington, DC, **17**	Buenos Aires, **24**
Anchorage, **3**	Dallas, **10**	Miami, **18**	Reykjavik, **25**
Vancouver, **4**	New Orleans, **11**	Bogotá, **19**	Dublin, **26**
San Francisco, **5**	Mexico City, **12**	Lima, **20**	London (Greenwich), **27**
Los Angeles, **6**	Toronto, **13**	Santiago, **21**	Lisbon, **28**
Edmonton, **7**	Ottawa, **14**	Caracas, **22**	Algiers, **29**
	Montreal, **15**		Paris, **30**
			Zürich, **31**

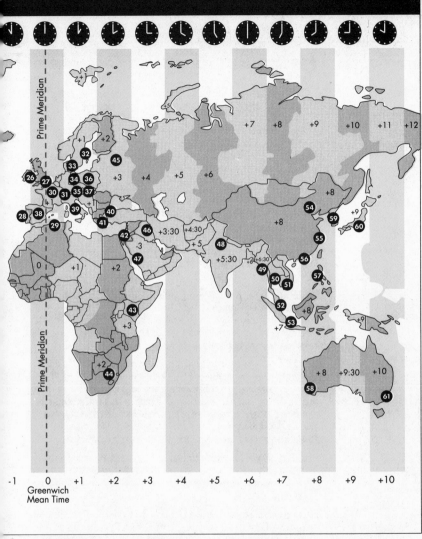

Stockholm, **32**
Copenhagen, **33**
Berlin, **34**
Vienna, **35**
Warsaw, **36**
Budapest, **37**
Madrid, **38**

Rome, **39**
Istanbul, **40**
Athens, **41**
Jerusalem, **42**
Nairobi, **43**
Johannesburg, **44**
Moscow, **45**
Baghdad, **46**

Mecca, **47**
Delhi, **48**
Rangoon, **49**
Bangkok, **50**
Saigon, **51**
Singapore, **52**
Djakarta, **53**
Beijing, **54**
Shanghai, **55**

Hong Kong, **56**
Manila, **57**
Perth, **58**
Seoul, **59**
Tokyo, **60**
Sydney, **61**

Introduction

When you fly to Hong Kong, try to get a window seat on the aircraft; the landing will take your breath away.

As the prelanding announcement is being made, you will probably still be out over the gray South China Sea. As you get closer to the coast of China, you will spot a few small, rocky islands, tiny fishing boats, and sailboats in the channels leading into Hong Kong Harbour—the most spectacular harbor you will ever see.

The final approach into Hong Kong's Kai Tak Airport is sudden and rather startling. If you come in over the sea, you follow the channel between Hong Kong Island and the mainland, on wings that seem close enough to touch the boats or the windows of the skyscrapers rising above the hills. If you fly in over Kowloon, the plane will seem dangerously close to the scrub-covered hills, and you will see children playing in schoolgrounds, and perhaps even read the advertisements on the sides of buses.

Close up, the streets are a jumble of brightly colored signs, most written in Chinese characters, and always crowded. Like ant hills that have been stirred up, the streets are filled with streams of people relentlessly going about their business—the restless, urgent need to make money.

Hong Kong is the ultimate capitalistic society, almost desperate in its urge to produce, earn, sell, and spend. You will find yourself caught up in this momentum, and wondering whether at heart the place is Western or Oriental. At first sight the character of the city will seem entirely Western, but this is only the veneer. Underneath the surface you will soon discover that Hong Kong is essentially Chinese, in heart and spirit.

In Cantonese, Hong Kong means "Fragrant Harbor," a name inspired either by the incense factories that once dotted Hong Kong Island or by the profusion of scented pink *bauhinias*, the national flower.

Hong Kong is both a British Crown Colony—one of the few left —and a "dependent territory" of Great Britain. Since New Territories, a major section of the colony, is leased from China, Hong Kong is also part of China.

Hong Kong is located on the southeast coast of China, at the mouth of the Pearl River, on the same latitude as Hawaii and Cuba. By air, it's 2¾ hours from Beijing, 17 from New York, 12¼ from San Francisco, and 13 from London.

It consists of three main parts: Hong Kong Island, roughly 32 square miles; Kowloon, 3.5 square miles; and New Territories, about 365 square miles.

The name Hong Kong refers to the overall colony as well as to its main island, Hong Kong Island, which is across the harbor from Kowloon. The island's principal business district is officially named Victoria, but everyone calls it Central. Also on the island are the districts of Wanchai, Causeway Bay, Repulse Bay, Stanley, and Aberdeen.

Kowloon includes Tsimshatsui, Tsimshatsui East, Hung Hom, Mongkok/Yaumatei, and the area north to Boundary Street. New Territories begins at Boundary Street and extends north to the border of China, encompassing the container port, the airport, most of the major factories, and the outlying islands.

Hong Kong is 98% Chinese. Other nationalities include British, American, Indian, and Japanese. Although the official languages are English and Cantonese, many other languages and dialects are spoken here, including Mandarin, Hakka (the language of a group of early settlers from China), Tanka (the language of the original boat people who came here some 5,000 years ago), Shanghainese, and Chinglish (a mixture of Cantonese and English). Some 30,000 Filipinos live and work in Hong Kong, so you're also likely to hear Philippine languages, especially near the Star Ferry and Statue Square park.

Buddhism, Taoism, ancestor worship, Christianity, and animism are the major religions, and you'll see signs of them everywhere. Pragmatism and money-making are such a part of the way of life here that you can almost call them religions, too. The distinctions are often blurred because Chinese people tend to be eclectic in their beliefs. It is not uncommon for the same Hong Kong citizen to put out food and incense for his departed ancestors at Spring Festival time, invite a Taoist priest to his home to exorcise unhappy ghosts, pray in a Buddhist temple for fertility, and take Communion in a Christian church.

Hong Kong is a delightful place to visit. It has the best shopping in the world, if you work at it; great Chinese food; mountains, beaches, harbors, and parks; and exotic festivals. You can experience firsthand an economic feat of superhuman proportions: some 5.5 million people living and working on 400 square miles of land with few natural resources other than a deep harbor on the Chinese coast. You can also experience history in the making, as the British prepare to hand over Hong Kong to the People's Republic of China when the New Territories lease expires in 1997. Feelings about this changeover are mixed, and most people are more than a little apprehensive.

Hong Kong is not entirely dependent on Britain, which pays only 25% of the colony's defense budget. The Hong Kong government picks up the rest of the tab. Britain, however, still makes most of the important decisions for Hong Kong, which is Britain's largest Asian market—a captive market for such British-made products as buses and railway cars. Hong Kong also trades with China, the United States, and Japan.

Part of Hong Kong's phenomenal success stems from its ties to the British government, which has given it political stability and a strong judicial system. These attributes have attracted local and foreign capital. The decision to make Hong Kong a duty-free port and a trading center was British. The territory has also benefited from Chinese entrepreneurial skills, hardworking Chinese refugee labor, and, of course, the harbor.

Hong Kong is also economically and politically dependent on China for markets, resources, and cooperation. China is Hong Kong's fourth largest trading partner, providing most of the food—including 1.8 million squealing pigs a year. About half of the water consumed in Hong Kong comes from China, which also provides the colony with relatively inexpensive pots, pans, blankets, sweaters, textiles, and beds.

In past years, Hong Kong has also been aptly described as "a pimple on China's behind" and "a gem in China's navel." Both descriptions fit—almost. The Communist Chinese have been very embarrassed by Hong Kong's blatant capitalism. But China has been earning an estimated 40% of its foreign exchange in Hong Kong, about U.S.$6 billion to U.S.$8 billion a year. Many Hong Kong businesspeople have also invested in China and, more particularly, in China's new Special Economic Zones. The largest, Shenzhen, is on Hong Kong's northern border. Financially, Hong Kong is worth more to China than it is to Britain.

Hong Kong is shamelessly capitalistic. But though it is the world's foremost example of a laissez-faire economy, it has many socialistic policies. Although Hong Kong has no minimum wage laws and no unemployment insurance, it has compulsory workmen's compensation laws, minimum working-age regulations, and nine years of compulsory education. About 2.5 million people—almost 50% of the population—live in government-subsidized housing. Government hospitals provide near-free medical care—an ambulance ride, X-rays, 14 stitches, an overnight hospital stay—and medicines cost less than U.S.$10.

Hong Kong is far from the classic image of a "colony" or a sweatshop based on cheap labor. It has an infant mortality rate lower than that of either Britain or the United States, more secondary students per capita than Britain, and one of the highest protein-consumption rates in the world. It also has hardly any unemployment.

Hong Kong has not just survived, it has thrived. It has the world's third largest financial center, third largest diamond and gold trading center, and the largest market for 24K gold jewelry. It is the second largest container port, and the world's largest manufacturer of toys, textiles, clothing, watches, clocks, and radios.

Major North American, European, and Japanese computer companies compete for customers here, sometimes at prices less than at home because of lower mark-ups, no sales taxes, and no duties. Computers not only keep track of customers and orders in Hong Kong, but they are also used to cut cloth into dresses in the most cost-efficient manner, to design machines, and to do other complicated tasks.

Hong Kong has hundreds of banks providing capital or facilitating financial transactions. Many publishing houses are in Hong Kong because world copyright and trademark registry are protected under British law, while costs are low. In addition, the government avoids interfering with editorial content (aside from pornographic and libelous material).

Some companies have departed, however, because of the incredibly high rents of the late 1970s and early 1980s—among the highest in the world for commercial and post-war residential property. Relatively new, modest (by American standards), three-bedroom apartments can cost as much as HK$25,000 a month, or more than U.S.$3,000.

Real estate is not only a principal money-maker for many Hong Kong citizens, it is the largest single source of revenue for the government. Ever since British Hong Kong began, the government has controlled practically all the land. People can buy buildings only on long-term leased land.

Hong Kong makes no pretense about being a democracy. It isn't. But it is more sensitive to its citizens than most "democratic" countries in Asia. Only illegal immigrants and criminals need fear the police.

Hong Kong's top political leader is the governor, who represents the British sovereign. In the absence of a "Colonial Office," the British foreign secretary is answerable to Britain's Parliament. Next in line to the governor are the chief secretary, financial secretary, and attorney general. The highest-ranking body is the 17-member Executive Council, which combines the functions of a cabinet and top advisory board. Since September 1985, as part of the plan to prepare the territory for self-rule under China in 1997, the Council has included 24 indirectly elected members.

The first semblance of popular government came with elections held in 1952 for seats on the Urban Council, which takes care of beaches, playgrounds, cultural centers, and garbage collection. In 1982, elections were held for the 18 newly created District Boards. After the District Boards were filled, the partially elected Regional Council, the rural version of the Urban Council, was created.

Citizen participation also takes the form of lively letters to the editors of newspapers and participation in open-line radio talk shows. Questions are usually answered by the government official concerned. District Offices have regular "Meet the Public" programs for citizens to make criticisms and offer suggestions directly to District Board members. Some 320 citizen advisory boards and councils give advice. Demonstrations and petitions to the governor also take place freely. Political stability, however, is a critical factor because it affects the entire economy.

Initially, Hong Kong's earliest visitors were believed to be boat people of Malaysian-Oceanic origin who came here about 5,000 years ago. They left geometric-style graffiti which is still visible on rocks in Big Wave Bay (on Hong Kong Island) and Po Toi Island. The earliest structure found so far is the 2,000-year-old Han Dynasty tomb at Lei Cheng Uk. More than 600 years later, the Tang Dynasty left lime kilns full of seashells—an archaeological mystery because there are no clues indicating how or why the lime was used.

There are also records from the 13th century, when Sung Dynasty loyalists fled China with their child-emperor to escape the invading Mongols. The last of the Sung Dynasty emperors, a 10-year-old boy, is said to have spent a night in the late 1270s near what is now the airport. One of his men is credited with naming Kowloon, which means "nine dragons" (he counted eight mountains that resembled dragons, and added one for the emperor, who was also considered a dragon). The boy was the only Chinese emperor believed to have set foot in what is now Hong Kong. However, many courtiers from his court settled here. Today, anyone visiting Po Lin Monastery, high in the mountains of Lantau Island, will pass Shek Pik reservoir, where innumerable Sung Dynasty coins were found during the reservoir's excavation. You can also get a feel for life during the period by visiting Sung Dynasty Village, a reproduction of a Sung village, in an amusement park in Lai Chi Kok near Kowloon. The village is small, but it demonstrates the highly developed Sung civilization with spirit and charm and is well worth a visit.

Western traders first appeared in the Hong Kong area in 1513. The first were Portuguese, soon followed by the Spanish, Dutch, English, and French. All were bent either on making fortunes trading porcelain, tea, and silk, or saving souls for their respective religions. Until 1757, the Chinese restricted all foreigners to neighboring Macau, the Portuguese territory 40 miles (25 km) across the Pearl River estuary. After 1757, traders—but not their families—were allowed to live just outside Canton for about eight months each year. (Canton, now known as Guangzhou, is only 20 minutes from Hong Kong by plane, or three hours by train or hovercraft.)

Trading in Hong Kong was frustrating for the foreigners. It took at least 20 days for messages to be relayed to the emperor, local officials had to be bribed, and Chinese justice seemed unfair. The Chinese confined foreign traders to a small, restricted zone and forbade them to learn Chinese. On top of that, the Chinese wanted nothing from the West except silver, until the foreigners, especially the British, started offering opium.

The spread of the opium habit and the growing outflow of silver alarmed high Chinese officials as early as 1729. They issued edicts forbidding the importation of the drug, but these were not strictly enforced until 1839. Then a heroic and somewhat fanatical Imperial Commissioner, Lin Ze-Xu (Lin Tse-hsu), laid siege to the foreign factories in Canton and detained the traders until they surrendered over 20,000 chests of the drug, almost a year's worth of trade. The foreigners also signed bonds promising to desist from dealing with it forever, upon threat of death. The opium was destroyed.

The traders did not find Lin's inflexible manner the least bit amusing. The resulting tension led to the Opium Wars and a succession of unequal treaties forced by superior British firepower. A bewildered, angry, and reluctant China had no choice but to open its doors to foreign trade and missionaries.

British-ruled Hong Kong flourished from the start of trade, especially the trade in opium, which was not outlawed in Hong Kong until after World War II. The population grew quickly, from 4,000 in 1841 to over 23,000 in 1847, as Hong Kong attracted anyone anxious to make money or just to live without the fetters of feudalism and family.

Each convulsion on the Chinese mainland—the Taiping rebellion in the mid-1800s, the 1911 republican revolution, the war lords of the 1920s, the 1937 Japanese invasion—resulted in another group of refugees here. Then Japan invaded Hong Kong itself. The population, which was 1.4 million just before the Japanese arrived, dropped to a low of 600,000 by 1945. Many Hong Kong residents were forced to flee to Macau and the rural areas of China. The Japanese period is still remembered with bitterness by many local residents.

The largest group of Chinese refugees came as a result of the civil war in China between the Nationalists and Communists that ended with a Communist victory in 1949. Many refugees, especially the Shanghainese, brought capital and business skills. The population of Hong Kong was 1.8 million in 1947. By 1961 it stood at 3.7 million. For 25 days in 1962, when food was short in China, Chinese border guards allowed 70,000 Chinese to walk into Hong Kong. Ordinarily, it is very difficult for Chinese citizens to get permission to leave China.

With the antilandlord, anticapitalist, and antirightist campaigns in China, and especially with the Cultural Revolution (1967–1976), more and more refugees risked imprisonment and the sharks in Mirs Bay to reach Hong Kong. Inspired by the leftist fanaticism of the Red Guards in China, local sympathizers and activists in Hong Kong set off bombs, organized labor strikes, and demonstrated against the British rulers and Hong Kong's Chinese policemen. They taunted the latter by saying, "Will the British take you when they go?" But the revolutionaries did not have popular support and the disruptions lasted less than a year.

In the late 1970s half a million Chinese refugees came to Hong Kong, disillusioned with Communism and eager for a better standard of living for themselves and their families.

Until October 1980, the Hong Kong government had a curious "touch-base" policy—a critical game of "hide and seek." Any Chinese who managed to get past the barbed wire, attack dogs, and tough border patrols to the urban areas was allowed to stay and work. Manpower was needed for local industries then. At first, a similarly lenient policy was applied to the Vietnamese boat people who arrived between 1975 and 1982. More than 100,000 of these refugees were allowed to work in Hong Kong pending transfer to permanent homes abroad, and 14,000 were given permanent resident status. As the number of countries willing to take them has dwindled, Hong Kong has been detaining recently arrived refugees indefinitely in closed camps, much like prisons, in the hope that no more boat people will come.

In the early 1980s jobs became less plentiful as a result of the worldwide recession. With an ever-increasing population, the standard of services in Hong Kong began deteriorating. After consulting China, the government decreed that everyone had to carry a Hong Kong identification card.

The future of Hong Kong after the expiration of the New Territories lease on June 30, 1997, was understandably the big question hanging over the colony from the moment Britain's prime minister, Margaret Thatcher, set foot in Peking in September 1982, to start the talks with China's top man, Deng Xiaoping. China stated from the beginning that it wanted to repossess all of Hong Kong. Officially, Britain was willing to return only New Territories, but no one believed a Hong Kong without them would be economically viable. New Territories consists of more than 97% of the land in Hong Kong and includes most of the manufacturing facilities, the airport, and the container port.

China proposed that Hong Kong become a Special Administrative Region under the Chinese flag, with a Chinese governor. The Chinese added a 50-year guarantee of autonomy, effective July 1, 1997, labeling the deal "One country/two systems."

The negotiations between China and Britain lasted for nearly two years, with China applying pressure by announcing that if a solution were not found by September 1984, it would declare one unilaterally. An agreement was inevitable.

Hong Kong's economy didn't react well to this political uncertainty. Land prices fell. The stock market plunged by as much as 50% from late 1981 to late 1983. The Hong Kong dollar careened to almost HK$10 to the U.S. dollar in September 1983, from HK$5.7 at the end of 1981. This forced the government to intervene reluctantly by stabilizing the local unit at HK$7.80 to U.S.$1. Emigration reached record levels.

The final agreement, both signatories say, gives Hong Kong as many safeguards and special freedoms as possible (very different from what is practiced and allowed across the border in the People's Republic of China). For the most part, the people of Hong Kong are resigned to a philosophy of, "it could have been worse." But Hong Kong's uncertainty about its future as a Special Administrative Region of China continues; no one can know what it will mean. Yet Hong Kong is still where the action is, where money can be made, and life goes on as usual.

The question of what will happen in 1997 is uppermost in everyone's mind. *See* The Hong Kong Way of Life in Portraits of Hong Kong.

1 Planning Your Trip

Before You Go

Visitor Information

Hong Kong For maps and additional information on travel to Hong Kong, contact the **Hong Kong Tourist Association (HKTA)**. There are three offices in the United States: 421 Powell Street, Suite 200, San Francisco, CA 94102, tel. 415/781–4582; 333 North Michigan Avenue, Suite 2323, Chicago, IL 60601, tel. 312/782–3872; and 548 Fifth Avenue, New York, NY 10036, tel. 212/869–5008.

Macau For information on travel to Macau from North America, contact the **Macau Tourist Information Bureau (MTIB)**. There are three offices in the United States: 608 Fifth Avenue, Suite 309, New York, NY 10020, tel. 212/581–7465; 3133 Lake Hollywood Drive, Box 1860, Los Angeles, CA 90078, tel. 213/851–3400; and 841 Bishop Street, Suite 2004, Honolulu, HI 96813, tel. 213/851–3400 (Los Angeles). In Canada: 475 Main Street, Vancouver, BC V6A 2T7, tel. 604/687–3316; and 150 Dundas Street West, Suite 3089, Toronto, Ont. M5G 1C6, tel. 416/593–1811.

Guided Tours

For a small island, Hong Kong is a big favorite with tour operators. Some 50 operators offer hundreds of packages, everything from intensive shopping and dining trips to tours pairing Hong Kong with Japan, China, Thailand, Singapore, Tibet, and even India. Listed below is a select sampling of packages to give you an idea of what is available. Your travel agent or regional HKTA office can provide more details.

When considering a tour, be sure to find out (1) exactly what expenses are included (particularly tips, taxes, side trips, additional meals, and entertainment); (2) government ratings of all hotels on the itinerary and the facilities they offer; (3) cancellation policies for you and for the tour operator; and (4) the single supplement, should you be traveling alone. Most tour operators request that bookings be made through a travel agent—there is no additional charge for doing so.

General-Interest Tours **Hemphill/Harris** (16000 Ventura Blvd., Suite 200, Encino, CA 90024, tel. 818/906–8086 or 800/421–0454) and **Abercrombie & Kent International** (1420 Kensington Rd., Oak Brook, IL 60521, tel. 312/954–2944) offer several deluxe tours at prices that reflect their high level of service. **InterPacific Tours International** (111 E. 15th St., New York, NY 10003, tel. 212/953–6010 or 800/221–3594) uses Hong Kong as its base of operations in the Orient and has a particularly wide range of packages (and prices) as a result. Other popular operators in the area include **Pacific Delight Tours** (132 Madison Ave., New York, NY 10016, tel. 212/684–7707) and **Japan and Orient Tours** (250 E. First St., Suite 912, Los Angeles, CA 90012, tel. 213/624–2866).

Special-Interest Tours **Shopping:** "Shop 'til you drop" is the motto of many a Hong Kong tour. **TBI Tours** (787 Seventh Ave., New York, NY 10019, tel. 212/489–1919) plunges a visitor into Hong Kong's many shops and outlets, as does **InterPacific Tours**. **Abercrombie & Kent** will even team up shopping in Hong Kong with a culinary tour of Bangkok, Thailand.

Sports: InterPacific Tours has a Hong Kong/China golf package as well as jogging and bicycling trips that include a stint atop the Great Wall.

Music: Dailey-Thorp Travel (315 57th St., New York, NY 10019, tel. 212/307–1555) offers deluxe opera and music tours set around special appearances by local or visiting performers.

Culture: Percival Tours (Box 6600, Tyler, TX 75711, tel. 817/ 870–0300 or 800/433–5656) arranges tours tied to special events such as the Hong Kong Food Festival. **Travel Concepts** (373 Commonwealth Ave., Suite 601, Boston, MA 02115, tel. 617/ 266–8450) offers the splash and fun of the Hong Kong Dragon Boat Festival and International Races. *See* Festivals and Seasonal Events.

Package Deals for Independent Travelers

Japan and Orient Tours (250 E. First St., Los Angeles, CA 90012, tel. 213/624–2866 or 800/421–0212) offers the "Hong Kong Travel Bargain"—with accommodations for six nights, round-trip airfare, and a sightseeing tour for less than $1,000. **Globus Gateway** (150 S. Los Robles Ave., Suite 860, Pasadena, CA 91101, tel. 818/449–0919 or 800/556–5454) has a nine-day Hong Kong/Tokyo package, a 10-day Hong Kong/Bangkok package, and others. **Cathay Pacific Airlines** (tel. 800/663–8833 or 800/663–8838 in San Francisco) has a number of air/hotel packages that can include destinations other than Hong Kong.

Tips for British Travelers

Passports and Visas You will need a valid passport (cost £15). Visas are not required. Vaccinations against typhoid are recommended. You will, however, need a visa if you plan a side trip to China. Apply for visas (£20) through the Chinese Embassy (31 Portland Pl., London W1N 3AG, tel. 01/636–5726).

Customs Returning to Britain you may bring home: (1) 200 cigarettes or 100 cigarillos or 50 cigars or 250 grams of tobacco; (2) two liters of table wine with additional allowances for (a) one liter of alcohol over 22% by volume (38.8 proof; most spirits), (b) two liters of alcohol under 22% by volume, or (c) two more liters of table wine; and (3) 50 grams of perfume and 1/4 liter of toilet water, and (4) other goods up to a value of £32.

Tourist Information For information on **Hong Kong**, contact the Hong Kong Tourist Association (4/F, 125 Pall Mall, London SW1Y 5EA, tel. 01/ 930–4775).

For information on **Macau**, contact the Portuguese National Tourist Office (New Bond Street House, 1/5 New Bond St., London W1Y 0NP, tel. 01/493–3873).

Insurance We recommend that you insure yourself against health and motoring accidents. **Europ Assistance** (252 High St., Croydon, Surrey CR0 1NF, tel. 01/680–1234) is a firm that offers this service. It is also wise to take out insurance to cover loss of luggage (though check that this isn't already covered in any existing homeowner policies you may have). Trip cancellation insurance is another wise buy. **The Association of British Insurers** (Aldermary House, Queen St., London EC4N 1TT, tel. 01/ 248–4477) will give comprehensive advice on all aspects of vacation insurance.

Here is a selection of companies offering packages to Hong Kong.

Tour Operators **Keith Kuoni Travel Ltd.** (Kuoni House, Dorking, Surrey RH5 4AZ, tel. 0306/885044) has a 10-day hotel package to Hong Kong and Bali, with an extra five nights on Bali free during certain periods. Prices per person are from £749. Kuoni also offers a range of half-day, full-day, and evening sightseeing tours, with prices ranging from £7 to £36.

Page & Moy Ltd. (136-140 London Rd., Leicester LE2 1EN, tel. 0533/552521) offers seven nights in Hong Kong with a choice of budget, first-class, or deluxe hotels. Prices (on a room only basis, per person sharing a twin room) range from £559 to £765.

Prowse Journeys (103 Waterloo Rd., London SE1 8UL, tel. 01/928-5511) has hotel packages for Hong Kong with prices (per person sharing a twin room) from £675 for seven nights. Keith Prowse also has a wide range of escorted extension tours into China with prices for three nights in Beijing from £600, and two nights in Guilin from £306.

Sovereign Holidays (Box 100, Hodford House, 17-27 High St., Hounslow, Middlesex TW3 1TB, tel. 01/748-7559) offers hotel packages similar to those of Page & Moy, with prices from £599. Sovereign also has combination tours to Hong Kong and Beijing, Xian, or Guilin (prices from £768 for seven nights), or to Hong Kong and Bali (prices from £977) for 14 nights.

Thomson Holidays Ltd. (Greater London House, Hampstead Rd., London NW1 7SD, tel. 01/387-1900) offers five-, 12-, or 19-day hotel vacations. Prices (per person on a room-only basis) range from £583 to £1,262. There is a choice of vacations on Bali (prices from £822) or combination tours (including the 17-night "Oriental Explorer" or the "Jalan Jalan" tour, both taking in Penang, Bangkok, Singapore, and Hong Kong), with prices per person from £1,099.

Voyages Jules Verne (10 Glentworth St., London NW1 5PG, tel. 01/723-6556) offers "The Oriental Journey," a 19-day escorted tour of Bangkok, Hong Kong, China, Singapore, and Pattaya. Prices, which include individual site tours, some meals, and an evening junk cruise, are from £1,195.

Contact **British Airways** (British Airways Holiday Centre, 65 Regent St., London W1R 7HG, tel. 0293/518-060) for information about their "Pound Stretcher" holidays that start at £650 for five nights.

When to Go

The high tourist season, October–late December, is popular for a reason: The weather is pleasant, with sunny days and comfortable, cool nights. January, February, and sometimes early March are not only cold but also dank, with long periods of overcast skies and rain. March and April can be either cold and miserable or beautiful and sunny. By May, the cold, damp spell has broken and the temperature is warm and comfortable. The months of June through September are the typhoon season, when the weather is hot and sticky, with lots of rain. All visitors to Hong Kong should know in advance that typhoons (called hurricanes in the West) must be treated with respect. Fortunately, Hong Kong is prepared for these blustery assaults. The front of every telephone book has emergency instructions and a listing of the typhoon warning signals used on the beaches and throughout the colony. If a storm is approaching, the airwaves will be crackling with information, and your hotel will make certain through postings in the lobby that you know the applicable signal. In addition, public places will have postings.

If a No. 8 signal is posted, Hong Kong and Macau close down completely. Head immediately for your hotel, and stay put. This is serious business—bamboo scaffolding can come hurtling through the streets like spears, ships can be sunk in the harbor, and large areas of the colony are often flooded.

Macau's summers are slightly cooler and wetter than Hong Kong's. In the 19th century, many Hong Kong residents summered in Macau to escape the heat.

Climate The following are average daily maximum and minimum temperatures for Hong Kong.

Jan.	64F	18C	**May**	82F	28C	**Sept.**	85F	29C
	56	13		74	23		77	25
Feb.	63F	17C	**June**	85F	29C	**Oct.**	81F	27C
	55	13		78	26		73	23
Mar.	67F	19C	**July**	87F	31C	**Nov.**	74F	23C
	60	16		78	26		65	18
Apr.	75F	24C	**Aug.**	87F	31C	**Dec.**	68F	20C
	67	19		78	26		59	15

Updated hourly weather information in 235 cities around the world—180 of them in the United States—is only a phone call away. Telephone numbers for **WeatherTrak** in the 12 cities where the service is available may be obtained by calling 800/247–3282. A taped message will tell you to dial the three-digit access code to any of the 235 destinations. The code is either the area code (in the United States) or the first three letters of the foreign city. For a list of all access codes send a stamped, self-addressed envelope to Cities, Box 7000, Dallas, TX 75209. For further information, phone 214/869–3035 or 800/247–3282.

Festivals and Seasonal Events

Top seasonal events in Hong Kong include Chinese New Year, around February and early March; the Hong Kong Arts Festival in January and February; the mid-June Dragon Boat Festival, probably the most colorful festival of all; the many lunar festivals celebrated throughout the year; and annual sporting events such as the Rugby Seven in late March or early April, and the Macau Grand Prix in November. For exact dates and further details about the following events, contact the HKTA *(see* Visitor Information).

Jan. 1: New Year's Day is a public holiday.
Mid-Jan.–early Feb.: Hong Kong Arts Festival takes place in theaters and halls throughout Hong Kong.
Late Jan.: Hong Kong Marathon is sponsored by the Hong Kong Distance Runner's Club.
Mid-Feb.: Chinese New Year is a time to visit friends and relatives and wear new clothes, and a time when the city virtually comes to a standstill.
Early Mar.: Spring Lantern Festival is on the last day of Chinese

New Year celebrations, when streets and homes are decorated with brightly colored lanterns.

Early Mar.: Hong Kong Open Golf Championship, at the Royal Hong Kong Golf Club in Fanling.

Late Mar. or early Apr.: The Invitation Sevens, a premier event, is a rugby tournament sponsored by Cathay Pacific and Hong Kong Bank.

Early Apr.: Easter holidays.

Early Apr.: Ching Ming Festival is the time when families visit the burial plots of ancestors and departed relatives.

Mid-Apr.: Hong Kong International Film Festival features films and film stars from several countries and is a busy, rewarding fortnight for film buffs.

Early May: Birthday of Tin Hau, goddess of the sea. Fishermen decorate their boats and converge on seaside temples to honor Tin Hau. Everyone even remotely connected with the sea happily participates, including some commuters who use the Hong Kong ferries. The busiest area is around the Tin Hau Temple in Junk Bay.

Late May: Birthday of Lord Buddha, when temples throughout the territory bathe the sacred Buddha's statue. The Po Lin Monastery on Lantau Island has ceremonies as elaborate as any.

Late May: Bun Festival on Cheung Chau Island is a three-day spirit-placating rite that culminates in a grand procession with young children taking part in tableaus. Thousands of people converge for the finale.

June 11: Birthday of Her Majesty the Queen is a public holiday.

Mid-June: Dragon Boat Festival pits dragon-head boats against each other in races to commemorate the hero, Ch'u Yuen. The long and many-oared boats are rowed to the beat of a drum. International races, sponsored by the HKTA, follow a week later.

Mid-Aug.: Seven Sisters (Maiden) Festival is a celebration for lovers and a time when young girls pray for a good husband.

Late Aug.: Hungry Ghosts Festival is a time when food is set out to placate roaming spirits temporarily released from hell. Offerings are made everywhere.

Late Sept.: Mid-Autumn and Lantern Festival brings families together. Mooncakes are eaten while the moon rises. More public and spectacular are the crowds with candle lanterns that gather in the park and other open spaces.

Oct. 7: Birthday of Confucius marks special remembrances of the revered philosopher.

Mid-Oct.: Chung Yeung Festival commemorates a Han Dynasty tale about a man taking his family to high ground to avoid disaster.

Late Nov.: Macau Grand Prix is unavoidable if you happen to be in Macau this weekend, as the racing is done in the streets and it's none too peaceful.

Mid-Dec.: Hong Kong Judo Championship takes place at Queen Elizabeth Stadium.

What to Pack

Whatever the time of year, it is wise to pack a folding umbrella. From May to September, lightweight short-sleeve or sleeveless clothes in cotton or linen are most suitable for the high humidity. Bring some comfortable shoes and loose-fitting cotton shorts for walking. Air-conditioning in hotels and restaurants can be glacial, so women should bring a sweater or shawl for evening use indoors. Don't forget your swimsuit and high-protection suntan lotion. Several hotels have pools, and you may want to spend some time on one of the many beaches. Dress in Hong Kong is fairly informal, but a few hotels and restaurants do insist on a jacket and tie for men in the evenings. It is best to pack a lightweight summer jacket.

In October, November, March, and April, a jacket or sweater should suffice, but during the winter months, December to February, you should bring a raincoat or a light overcoat. It never really gets cold enough to wear furs, but you will see them worn by fashion-conscious Hong Kong women as soon as the first winter breezes blow.

Taking Money Abroad

The safest way to carry money abroad is in the form of traveler's checks, which are insured by the issuing company against loss or theft. The most recognized traveler's checks are American Express, Barclays, Thomas Cook, and those issued through major commercial banks such as Citibank and Bank of America. Some banks will issue checks free to established customers, but most charge a 1% commission fee. Be sure to keep a note of the check numbers in a separate place from the checks themselves so you have a record if they are lost.

Buy some of the traveler's checks in small denominations to cash toward the end of your trip. This will save you from having to cash a large check and ending up with more foreign money than you need.

All major credit cards are widely accepted, except in some of the smaller restaurants and shops.

Although you won't get as good an exchange rate at home as abroad, it's wise to change a small amount of money into Hong Kong dollars before you go to avoid long lines at airport currency exchange booths. Most U.S. banks will exchange your money into Hong Kong dollars. If your local bank can't provide this service, you can exchange money through Deak International. To find the office nearest you, contact them at 630 Fifth Avenue, New York, NY 10011, tel. 212/635–0515.

Getting Money from Home

There are at least three ways to get money from home:

(1) Have it sent through a large commercial bank with a branch in Hong Kong. The only drawback is that you must have an account with the bank; if not, you'll have to go through your own bank and the process will be slower and more expensive.

2) Have it sent through American Express. If you are a cardholder, you can cash a personal check or a counter check at an American Express office for up to $1,000; up to $200 will be in cash and the rest in traveler's checks. There is a 1% commission on the traveler's checks. American Express has a new service that should be available in most major cities worldwide by January 1989, called American Express MoneyGram. Through this service, you can receive up to $5,000 cash. It works this way: you call home and ask someone to go to an American Ex-

press office or an American Express MoneyGram agent (located in a retail outlet) and fill out an American Express MoneyGram. It can be paid for with cash or any major credit card. The person making the payment is given a reference number and telephones you with that number. The American Express MoneyGram agent calls an 800 number and authorizes the transfer of funds to an American Express office or a participating agency in Hong Kong. In most cases, the money is available immediately on a 24-hour basis. You pick it up by showing identification and giving the reference number. Fees vary according to the amount sent. To send $300, the fee is $22; for $5,000, $150. For the American Express MoneyGram location nearest your home, and to find out where the service is available overseas, call 800/543–4080. You do not have to be a cardholder to use this service.

3) Have it sent through Western Union. The U.S. number is 800/988–4726. If you have a MasterCard or Visa, you can have money sent for any amount up to your credit limit. If not, have someone take cash or a certified cashier's check to a Western Union office. The money will be delivered in two business days to a bank in Hong Kong. Fees vary with the amount of money sent: for $1,000 the fee is $67; for $500, $57.

Currency

The units of currency in Hong Kong are the Hong Kong dollar ($) and the cent. There are bills of 1,000, 500, 100, 50, 20, and 10 dollars. Coins are 5, 2, and 1 dollars and 50, 20, and 10 cents. The Hong Kong dollar is fixed at 7.8 dollars to the U.S. dollar. At press time (mid-1988), it is 6.14 to the Canadian dollar, and 13.7 to the pound sterling.

There are no currency restrictions in Hong Kong. Money-changing facilities are available at the airport, in hotels, in banks, and at private money changers scattered through the tourist areas. You will get better rates from a bank or money changer than from a hotel. However, beware of money changers who advertise "no selling commission" and do not mention the "buying commission" you must pay when you exchange foreign currency or traveler's checks for Hong Kong dollars.

The official currency unit in Macau is the pataca, which is divided into 100 avos. Bank notes come in five denominations: 500, 100, 50, 10, and 5 patacas; coins are 5 and 1 patacas and.50, 20, and 10 avos. The pataca is pegged to the Hong Kong dollar (within a few cents). Hong Kong currency circulates freely in Macau but not vice versa, so remember to change your patacas before you return to Hong Kong.

What It Will Cost

Hotels Aside from a few guest houses and hostels (*see* Student and Youth Travel), prices start at the equivalent of U.S.$50 to U.S.$60 per night; a 10% service charge, and a 5% government service charge are added.

Food It is still possible to go into a small Chinese restaurant and have a bowl of noodles and Chinese tea for the equivalent of about U.S.$1. Portions of dim sum, a smorgasbord of Chinese specialties served in small portions, plate by plate, can be had for as low as HK$3 to HK$4. You could have a splendid meal, with a couple of beers and Chinese tea, for about HK$40, or the equivalent of U.S.$5. Posh Western and Chinese restaurants, in contrast, are expensive. A three-course steak meal at your hotel grill could easily set you back HK$300 to HK$400 (U.S.$38–U.S.$51), plus a 10% service charge, excluding cocktails and wine.

Shopping Clothing is high on everyone's shopping list. Foreign brands will be a big bargain if you shop in street markets such as the one in Stanley Village, less so in luxury shopping complexes such as The Landmark or the hotel arcades. That famous Hong Kong made-to-measure suit is still a very good deal. Remember that goods (with the exception of alcohol, tobacco, petroleum products, perfume, and soft drinks) are duty-free, everywhere in Hong Kong, not just in stores touting that they are duty-free. Also, there are no sales taxes or Value Added Taxes, except for the 5% hotel room tax and the airport departure taxes. Bargaining, particularly at street markets and at small camera and hi-fi shops, is a must.

Tipping Hotels and major restaurants add a 10% service charge. In many of the more traditional Chinese restaurants, a waiter will bring small snacks at the beginning of the meal and charge them to you, even if you did not order them. This money is in lieu of a service charge. It is customary to leave an additional 10% tip in all restaurants, and in taxis and beauty salons.

Sample Prices
Cup of Coffee HK$14 to HK$20/U.S.$1.80 to U.S.$2.50, plus 10% (hotel coffee shop).
HK$3/U.S.$.40 (McDonald's).

Hamburger HK$40 to HK$45/U.S.$5 to U.S.$5.75 (hotel coffee shop).
HK$3.50/U.S.$.45 (McDonald's).

Soft Drink HK$16 to HK$20/U.S.$2 to U.S.$2.50, plus 10% (hotel bar).
HK$3/U.S.$.40 (McDonald's, small).

Beer HK$11 to HK$17/U.S.$1.40 to U.S.$2.15 (pub, hotel bar).
HK$20 to HK$50/U.S.$2.50 to U.S.$6.40 (bar, hostess club).

Whiskey HK$15–HK$20/U.S.$2 to U.S.$2.50 (pub, hotel bar).

Taxi HK$5.50/U.S.$.70 first 2 km (1.25 mi).

Subway HK$2–HK$2.50/U.S.$.25 to U.S.$.70.

Double Room HK$230/U.S.$29.50 (budget guest house).
HK$400–HK$600/U.S.$51 to U.S.$77 (moderate hotel).

Tailored Suit HK$1,000–HK$2,500/U.S.$128 to U.S.$320.50.

Passports and Visas

U.S. citizens holding valid passports may visit Hong Kong for one month without a visa, provided they have an onward or return ticket and enough money for their stay. Europeans, South Americans, most Asians, Commonwealth citizens, and nationals of non-Communist countries may visit for one to three months without a visa under the same conditions. Canadians are usually granted stays of two months. Holders of British passports issued in the United Kingdom may visit Hong Kong for six months; no visas are required. As a rule, extensions are readily granted. Questions about visas, once you're in Hong Kong, should be directed to: Department of Immigration (Mirror Tower, 61 Mody Rd., Tsimshatsui East, tel. 3/733–3111).

To enter the neighboring territory of Macau, visas are not required for citizens of the United States, Canada, the United Kingdom, Australia, and most Western European countries. Nationals of countries that do not maintain diplomatic relations with Portugal may not obtain visas upon arrival, but must obtain them from Portuguese consulates overseas. Contact the Portuguese Consulate (1001-2, Tower II, Exchange Sq., 8 Connaught Pl., Hong Kong, tel. 5/231–338) which is open weekdays 9–3.

Customs and Duties

On Arrival   Except for the usual prohibitions against narcotics, explosives, firearms, and ammunition, and modest limits on alcohol, tobacco products, and perfume, you can bring anything you want into Hong Kong, including an unlimited amount of money.

Nonresident visitors may bring in, duty free, 200 cigarettes or 50 cigars or 250 grams of tobacco, and one liter of alcohol.

On Departure   With the exception of narcotics, explosives, firearms, and ammunition, you can take anything you want out of Hong Kong. There are no restrictions on currency.

Traveling with Film

Don't pack your unprocessed film in your checked luggage; if your bags get X-rayed, you may be saying goodbye to your photographs. Carry the undeveloped film with you through security and ask to have it inspected by hand. It helps if you keep your film in a separate plastic bag, ready for quick inspection. Inspectors at U.S. airports are required by law to honor requests for hand inspection; abroad, you'll have to depend on the kindness of strangers. The danger is that the old airport scanning machines—still in use in some third-world countries—use heavy doses of radiation that can turn a family portrait into an early morning fog. The newer models—used in all U.S. airports—are safe for anything from five to 500 scans, depending on the speed of your film. The effects are cumulative; you can put the same roll of film through several scans without worry. After five scans, you're asking for trouble.

If your film gets fogged and you want an explanation, send it to: National Association of Photographic Manufacturers (600 Mamaroneck Ave., Harrison, NY 10528). They will try to determine what went wrong. The service is free.

Language

The official languages of Hong Kong are English and Chinese. The most commonly spoken Chinese dialects are Cantonese and Mandarin. In Macau, the languages are, officially, Portuguese and Chinese, but many people speak some English.

In hotels, major restaurants, shops, and tourist centers, almost everyone speaks fluent English. However, this is not the case with taxi drivers and workers in small shops and market stalls. In a local street cafe, you may not find anyone who speaks English, or an English-language menu, and you will have to resort to pointing at the food on someone else's table.

Staying Healthy

There are no serious health risks associated with travel to Hong Kong, but you should remember that you are in the tropics and need to protect yourself from the fierce midday sun, from 11 AM to 3 PM. Wear a hat and try not to rush around. Drink plenty of liquids and if you feel tired, *rest*. In the summer, try to do your walking and sightseeing in the early morning and late afternoon.

The **International Association for Medical Assistance to Travelers** (IAMAT) is a worldwide association offering a list of approved doctors whose training meets very high standards. For a list of Hong Kong physicians and clinics that are part of this network, contact IAMAT (736 Center St., Lewiston, NY 14092, tel. 716/754–4883; in Canada, 188 Nicklin Rd., Guelph, Ont. N1H 7L5; in Europe, Gotthardstrasse 17, 6300 Zug, Switzerland). Membership is free.

Shots and Medications Inoculations and antimalaria drugs are not needed for Hong Kong. If you have a health problem that might require purchasing prescription drugs while in Hong Kong, have your doctor write a prescription using the drug's generic name.

Water Although the Hong Kong government declares that the water is safe to drink, even locals prefer to boil it or to drink mineral water in bottles.

Insurance

Travelers may want insurance coverage in three areas: health and accident, loss of luggage, and trip cancellation. Your first step is to review your existing health and homeowner policies; some health insurance plans cover health expenses incurred while traveling, some major medical plans cover emergency transportation, and some homeowner policies cover the theft of luggage.

Health and Accident Several companies offer coverage designed to supplement existing health insurance for travelers:

Carefree Travel Insurance (Box 310, 120 Mineola Blvd., Mineola, NY 11501, tel. 516/294–0220 or 800/645–2424) provides coverage for medical evacuation. It also offers 24-hour medical phone advice.
Health Care Abroad, International Underwriters Group (243 Church St. W, Vienna, VA 22180, tel. 703/281–9500 or 800/237–6615) offers comprehensive medical coverage, including emergency evacuation for trips of 10 to 90 days.
International SOS Insurance (Box 11568, Philadelphia, PA 19116, tel. 215/244–1500 or 800/523–8930) does not offer medical insurance but provides medical evacuation services to its clients, who are often international corporations.
Travel Guard International, underwritten by Cygna (1100 Centerpoint Dr., Stevens Pt., WI 54481, tel. 715/345–0505 or 800/782–5151), offers medical insurance, with coverage for emergency evacuation when Travel Guard's representatives in the United States say it is necessary.

Loss of Luggage Luggage loss is usually covered as part of a comprehensive travel-insurance package that includes personal accident, trip cancellation, and sometimes default and bankruptcy insurance. Several companies offer comprehensive policies, including

Access America, Inc., a subsidiary of Blue Cross-Blue Shield (Box 807, New York, NY 10163, tel. 800/851–2800).
Near, Inc. (1900 N. MacArthur Blvd., Suite 210, Oklahoma City, OK 73127, tel. 800/654–6700).
Travel Guard International *(see* Health and Accident Insurance).
Tele-Trip (tel. 800/228–9792), a subsidiary of Mutual of Omaha, and **The Travelers Insurance Co.** (Ticket and Travel Dept., 1 Tower Sq., Hartford, CT 06183). Tele-Trip operates sales booths at airports and issues insurance through travel agents. It will insure checked luggage for up to 180 days and for $500 to $3,000 valuation. For one to three days, the rate for a $500 valuation is $8.25; for 180 days, $100. The Travelers Insurance Co. will insure checked or hand luggage for $500 to $2,000 valuation per person, and also for a maximum of 180 days. Rates for one to five days for $500 valuation are $10; for 180 days, $85.

Before you go, itemize the contents of each bag in case you need to file an insurance claim. If your luggage is stolen and later recovered, the airline must deliver the luggage to your home, free of charge.

Trip Cancellation Flight insurance is often included in the price of a ticket when paid for with American Express, Visa, or other major credit cards. It is usually included in combination with travel-insurance packages available from most tour operators, travel agents, and insurance agents.

Renting Cars

It is unlikely you will want to rent a car in Hong Kong. The driving conditions are difficult, traffic is constantly jammed, and parking is usually impossible. Public transportation is excellent and the taxis are inexpensive. If you do decide to rent a car, take one *with* a driver. Several operators offer such services, which can be arranged through your hotel. Charges are from HK$400 for the first three hours, and from HK$130 for each subsequent hour.

If you are determined to drive yourself, you'll need an international driver's license. Car rental companies in Hong Kong include: **Avis** (50 Po Loi St., Zung Fu Car Park, Hung Hom, Kowloon, tel. 3/346–007), **National Car Rental** (Intercontinental Plaza, 94 Granville St., Tsimshatsui East, Kowloon, tel. 3/671–047), **Fung Hing Hire Co.** (4 Tsui Man St., Happy Valley, Hong Kong, tel. 5/720–333), and **Mutual Transport & Trading Co.** (39 Tak Wan Shopping Arcade, 1st fl., 12 Pak Kung St., Hung Hom, Kowloon, tel. 3/636–939).

Student and Youth Travel

Although there are few student discounts available, Hong Kong is within the budget of the student traveler once accommodations have been found. Inexpensive digs include the **Chungking Mansions** (Nathan Rd., Tsimshatsui, Kowloon), offering a rabbit warren of not-so-clean rooms for about U.S.$25 to U.S.$30. Holders of **International Youth Hostels** cards may contact Room 1408A, Watson's Estate, Watson's Road, North Point, Hong Kong, tel. 5/706–222, to see if there is space in the territory's very crowded hostels. The **YMCA** (41 Salisbury Rd.,

Tsimshatsui, Kowloon, tel. 3/692–211), across from the Peninsula Hotel, is the most popular place for inexpensive accommodations, but it is hard to get a booking.

An International Student Identity Card is of value at the **Hong Kong Student Travel Bureau** (1024 Star House, Star Ferry Concourse, Kowloon, tel. 3/722–3269). They can help you with travel discounts and sometimes with discounted lodging rates.

Traveling with Children

Publications *Family Travel Times* is an eight- to 12-page newsletter published 10 times a year by **Travel With Your Children** (TWYCH; 80 Eighth Ave., New York, NY 10011, tel. 212/206–0688). Subscription includes access to back issues and twice-weekly opportunities to call in for specific advice.
Hong Kong for Kids is a free brochure published by the HKTA (548 Fifth Ave., New York, NY 10036, tel. 212/869–5008).

Family Travel Organizations **American Institute for Foreign Study** (102 Greenwich Ave., Greenwich, CT 06830, tel. 203/869–9090) offers a family vacation program in Hong Kong and China specifically designed for parents and children.
Rascals in Paradise Family Vacation (Adventure Express, 185 Berry St., Suite 5503, San Francisco, CA 94107, tel. 800/443–0799) organizes tours to Hong Kong and China accompanied by a preschool teacher (depending on the age of the children) and emphasizes cultural exchange with visits to schools and lessons on such things as how to write your name in Chinese.

Hotels The **Shangri-La Hong Kong** (64 Mody Rd., Tsimshatsui East, Kowloon, tel. 3/721–111) allows children under 18 to stay free in the same room with their parents. It also features a children's menu and English-language color TV. For reservations from the United States, call Westin Hotels (tel. 800/228–3000).

Getting There On international flights, children under two not occupying a seat pay 10% of adult fare. Various discounts apply to children two to 12 years of age. If you're traveling with an infant, reserve a seat behind the bulkhead of the plane, which offers more leg room and can usually fit a bassinet (supplied by the airline). Also inquire about special children's meals or snacks, and whether you can take your child's car seat aboard. See "TWYCH's Airline Guide," in the February 1988 issue of *Family Travel Times* for a rundown on children's services offered by 46 airlines. For the booklet, "Child/Infant Safety Seats Acceptable for Use in Aircraft," write Community and Consumer Liaison Division (APA-400 Federal Aviation Administration, Washington, DC 20591, tel. 202/267–3479).

Baby-sitting Services Child-care arrangements are usually easy to make through the hotel concierge.

Hints for Disabled Travelers

Hong Kong is not the easiest of cities for people in wheelchairs because there are few ramps or special accesses. Progress is being made, however, and the airport, City Hall, Hong Kong Arts Centre, and the Academy for Performing Arts all have made efforts to assist people in wheelchairs. *A Guide for Physically Handicapped Visitors in Hong Kong* is available through the HKTA, and will prove invaluable. Not only does it list those rare places that have special facilities for the handicapped, but it also explains the best access to hotels, shopping centers, government offices, consulates, restaurants, and churches.

The Information Center for Individuals with Disabilities (20 Park Plaza, Room 330, Boston, MA 02116, tel. 617/727–5540) offers useful problem-solving assistance, including lists of travel agents that specialize in tours for the disabled.

Moss Rehabilitation Hospital Travel Information Service (12th St. and Taber Rd., Philadelphia, PA 19141, tel. 215/329–5715) provides information on tourist sights, transportation, and accommodations in destinations around the world. The fee is $5 for each destination. Allow one month for delivery.

Mobility International (Box 3551, Eugene, OR 97403, tel. 503/343–1284) has information on accommodations and organized study.

The Society for the Advancement of Travel for the Handicapped (26 Court St., Brooklyn, NY 11242, tel. 718/858–5483) offers access information. Annual membership costs $40, or $25 for senior travelers and students. Send a stamped, self-addressed envelope.

The Itinerary (Box 1084, Bayonne, NJ 07002, tel. 201/858–3400) is a bimonthly travel magazine for the disabled.

Access to the World: A Travel Guide for the Handicapped by Louise Weiss is useful but out of date. Available from Facts on File (460 Park Ave. S, New York, NY 10016, tel. 212/683–2244). *Frommer's Guide for Disabled Travelers* is also useful but dated.

Hints for Older Travelers

The American Association of Retired Persons (AARP, 1909 K St. NW, Washington, DC 20049, tel. 202/662–4850) has two programs for independent travelers: (1) *The Purchase Privilege Program*, which offers discounts on hotels, airfare, car rentals, and sightseeing; and (2) the *AARP Motoring Plan*, which offers emergency aid and trip routing information for an annual fee of $29.95 per couple. The AARP also arranges group tours, including apartment living in Europe, through two companies: **Olson-Travelworld** (5855 Green Valley Circle, Culver City, CA 90230, tel. 800/227–7737) and **RFD, Inc.** (4401 W. 110th St., Overland Park, KS 66211, tel. 800/448–7010). AARP members must be 50 or older. Annual dues are $5 per person or per couple.

When using an AARP or other identification card, ask for a reduced hotel rate at the time you make your reservation, not when you check out. At restaurants, show your card to the maitre d' before you're seated, since discounts may be limited to certain set menus, days, or hours. When renting a car, remember that economy cars, priced at promotional rates, may cost less than cars that are available with your ID card.

Elderhostel (80 Boylston St., Suite 400, Boston, MA 02116, tel. 617/426–7788) is an innovative 13-year-old program for people 60 and older. Participants live in dorms on some 1,200 campuses around the world. Mornings are devoted to lectures and seminars; afternoons, to sightseeing and field trips. The all-inclusive fee for two to three week trips, including room, board, tuition, and round-trip transportation, is $1,700–$3,200.

Travel Industry and Disabled Exchange (TIDE, 5435 Donna Ave., Tarzana, CA 91356, tel. 818/343–6339) is an industry-based organization with a $15 per person annual membership fee. Members receive a quarterly newsletter and information on travel agencies and tours.

National Council of Senior Citizens (925 15th St. NW, Washington, DC 20005, tel. 202/347–8800) is a nonprofit advocacy group with some 4,000 local clubs across the country. Annual membership is $10 per person or $14 per couple. Members receive a monthly newspaper with travel information and an ID card for reduced-rate hotels and car rentals.

Mature Outlook (Box 1205, Glenview, IL 60025, tel. 800/336–6330), a subsidiary of Sears Roebuck & Co., is a travel club for people over 50, with hotel and motel discounts and a bimonthly newsletter. Annual membership is $7.50 per couple. Instant membership is available at participating Holiday Inns.

"Travel Tips for Senior Citizens" (U.S. Dept. of State Publication 8970, revised Sept. 1987) is available for $1 from the Superintendant of Documents, U.S. Government Printing Office, Washington, DC 20402.

Golden Age Passport is a free lifetime pass to all parks, monuments, and recreation areas run by the federal government. People over 62 should pick them up in person at any national park that charges admission. A driver's license or other proof of age is required.

Further Reading

James Clavell's *Taipan* and *Noble House* are blockbuster novels covering the early history of the British colony and the multifaceted life found there around the 1950s. Both books provide insights, sometimes sensationalized, sometimes accurate. Robert S. Elegant's *Dynasty* is another epic novel tracing the development of a powerful Eurasian family. It has some simplified history, but it does reveal a lot about the way that locals think. Another bestseller set in Hong Kong is John LeCarre's *The Honorable School Boy*, a superb spy thriller. On a smaller scale is Han Suyin's *A Many Splendoured Thing*. Another classic novel is Richard Mason's *The World of Suzy Wong*, which covers an American's adventures with a young woman in the Wanchai bar area. Austin Coates's *Myself a Mandarin* is a lively and humorous account of a European magistrate handling Chinese society, and his *City of Broken Promises* is a rags-to-riches biography of an 18th-century woman from Macau.

Maurice Collis's beautifully written classic, *Foreign Mud*, covers the early opium trade and China wars. G.B. Endicott's *History of Hong Kong* traces Hong Kong from its beginnings to the riot-wracked 1960s. Trea Wiltshire's *Hong Kong: Improbable Journey* focuses exclusively on recent times. Richard Hughes's *Borrowed Time, Borrowed Place* looks at Hong Kong immediately before the signing of the 1984 Sino-British Agreement that will give Hong Kong back to the People's Republic of China in 1997. David Bonavia's *Hong Kong 1997: The Final Settlement* provides history and analysis of the agreement.

Getting to Hong Kong

From North America by Plane

The Airlines **United Airlines** (tel. 800/421–4655) flies daily out of New York and Chicago, with stops on the West Coast and in Tokyo. It also flies out of Los Angeles, with stops in Honolulu and Tokyo, and has nonstop flights from Seattle and San Francisco. **Northwest** (tel. 800/225–2525) has departures from New York and Chicago that go via the West Coast and Tokyo. It also has flights from Seattle, San Francisco, and Los Angeles via Tokyo. **Cathay Pacific Airways** (tel. 800/663–8833 in the USA; in CA 800/663–8838; in British Columbia and Alberta 800/663–9393; and in the rest of Canada 800/663–1252) has daily nonstop service out of Vancouver and one-stop service via Vancouver leaving from San Francisco. **Canadian Airlines International** (tel. 800/387–2737) flies six times a week out of Vancouver, all flights via Tokyo. **Singapore Airlines** (tel. 800/387–2737) flies daily out of San Francisco and three times a week from Los Angeles, all via Honolulu.

Flying Times From New York, via Tokyo, 24 hours; from Chicago, via Tokyo, 24 hours; from Los Angeles, via Honolulu, 17 hours; and from San Francisco, direct, 13 hours.

Luggage Regulations *Carry-on Luggage* If you are flying to and from Hong Kong directly, you will be able to take two bags. The heaviest cannot weigh more than 70 pounds. The total dimensions cannot exceed 107″ (length + width + height), and the largest bag cannot be more than 62 inches. You are allowed one carry-on piece of luggage, plus a handbag. If you stop en route, you can only check luggage totaling 44 pounds if you are flying economy class, 66 pounds if flying business class, and 88 pounds, first class. You will be allowed one piece of carry-on luggage in addition to a handbag, duty-free shopping bag, or camera case. Leaving Hong Kong, the carry-on piece must be able to fit inside a 22″ × 14″ × 9″ box, unless it is a garment bag. If you can't meet these regulations, ask an airline supervisor for an exemption. You can usually get one, but don't count on it.

Checked Luggage U.S. airlines allow passengers to check in two suitcases whose total dimensions (length + width + height) do not exceed 60″. There are no weight restrictions on these bags.

Rules governing foreign airlines vary from airline to airline, so check with your travel agent or the airline itself before you go. All the airlines allow passengers to check in two bags. In general, expect the weight restriction on the two bags to be not more than 70 pounds each, the size restriction of the first bag to be 62″ total dimensions, and that on the second bag to be 55″ total dimensions.

Labeling Luggage Be sure to put your business address on each piece of luggage, including hand luggage.

Enjoying the Flight The key to successful, long-haul flying is comfort. Loose-fitting casual clothes are a must unless business formality requires otherwise. Your carry-on luggage should have enough toiletries to help you freshen up before arrival and to hold you over in an airport. Feet swell at high altitudes, so consider taking off your shoes. Jet lag will be eased by going easy on food and alcohol. It's important, though, to drink plenty of nonalcoholic liquids. For sleeping, there are those who swear by an aisle seat for leg room, and others who prefer window seats for something to lean against. Middle seats are to be avoided. Pipes and cigars are forbidden on all flights. Nonsmokers should ask for seats as far away from the smoking section as possible. U.S. airlines are required by law to find nonsmoking seats for all passengers who request them.

From North America by Ship

P&O Princess Cruises (2029 Century Pk. E, Los Angeles, CA 90067, tel. 213/553–1770; 355 Burrard St., Vancouver, BC V6C 2H7, tel. 604/685–4541) sail regularly to the Orient in the fall from Vancouver. While **Royal Viking** (750 Battery St., San Francisco, CA 94111, tel. 415/398–8000) sails from Vancouver and San Francisco. Ask your travel agent for details. Other cruise lines that include Hong Kong as a port of call are **Lindblad Travel, Cunard, Princess,** and **Holland America.** Ask your travel agent for a complete list.

From the United Kingdom by Plane

Cathay Pacific Airways (tel. 01/930–4444) and **British Airways** (tel. 01/897–4000) have daily flights from London to Hong Kong. **British Caledonian** (tel. 01/668–4221) has flights six times a week, all via the Middle East, with departures from both Heathrow and Gatwick. Various Asian national airlines fly to Hong Kong via their capital cities, usually at reasonable rates. There are some direct flights on Cathay Pacific and British Airways. The flying time is usually 16 to 17 hours with a stopover, or 12 to 13 hours nonstop.

From the United Kingdom by Ship

Hong Kong is a major port of call for around-the-world cruises. Fabulous floating palaces, such as **Cunard's** *Queen Elizabeth II* and **P&O's** *Canberra* still pull away from Southampton regularly, and dock in Hong Kong for a day or two. *Cunard Line, 30A Pall Mall, London SW1Y, tel. 01/491–3930. P&O, 77 New Oxford St., London WCIA 1PP, tel. 01/831–1881.*

2 Portraits of Hong Kong

Doing Business in Hong Kong

by Saul Lockhart

An American based in Hong Kong since 1967, Saul Lockhart is the author or co-author of six guidebooks on Asia. He has written numerous articles over the years for a variety of American, Asian, and European publications.

Made in Hong Kong. That familiar phrase—seen on everything from designer fashions and computers to toys, radios, and the proverbial left-handed widget—is the clue to the territory's export-oriented, manufacturing economy. The spirit of Hong Kong is the spirit of entrepreneurship; with people as its only natural resource, this tiny island is the world's 13th largest trading entity outside OPEC and COMECON.

Hong Kong is one of the rare places on earth that plays the free-trade game according to the classical rules, with only one or two peculiarities arising out of its colonial past. It is a free port —that is, there are no import duties or export levies, although there are domestic excises on alcohol (therefore on alcoholic beverages and perfumes), tobacco and tobacco products, petroleum products, and soft drinks. Some articles, such as firearms, ammunition, certain toxic drugs and, of course, narcotics, are controlled. There are limited controls on banking and finance, and on stock, futures, and commodities exchanges. But, by and large, these are minimal and usually implemented only after some calamitous, often illegal, happening. The territory's bankers practice confidentiality, though it is not codified, as in Switzerland. The Independent Commission Against Corruption has the power to force banks to disclose all accounts and transactions.

With a few historical exceptions, you cannot own land in Hong Kong; it all belongs to the Crown (the government), but long- and short-term leases are auctioned off to all comers. With the signing of the 1984 Sino-British Agreement, which will return sovereignty to the People's Republic of China at the end of June 1997, land leases and mortgages are to extend past the magic 1997 mark as if it were not there. Otherwise, there are no business ownership limitations. A national of any country may do business or set up business, although nationals of countries that, for the time being, are not politically friendly with either Great Britain or China may be refused entry, working visas, or residence permits—most particularly those from the Eastern bloc who were not here before the Sino-Russian split.

The Law

Until midnight, June 30, 1997, Hong Kong will closely follow English Common Law, with modifications for Hong Kong's unique circumstances. Barristers and solicitors make up a two-tier legal system. The judiciary is separate and independent from the rest of government and the governor appoints all judges and magistrates, who, unlike their counterparts in Britain, are part of the civil service. Ultimate appeal is to the Judicial Committee of the Privy Council in London. As in Britain, the defendant is assumed innocent until proven guilty, except in cases of corruption, pornography, and dissemination of false news, in which the onus of proof rests with the defendant.

Hong Kong's rule of law has always been a great attraction to the international business community. Since 1841, with few exceptions, Hong Kong has offered full redress in its civil and criminal courts. The government is held in check by the very people whose salary it pays.

Part of Hong Kong's attraction as an international business center is its proximity to the People's Republic of China. Hong Kong's China-watching role naturally decreased once China opened up, but because of the hassles of living, working, negotiating, and doing day-to-day business in the PRC, Hong Kong's overall role in the worldwide China trade has increased. Hong Kong also shares a border with the Shenzhen Special Economic Zone (SEZ), the most successful of the SEZs China has created to funnel in foreign investment. In short, Hong Kong is still China's foreign-exchange window and a very good place to position yourself if you are interested in trade with China, or just learning what business in Asia is all about.

The Future After 1997

As we go to press, the Basic Law Drafting Committee of the People's Republic of China is toiling away at the territory's post-1997 miniconstitution, putting in writing the guarantees set down in the 1984 Sino-British Agreement, and ratified by both parties in May 1985. Many prominent Hong Kong natives sit on these committees to insure Hong Kong's input.

Although there is considerable uncertainty in Hong Kong about life after 1997, Chinese premier Deng Xiaoping has given Hong Kong a half-century guarantee from July 1, 1997. This promise will allow the territory to exist as a Special Administrative Region (SAR) of the People's Republic, with separate laws and a high degree of autonomy in domestic affairs. The SAR will be vested with executive, legislative, and independent judicial powers, including the authority of final adjudication. The laws currently in force will remain basically unchanged.

Rights and freedoms, including those of person, speech, press, assembly, association, travel, movement, correspondence, strike, occupation, inheritance, and religion, will be ensured, as will the right of academic research. Private property and foreign investment will be protected. Hong Kong will retain its status as a free port with its own shipping registry, a separate customs authority, and an international financial center. Foreign exchange, gold, securities, and futures markets will continue. The Hong Kong dollar will continue to circulate as a separate, freely convertible currency, distinct from China's *renminbi;* there will be no exchange controls. Hong Kong will manage its own finances and China will not levy any taxes on the SAR.

Hong Kong will be allowed to maintain and develop independent economic and cultural relations and to conclude agreements with foreign countries and trade organizations, such as the GATT and MFA, and air and tax agreements.

China will hold sway over foreign and defense matters, and Chinese troops will replace the British garrison. A Chinese-appointed governor, who may or may not be Hong Kong Chinese, will be responsible to Peking, much as the current governor is responsible to London. Whether he'll be as independent as Hong Kong's British governors have traditionally been is a moot point. A special tripartite Joint Liaison Group, with members from Hong Kong, Britain, and China, meets regularly to hammer out the fine points necessary for a smooth handover. The Basic Law is due to be published in 1990.

For its part, the Hong Kong government is reviewing the way things are run with a view to instituting changes to prepare this huge populace for the future. In November 1984, it issued a White Paper (statement of policy) called *The Future Development of Representative Government in Hong Kong*, followed in May 1987 by a Green Paper (nonbinding suggestions on policy meant for public debate) called *The 1987 Review of Developments in Representative Government*. In February 1988, the White Paper on future policy, *The Development of Representative Government: The Way Forward*, was published. The controversy over whether direct elections to the Legislative Council should be introduced in 1988 or delayed until 1991 was decided in favor of the latter. Behind all these papers is the desire that Hong Kong citizens have a greater say in government before 1997, so that everything will be in situ come the changeover.

Economy

Economist Milton Friedman called Hong Kong's the "last *laissez faire* economy," which must have been music to the ears of the local government. Hong Kong is living proof that Rudyard Kipling's statement about East and West—"ne'er the twain shall meet"—was wrong. Not only do East and West meet in Hong Kong, but each side also generally makes a profit on the relationship.

Profit making starts at the top. Only in the most adverse of times has the Hong Kong government's budget gone into the red. Annual surpluses are planned and expected; deficit spending is anathema. In fact, an intentional game is played each year at budget time, when the economic performance for that year is always underestimated; 6.2% was the growth-rate prediction for 1987, while at the year's end, the figure stood at 13.6%.

This mercantile community has a light-industrial and manufacturing-based economy. It is the world's largest exporter of clothing, furs, toys and games, watches and clocks, imitation jewelry, metal watchbands, electrical hair-dressing apparatus, artificial flowers, flashlights, and electric lamps. On-shore and off-shore financial and business services fill out the rest of the economic equation.

To support this thriving export manufacturing economy, Hong Kong imports—to the tune of US$48.5 billion in 1987—make it the world's 13th largest importer. With the exception of narcotics and firearms—which are illegal—and duty on liquor, perfumes, petroleum products, and soft drinks, any and all goods can be brought into the colony without hindrance. That is why Hong Kong cries "foul" when it is thrown into the same basket —particularly by the United States and the European Economic Community (EEC)—as Japan, Korea, and Taiwan, countries going to great lengths to block the importation of foreign goods.

With little land and no natural resources, Hong Kong's heavy industry is negligible. The territory's greatest asset is a hardworking and entrepreneurial people, who share with Singaporeans the highest living standard in Asia outside Japan.

Recent arrivals are stunned by the pace of Hong Kong, and staggered by cocktail chitchat from perfect strangers who want to know, after a two-minute acquaintance, how much rent you pay, how much you make, how much your car costs, etc. Natives are direct in situations in which Westerners are more circumspect. But that is because everyone in Hong Kong is in a rush to make his or her pile. The mentality is probably due to the historical uncertainty of Hong Kong's status—everyone knew that one day China would deal in her own way and in her own time with what she always considered an internal matter. That is precisely what happened, much to the chagrin of Prime Minister Thatcher, who had her own ideas about Britain staying on to run the place when she initiated the September 1982 negotiations that led to the agreement two years later.

Novelist Han Suyin summed it all up in a 1959 *Life* magazine article. Hong Kong, she said, "works splendidly on borrowed time in a borrowed place." Add to the mixture a bit of the refugee syndrome—more than half of the 5.5 million people have fled the Middle Kingdom, the Motherland, at one time or another since 1949—and Hong Kong's business (and social) pace is more understandable.

Finance

Hong Kong is the world's third largest financial center, after New York and London, and the third leg of the 24-hour trading triangle. Hong Kong has a three-tier banking system—156 licensed, full-service banks are followed by 35 licensed and 231 registered deposit-taking companies (DTCs). Different regulations govern issued share capital and paid-up capital for each type of DTC. Interest rates for both are unrestricted and very competitive. Interest rates for the licensed banks, by contrast, are set up by the Hong Kong Association of Banks, to which all licensed banks must belong.

Registered DTCs, with a minimum deposit of HK$100,000, are smaller operations, specializing in mortgages, hire purchase, and stock-market financing. Licensed DTCs, most often affiliated with foreign banks, have a minimum deposit of HK$500,000, and tend to go for project finance, syndicated loans, underwriting, corporate advice, investment, and related financial services.

There is no central bank in Hong Kong, though many believe the Bank of China may take over that role after 1997. Supervisory functions and management of the foreign exchange reserves are shared by various government departments—including the Commissioner of Banking, the Commissioner of Securities and Commodities Trading, and the Secretary for Monetary Affairs—and private institutions, particularly the Hongkong and Shanghai Banking Corporation (HKSBC), the government's banker. The HKSBC and its neighbor, the Chartered Bank, are the two note-issuing banks, although it is assumed the Bank of China will issue currency after 1997.

Currency

The Hong Kong dollar is freely convertible. There are no restrictions whatsoever on the movement of currency in or out of the colony. Since October 15, 1983, the Hong Kong dollar has been pegged to the U.S. dollar at U.S.$1:HK$7.80. The Hong Kong Exchange Fund, the territory's reserve fund, issues and redeems Certificates of Indebtedness to the two note-issuing banks, the Hongkong and Shanghai Banking Corporation and the Chartered Bank. For their part, the two institutions buy and sell banknotes to other licensed banks, in effect acting as agents for the fund.

The government has not made the HK$7.80 conversion facility available to the nonbanking public, and has given no guarantee of the foreign-currency price of deposits or cash held by the public, that is free to trade at market rates. The spread between the official and the free-market rates is where the industry makes its profit or takes its loss.

But for the trading public—and that includes business—the stable rate has given an impetus to Hong Kong's economy by allowing the United States a steady position as the territory's largest trading partner besides China. When the greenback is high, the Hong Kong dollar is high against other currencies, and vice-versa, tending to be more competitive vis-à-vis other currencies when the U.S. dollar is low.

The Markets

The Hong Kong Stock Exchange, which opened trading on April 2, 1986, is one of the most modern and sophisticated in the world. Its vast trading floor holds 800 booths and has room for more. At the end of 1987, 276 public companies were listed, with a total capitalization of HK$420 billion. The Exchange had 85 corporate members and 688 individual members at the end of 1987. The Hang Seng Index, calculated every quarter hour, measures performance.

The Hong Kong Futures Exchange offers contracts in five markets: cotton (though no trading has taken place in recent years), sugar, soybeans, gold, and the Hang Seng Futures Index. The last of these, which began on May 6, 1986, allows investors to hedge their share portfolios against adverse price fluctuations, and is now the most active stock-futures index market outside the United States. By the end of 1986, the Futures Exchange had 96 members.

There are two gold markets. The Chinese Gold & Silver Exchange Society operates a gold bullion market, one of the most active in the world. The gold is of 99% fineness and traded in *taels*, traditional Chinese measurement equal to about 1.2 troy ounces. The 193-member firms closely follow the markets in London, Zurich, and New York. The other gold market is called "loco-London" and its participants are, in the main, the major gold-trading companies. Dealings take place in U.S. dollars per troy ounce of 99.5% fineness, with deliveries in London.

The Layout of the Territory

Hong Kong Island is where the big-time commerce is: the bank HQs, the big company HQs, the lawyers, accountants, public relations, and advertising people, etc. Central District, as the name implies, is where the giants live.

Kowloon is where the industry is, and also the main tourist activity. In any case, you can get to and from the Island and Kowloon by road (through an undersea tunnel) in about 20 to 30 minutes, or by passenger ferry (the famous Star Ferry) in 10 minutes, except during rush hours.

In New Territories there are *seven* new towns being built, with new factories, offices, dwellings, schools, hospitals, hotels, and other facilities. Finally, a number of the outlying islands are also developing fast, with new incomes and market possibilities. Visit at least one (and also Macau which, after many decades of sleepy stagnation, is busting out all over in development; you can get there in 45 minutes by jetfoil).

Business Centers

Most of the major hotels have business centers, which provide secretarial, translation, courier, and printing services—even word processors. Charges vary from hotel to hotel, but secretaries run HK$50–HK$75 per hour, typing HK$25–HK$30 per page, and word processing about HK$75 per hour. Each hotel has a business-center tariff, so check before you act.

In a mercantile community such as Hong Kong, you'd expect business centers outside the hostelries, and there are many. Some are considerably cheaper than those in hotels. Others cost about the same but offer private desks (from HK$500 to HK$1,000 weekly for private offices and meeting facilities).

Other amenities include a private address and personal answering and forwarding services. Many service centers are tied in with accountants and lawyers for those who want to register a company quickly. Some will even process visas and wrap gifts for you.

One hotel business center, equipped like those normally found outside the hostelries, is the **China Traders Centre** in the Regal Meridien Airport Hotel. A short walk across a footbridge from the passenger terminal, it has offices and conference rooms. It is popular with transient businesspersons who need only the daylight hours to transact business before winging their way out again. Their club, the China Traders Circle, which has free membership, offers discounts on offices that can be rented by the hour, day, week, or month.

The **American Chamber of Commerce** (1030 Swire House, Central, Hong Kong Isl., tel. 5/260–165. Telex: 83664 AMCC HX. Fax: 5–8101289. Cable: AMCHAM) not only offers short-term rental of office and conference space, but also has a splendid and succinct Business Briefing Program (U.S.$200 members/ U.S.$300 nonmembers). The chamber also has a library and a *China Trade Services* section.

Other organizations of note:

Hong Kong Business Centre (Bank of Canton Building, 6th Fl., 6 Des Voeux Rd., Central, Hong Kong Island, tel. 5/212–511. Telex: 65779 HKBC HX. Fax: 852–5–8100235. Cable: HKBZCTR).

Margaret Sullivan Secretarial Services (13 Duddell St., Central, Hong Kong Island, tel. 5/265–946. Telex: 63210 ALAYE HX. Fax: 852–5–845–0989) also runs the Business Centre at the Garden Hotel in Canton.

Pacific Centre (Bank of America Building, 10th Fl., 1 Kowloon Park, tel. 3/721–0880. Telex: 56443 WATC HX).

British Business Centre (run by British Chamber of Commerce; Sing Pao Centre, 8th Fl., 8 Queen's Rd., Central, Hong Kong Island, tel. 5/810–8118. Telex: 82759 BRIT HX. Fax: 5–845–0404).

Language

Hong Kong, it should be realized, is a Chinese city, not an English city. The great bulk of the population speaks Cantonese, though Poutongua (Mandarin) is becoming more widely spoken. Even the taxi drivers often have little English. But the international communications, the hotels, and the Western-style entertainments are conducted multilingually, and it is possible to do business for years without knowing more than a few politesses in Chinese and a snatch of taxi-driver's lingo. But, in an office, you must have at least one good bilingual secretary.

Translations and Translators

There may come a time when you need an official translator or an official translation of a document. The hotel business centers can be of assistance as can those outside the hotels. *See* Business Centers above. For specialist work in all languages, try **Translanguage Center** (1604 Tung Wah Mansion, 199 Hennessy Rd., Wanchai, Hong Kong Island, tel. 5/732–728) or **Polyglot Translations** (1701 Chinese Bank Bldg., 61 Des Veoux Rd., Central, Hong Kong Island, tel. 5/215–689).

Style

Business in Hong Kong is cosmopolitan and formal. Despite the summer heat, a suit is necessary when calling on people. When you have become a familiar face, then more casual attire is suitable for daytime factory visits. Meetings with Chinese businesspersons can become very formal and very alcoholic. Be sure to have bilingual business cards printed—hundreds of them. Many in the West may laugh at the Asian penchant for whipping out their cards, but it is the preferred way of keeping track of people in Hong Kong.

Transportation

Hong Kong International Airport—known so widely as "Kai Tak," the name of the previous owners of the land, that if you gave the official title to a taxi driver he would not know where to go—is one of the major hubs in Southeast Asia, in terms both of its 12.6 million annual passengers and of its air cargo terminal with its 610,000 tons throughout (the sixth busiest in the world, outperforming London's Heathrow). Hong Kong is served by 38 scheduled airlines, operating about 1,100 flights weekly between Hong Kong and 70 cities throughout the world. And the best part of Kai Tak is the beautiful landing, over either Kowloon or the harbor. Even hardened pilots enjoy "turning left at the Hitachi sign and right when you spot Mrs. Wong's bloomers drying on a bamboo pole stuck out her 20th floor window."

Road traffic conditions are Hong Kong's perpetual problem. The government barely keeps up with needs, even though new roads are being built day and night.

Public transportation is excellent and offers a wide choice; swaying double-decker buses and minibuses are the most prevalent. Hong Kong Island also sports ancient trams rattling across the northern shore and an equally ancient funicular (the Peak Tram). The colony is inundated with taxis, except when you want one. A superb Mass Transit Railway (subway, tube, metro, U-Bahn, depending on your language) covers 24 air-conditioned miles (38.6 km) with 37 stations connecting Hong Kong Island with Kowloon and New Territories, and interchanging with the Kowloon Canton Railway, a commuter train running from Hung Hom in Kowloon to the Chinese border. The Star Ferry, of course, is Hong Kong's most famous mode of transport, but there are many smaller ferries—*walla-wallas*—to take you across the harbor if you can't find a taxi to take you through the cross-harbor tunnel when the Star Ferry closes.

One word of warning: Hong Kong is not the place to pick up a car at the airport and drive off. You can rent self-drive cars, from **Avis** and **National** (from HK$290 and HK$320 respectively, per day, no mileage), and some local agencies, and all you need is an International Driving License, but you'd have to be crazy to try it. Hong Kong's traffic is lethal and parking is irritating. It takes a while to get accustomed to Hong Kong drivers' terrible habits and lack of courtesy, and surely no businessperson would travel all this way to upset both mind and body on the road.

The answer is to rent a car *with* a driver and leave the problems to him. All the major hotels offer such a service, ranging from a low of HK$120 per hour (usually a minimum of 2 hours) to the posh Roll-Royces of the Peninsula Hotel at HK$600 per hour (no minimum). For a listing of car hire agencies *see* Renting Cars in Planning Your Trip.

All in all, there are 20 varieties of transport in Hong Kong, from a few old rickshaws and trams to helicopters and jetfoils. Transport will get even more crowded as time goes by, because the Chinese economy next door is opening up rapidly to trade, commerce, and finance, and most of that will be through Hong Kong. Already an additional transit point has been developed over the border; a multilane highway is being built from Hong Kong through to Canton and Macau. But that is another story —the whole new business ballgame with China, which requires another book for itself.

Meeting Places

At the end of 1988 there were some 24,400 hotel rooms available in 65 hotels, ranging from world-class establishments like the Peninsula, Mandarin, and Regent and those belonging to the major chains (Hilton, Sheraton, Holiday Inn, Hyatt Regency, Inter-Continental, Marriott, Ramada, Regal Meridien, and Nikko) to more modest hostelries. By the end of 1989 there should be an additional 4,000 rooms in eight new hotels. Many have ballrooms and most have smaller function meeting rooms. For an overview of Hong Kong meeting, convention, and incentive facilities, contact the **Convention and Incentive Department,** Hong Kong Tourist Association, 35th Floor, Connaught Centre, Central, Hong Kong Island, tel. 5/244–191.

The end of 1988 will see the opening of the **Hong Kong Convention and Exhibition Centre,** a state-of-the-art, completely integrated, 4.4 million-square-foot complex on the Wanchai waterfront. There will be two exhibition halls of 97,000 square feet each, with a main convention hall capable of seating 2,600. The complex, Asia's largest, will house two hotels, a 600-room Grand Hyatt and a 900-room New World, an apartment block, and a 54-story trade-mart/office building. *Hong Kong Convention and Exhibition Centre, Harbour Rd., Wanchai, Hong Kong Island, tel. 5/864–8888.*

Social and Health Clubs

Hong Kong is very much a club town and visitors quite often feel left out, particularly at lunchtime or on weekends. Quite obviously, you will not be able to join a social or sporting club just for your few days here, but there still may be a way to partake by checking on your own memberships before you depart. Most of Hong Kong's private social and sporting clubs have reciprocal arrangements with clubs overseas. For example, membership in the Club Corporation of America, with its more than 200 clubs in the United States, can gain you entrance to the Pacific Club in Central, the Tower Club in Kowloon, or the Marina Club in Aberdeen on the south side of the island for a bit of weekend recreation. The American Club has reciprocal rights with other American Clubs in Asia, the World Trade Centre Club has sister clubs in the United States, and Foreign Correspondents' Club members can use about two dozen press clubs around the world. Many country clubs, private clubs, eating clubs, and cricket, golf, and sailing clubs have reciprocal rights. A little forethought before you depart could make the difference between a lonely and an enjoyable trip. Have your club write ahead and be sure to bring an introductory letter. Here is a list of major clubs with reciprocal facilities. **Royal Hong Kong Jockey Club:** free entry to the members enclosure during racing season, no use of the recreational facilities. **Royal Hong Kong Golf Club:** free greens fees 14 times a year. Other clubs: **Royal Hong Kong Yacht Club, Hong Kong Cricket Club, Kowloon Cricket Club, Hong Kong Football Club, Hong Kong Country Club, Kowloon Club, Hong Kong Club.**

Health clubs are another matter. With the exception of the **Tom Turk Fitness Clubs** (Bond Centre, West Wing, 13th Fl., Queensway, Hong Kong Isl., tel. 5/214–541); and Albion Plaza, 2 Granville Rd., Tsimshatsui, Kowloon, tel. 3/680–022), you must be a member to use a club's facilities. Guests of the Mandarin and Excelsior can use the facilities of the **Spa on the Square** in Exchange Square.

Hotels

More than four million people visited Hong Kong in 1988, a healthy percentage of whom were conducting business of one sort or another. The hotels in Hong Kong realize this and, like the airlines with Business Class, many have created a business oasis within their establishments to pamper their business guests, and most have some sort of "guest recognition program." The **Hyatt-Regency,** for example, has its Regency Club floors while the **Hilton** has special Executive Floors. Recognition at the **Sheraton** is through its Sheraton Club International, at the **Furama Inter-Continental** through its Six Continents Club, and at the **Holiday Inns** through their Insider Club. Some hotels, like the Kowloon Hotel, even have word processing facilities in the room. Have your travel agent or company make it known in advance that you are a businessperson; in Hong Kong, which thrives on commerce, that makes you a VIP.

Timing

Busiest business seasons are January through May and October through early November; October is the top foreign-buying and commercial-show season. But much business works round the clock, except for Chinese New Year. Most banks are open 10 AM to 4 PM, but some open in the evening and even on Sundays for special purposes; there is 24-hour automated banking in many branches. Office hours are more or less the same as in the West, 9 AM–5 or 6 PM, but the shops usually open about 10 AM and stay open until late at night, especially in the tourist and residential areas.

Trade Information

Hong Kong Trade Development Council (Great Eagle Centre, 31st Fl., 23 Harbour Rd., Hong Kong Isl., tel. 5/833–4333. Telex: 73595 CONHK HX; Cable: CONOTRAD HONGKONG). The TDC has 23 overseas offices, including four in the United States and one in the United Kingdom.

Trade Department (Ocean Centre, ground, 1st, 13th, 14th, and 15th floors, 5 Canton Rd., Kowloon, tel. 3/722–2333. Telex: 75126 HX).

Industry Department (Ocean Centre, 14th Fl., 5 Canton Rd., Kowloon; tel. 3/722–2573).

Chambers of Commerce

Hong Kong General Chamber of Commerce (United Centre, 22nd Fl., Queensway, Hong Kong Island, tel. 5/299–229. Telex: 83535 HX; Cable: CHAMBERCOM HONGKONG).

American Chamber of Commerce in Hong Kong (1030 Swire House, Connaught Rd., Hong Kong Island, tel. 5/260–165. Telex: 83664 HX; Cable: AMCHAM HONGKONG).

Federation of H.K. Industries (408 Hankow Centre, 5–15 Hankow Rd., Kowloon, tel. 3/723–0181. Telex: 84652 HKIND HX; Cable: FEDINDUSTR HONGKONG).

Chinese Manufacturers Association (Chinese Manufacturers Assoc. Bldg., 64–66 Connaught Rd., Hong Kong Island, tel. 5/456–166. Telex: 63526 HX; Cable: MAFTS HONGKONG).

Hong Kong Productivity Council (World Commerce Centre, 12th and 13th Fls., 11 Canton Rd., Kowloon, tel. 3/723–5656. Telex: 32842 HX; Cable: PROCENTRE HONGKONG).

The Indian Chamber of Commerce Hong Kong (Hoseinee House, 2nd Fl., 69 Wyndham St., Hong Kong Island, tel. 5/233–877. Telex: 64993 HX; Cable: INDCHAMBER HONGKONG).

The Hong Kong Japanese Chamber of Commerce and Industry (Hennessy Centre, 38th Fl., 500 Hennessy Rd., Hong Kong Island, tel. 5/776–129).

British Chamber of Commerce (Sing Pao Centre, 6th Fl., 8 Queen's Rd., Central, Hong Kong Island, tel. 5/810–8118. Telex: 82759 BRIT HX).

Swedish Chamber of Commerce (3607 Gloucester Tower, Pedder St., Central, Hong Kong Island, tel. 5/250–349. Telex: 85946).

Travel Information

Hong Kong Tourist Association (HKTA) (Connaught Centre, 35th Fl., Hong Kong Island, tel. 5/244–191. Telex: 74720 HX; Cable: LUYU HONGKONG). Eleven overseas offices, including three in the United States and one in the United Kingdom.

Area Travel

Hong Kong is a hub for travel in the area. In fact, it takes longer to drive to Kai Tak Airport and proceed through the facilities than it does to fly to Manila and Taipei. Most Asian countries have a National Tourist Office here. The cost of tickets or holiday packages is cheaper in Asia than in the United States or Europe, and Hong Kong is no exception to the rule. See the classified ads in the *South China Morning Post* for up-to-date listings. The most crowded times to travel in and out of the colony are Chinese New Year, the Easter/Ching Ming holidays, especially when they fall together (*see* Public Holidays in the front of the book), and the year-end. "Crowded" takes on meanings in Hong Kong you would never contemplate elsewhere. Picture 25%–30% of the colony on the move to China or Macau, and you will get the picture.

Useful Tips

Publications Hong Kong is the international publishing center of Asia, not only because of its excellent business environment, but because, with the exception of libel and pornographic regulations, publishers are free to print what they like whether or not the Hong Kong or Chinese governments, or any other government, likes it. In other words, even though Hong Kong is a colony, there is more freedom of the press here than in most independent countries.

Aside from the myriad of guidebooks and picture books on Hong Kong, there are many specialist publications available. Most of the banks and major realty companies, for example, publish economic newsletters for their customers. The Hong Kong Trade Development Council publishes eight product magazines that are on sale in Hong Kong or free to qualified companies. The Asian Sources series has 11 product magazines and one newsletter. Business International has newsletters and studies on China and Asia. Asia Letter also has a series of newsletters on Asia and specific countries. The American Chamber of Commerce publishes books on Hong Kong and China, including *Living in Hong Kong, Doing Business in Hong Kong, Establishing an Office in Hong Kong*, which are available to members and nonmembers. The *Far Eastern Economic Review Yearbook* and the Hong Kong Government *Yearbook* are required reference books; the *Monthly Digest* from the government's Census & Statistics Department may also be useful. *Hong Kong Tax Planning*, as the name implies, is a useful book to cut through all the legalese of Hong Kong's tax codes. The China Phone Book Co. publishes a slew of useful publications on China in addition to their telephone and telex directories.

Newspapers and magazines from all over the world are readily available in Hong Kong. Both the *Asian Wall Street Journal* and the *International Herald Tribune* print international editions in Hong Kong to supplement the two excellent English-language daily newspapers, *The South China Morning Post* and the *Hong Kong Standard*, both of which carry a great deal of international news. The *Far Eastern Economic Review* leads the pack in business publications. *Time* and *Newsweek* both print in Hong Kong and the newsweekly *Asiaweek* is also here.

With satellite feeds on both radio and TV, you will never be starved for information during your stay in Hong Kong.

Accountants It should be little surprise to find that all the big accounting firms—**Arthur Anderson; Arthur Young; Coopers and Lybrand; Deloitte, Haskings & Sells; Ernst & Whinney; Peak Marwick Mitchell; Price Waterhouse**, etc.—have offices here.

Stockbrokers Because of Hong Kong's geographical location, you can play the market 24 hours a day. All the major stockbrokers from all countries are represented in Hong Kong.

Couriers The Post Office runs a **Speedpost** service akin to the overnight express service run by the U.S. Postal Service. Large international couriers, like **DHL, Federal Express, TNT Skypak,** and **Purolator,** all have large operations here.

Hotel "Home Delivery"	If you've been away so long that you're dreaming of hot corned beef sandwiches, call the **Beverly Hills Deli** (tel. 3/698–695 or 5/265–809). For pizza, those staying on Hong Kong Island can call **Marco Polo Pizza** (tel. 5/216–679).
Florists	Use the ones in major hotels. It's easier and they all deliver. Hosts and hostesses here appreciate flowers as gifts, as do their counterparts around the world.
Chocolates	Hong Kong natives have a sweet tooth, too. **See's Candies,** flown fresh from California daily, are available in their outlets in Landmark (Central District), Ocean Terminal (Kowloon), and City-Plaza (Quarry Bay, Hong Kong Island) seven days a week. **Peninsula Chocolates,** from the hotel of the same name, are also sold in the Lucullus outlets and have an excellent reputation.
Telex	Most hotels have telexes and will send messages for guests. All the business centers have them, too. However, if you want to avoid the hotel surcharge or your business is closed, the public telex for sending is through **Cable & Wireless (C&W)**. There are many offices throughout the territory, but the two 24-hour ones are Exchange Square in Central, Hong Kong Island, and Hermès House, Middle Rd. (across the street from the Sheraton), Tsimshatsui, Kowloon. The public C&W facility at the airport is open from 8 AM to 11 PM.
Telephone	You can, of course, make long distance (person-to-person, station-to-station, or direct dial) calls from your hotel or business center. They can also be made from C&W.
Facsimile	In Hong Kong, facsimile (fax, telecopying) has grown by leaps and bounds because local calls, hence local faxes, are free. The Chinese language, which cannot be used on a telex, lends itself to the pictorial. For a public fax service, the Post Office and C&W offer a joint service called "Postfax." Check the **General Post Office** (tel. 5/231–071) to find out which post offices have the service in addition to the main ones. At C&W it is only available at their two main, 24-hour offices.
Photocopying	All hotels and business centers have photocopy machines, as do many stores, particularly stationery stores, scattered throughout the territory. However, for some heavy-duty copying, including oversize pages (architectural drawings) or color reproduction, **Rank Xerox** has Copy Service Centres operating during office hours (New Henry House, 10 Ice House St. and Chung Hing Commercial Bldg., 62–63 Connaught Rd., both in Central District, and Wah Kwong Bldg., 48–66 Hennessy Rd., Wanchai, all on Hong Kong Island). In Kowloon, there is one at 4 Canton Road in Tsimshatsui and another in the Peninsula Centre, Tsimshatsui East.
Local Messengers/ Courier Services	In the posher hotels, deliveries can be arranged through the concierge. Most business centers offer a service, too. However, there is a good chance that both of them will contact **DHL's** local courier service, run simultaneously with their international one. They have numerous **Express Centres** located in major buildings and various Mass Transit Railway Stations. For the one nearest you, call 3/770–1008. They will also pick up from your hotel. The minimum charge is HK$50 for under one kilogram, but of course weight and distance determine price. If the

timing is right at the Express Centre, you should be able to get same-day delivery.

Dry Cleaning   Hotels have dry cleaning services, but if you spill something on your shirt at lunch and want it in a pristine condition for your 3 PM appointment, head for **Martinizing Dry Cleaning** and its one-hour service. The head plant is at 7 Glenealy Road, Central. The other pick-up offices are at Bank of America Tower and World Wide House, both in Central; Causeway Centre, Harbour Road, in Wanchai; and in Harbour City, Canton Road, Tsimshatsui, Kowloon.

The Hong Kong Way of Life: Living with an Uncertain Future

by Donald Wise

A part-time resident of Hong Kong for many years, Donald Wise was based in Africa, the Middle East, and Asia for 26 years as a correspondent for the world's largest-circulation morning papers: the Daily Express *and the* Daily Mirror, *both of London.*

Although tourists might not be aware of it during a brief visit, the question uppermost in everyone's mind is: What will happen to Hong Kong and its people when Britain hands over control of its last major colony to China in 1997?

The governments in both Beijing and London have remained remarkably close-lipped about details of the agreement and the sort of life Hong Kong's (by then) more than six million people can expect when the gold-starred red flag replaces the Union Jack over Government House. Predictably, anyone financially able to do so is making arrangements to emigrate—now or later, if conditions become unpleasant.

The guesstimate is that one in 24 of Hong Kong's 5.5 million citizens is planning to leave. Hong Kong Island was ceded to Britain in 1841, but Britain had actually occupied it since the First Opium War between China and Britain (1839–1841). Some 3.75 square miles (1.4 sq km) of the Kowloon Peninsula and Stonecutters Island were added in 1860 after the Second Opium War (1856–1858). Much later, in 1898, Britain obtained a 99-year lease of the mainland area, New Territories, and another 235 islands, giving Britain a total of 370 square miles (976 sq km).

The Crown Colony is, in reality, a city-state such as Singapore, populated mostly by refugees from China. Many of today's Hong Kong citizens reached the colony by swimming past sharks, being smuggled in so-called "snake boats" for large sums of money or gold, or by sneaking across the border, avoiding police, Gurkha troops, or British squads. The best bet has been to slip past British troops, many of whom served in Berlin, where they were officially encouraged to help East Bloc refugees through the wires and booby traps to reach the West: British troops do not like keeping people out of democratic Hong Kong and its Union Jack brand of justice.

Refugees themselves remember, or have had described to them, what happened in China when Mao Zedong's antiright, anticapitalist Communists took over the country from General Chiang Kai-shek in 1948. There were denunciations of landlords by peasants, with attendant firing squads. Property was confiscated and bank accounts frozen or appropriated. Life was ruled by block leaders, street cadres, secret police, and army troops. But under Mao all (at that time) 650 million Chinese were fed regularly, many for the first time. Despite his merciless methods, he taught them to be proud of their nationality, after living for centuries blackguarded by emperors and empresses, warlords, invading Japanese, and invading Westerners.

Today, Hong Kong Chinese are prouder than ever of their heritage, delighted that their 1.2 billion brothers and sisters ruled by Beijing are well fed and can visit their families outside of

China during holidays. Most Hong Kong Chinese have been to China to see for themselves what goes on there, and have come back prouder than ever of being Chinese. But at the same time, they want little to do with China, and they especially do not want to live there, ruled Beijing-style.

Hong Kong is dependent on China for water, pork, and vegetables, and is worth more to China than to Britain. About 40% of every incoming U.S. dollar is remitted to China. In this curious way the *hongs* (business houses) and the Beijing government are allied against any sudden bursts of democracy being introduced before 1997.

But the freewheeling "good times" are likely to be circumscribed politically, financially, and socially after 1997. The present total of almost four million visitors a year to Hong Kong is likely to slack off, and the supercharged, three-night shore leaves of Western sailors may no longer brighten the lights of Wanchai, the "Suzy Wong" district. The paltry personal income tax (15.5%) and tax-free earnings from unearned income may be readjusted by the Beijing bureaucrats. These could be the last freewheeling years for Hong Kong.

Derek Davies, editor of the prestigious Hong Kong weekly, *The Far Eastern Economic Review*, noted that ever since Britain and China started negotiating the 1997 issue, standards have plummeted in every area of Hong Kong life, both public and private.

Said Davies: "The hugely successful city, which once encapsulated capitalist optimism and confidence, is dwindling into a third-rate place where worries are paramount, the profit motive has been superseded by myopic greed, and men and women of principle feel at odds with the rest of society. The general decline has been most visible in standards of government, while the main reason is obvious: the difficulty of recruiting first-class men and women, even on contractual terms, to serve a dying colonial possession. Those still in harness have lost much of their former sense of mission and service—a trend illustrated by the large number of retired civil servants, still drawing generous pensions, who have taken jobs in the private sector." Many also criticize the lackluster leadership from Government House, which Davies calls the "quackery of lame-duckery."

It appears to an increasing number of onlookers that, while the Hong Kong government has never claimed to be able to guide the economy or influence the policies of businesspeople, it has, until now, been able to hold the ring in which market forces operate and compete most efficiently.

Because almost no Chinese "Belonger" (legal resident) holding a Hong Kong identity card will be eligible for residence or citizenship in the United Kingdom, the fears of the Chinese for the future of their children have been heightened. An estimated 220,000 Hong Kong Chinese are in a position, financially, legally, or physically, to emigrate. Many are already sending their children to school overseas, while others are leaving to get blue, green, gray, or whatever color cards they might need to live in the country of their choice. Older people are going to places such as the Dominican Republic in hopes that, inside two years or so, they will be part of a West Indian quota system that will give them a foothold in the United States earlier than if they started their paperwork in Hong Kong. Others have bought Latin American passports for U.S.$50,000 only to find that the seller did not mention that such documents are valid only for two years. The one thing that would-be emigrants from Hong Kong have in common is that everyone wants to stay in Hong Kong as long as possible or return to Hong Kong and live here as long as living here is tolerable after 1997.

It is getting easier to leave, according to both the Chinese- and English-language press. They report that Canada issued 16,500 visas to Hong Kong immigrants in the first nine months of 1987, up 5,752 over the same period in 1986. The number of working people emmigrating to Australia was estimated at 10,000 in 1987, double that of the previous year. For the United States, the number of immigrants in 1987 was 7,400. A bill was presented in 1988 in the United States Congress which, if passed, would double the number of Hong Kong residents allowed into the country.

The United States, Canada, and Australia seem to be the three favorite countries of Hong Kong emigrants. A few with Indo-Chinese backgrounds go to France. Few opt for Britain. They know that because there are already many West Indians and Asians in Britain, there is little hope that any British politician would champion Hong Kong Chinese immigration —it would be political suicide, even though the prevailing feeling among the electorate is that it was a great pity the Hong Kong Chinese didn't start flooding into Britain ahead of the other Asians and West Indians.

Watching all this, eyes widening at the size of the brain drain, are the government functionaries of London and Beijing. The flood of emigrants was immediately pooh-poohed by the Chinese, who blamed it on British scare tactics. But by year-end 1983, the Hong Kong stock market had plunged by as much as 50%, and the Hong Kong dollar slumped from $5.70 against U.S.$1 in 1981 to $10 against U.S.$1 in 1983. The government intervened, reluctantly, by stabilizing the Hong Kong dollar at $7.80 against U.S.$1. The drain became a torrent.

Both governments are keeping a close watch on the territory's emigration profile. For the moment there is apparently no desire on either side to take action that might be seen as infringing individual freedom of movement, thus making matters worse. The Hong Kong government and the Xinhua News Agency of the Beijing government are each researching the size and strength of the exodus and its impact on life in the colony. It is thought that both sides do not yet feel that the flow of young, educated people has reached panic proportions. According to the Hong Kong *South China Morning Post*, applications are soaring for certificates of "non-criminal" records, which would-be emigrants must send to host countries.

There is little doubt that if hundreds or thousands of young Chinese businesspersons or professionals pack up and move off before the colony is handed over to China, the effect would be catastrophic. The one positive move by both sides has been to go public with concern at what is currently happening. The exodus of talent is no longer seen as simply a British-inspired scare tactic, but as an official fact of life, recognized by both Sir David Wilson, the governor, and leaders of the People's Republic of China.

The Hong Kong police received some 53,500 "non-criminal" record applications in 1987, up 41% over the previous year. But there is no breakout of how these applications were used. Since these certificates are required not only by the police but also by students who want to study abroad, the figures do not provide a totally reliable emigration indicator. Right now, employment in Hong Kong is nearly 100%, so the exodus has not yet sparked further scrutiny.

In February 1988, the British government produced a major policy on Hong Kong, known as a White Paper, which outlined a timetable for political reform in the years leading to 1997. It ruled out any major political changes before 1991, until China promulgates the Basic Law, its constitution for Hong Kong after the takeover. The White Paper confirmed the necessity of directly elected members to the Legislative Council (Legco), an advisory group without veto power, selected by the colonial government. But the White Paper said flatly that there would be no such elections until 1991 and that the elections would then apply only to fewer than one member in five of Legco. The most vociferous local politicians, aiming at the elections of 1988, were dismayed, saddened, and infuriated. The British opposition Labour Party in London kept silent on the issue. After all, the reasoning went, in past years the Hong Kong Chinese made money while the British supplied an efficient administration. Therefore, it was argued, more time was needed before local elections could be held—all in the spirit of evolutionary, rather than revolutionary, change.

The policy of the Hong Kong government is decided by the Executive Council (Exco), made up of heads of government departments and prominent local citizens appointed by the governor who, in turn, is appointed by London. Under a 1984 agreement, Hong Kong will become a Special Administrative Region (SAR) of China for 50 years after 1997. During that time it is to retain its capitalist style while enjoying a high degree of autonomy with a locally elected legislature. How such elections are to be carried out has not been explained.

It means, though, that some local people on the British side of the Anglo-Chinese team helping to formulate the Basic Law are known to have little intention of staying on past 1997. According to Beijing, there will be a "one country, two systems" form of government, a novel idea in itself. In theory, Hong Kong will be able to ease out of its high-octane lifestyle in the first 50 years after the British leave.

Writing in the London magazine, *The Spectator*, William McGurn of the *Asian Wall Street Journal* pointed out that although it did not use the word "democracy," the 1984 accord did promise that the legislature "shall be constituted by elections." He said the concept was sold to the British Parliament and the people of Britain in another White Paper addressing the issue of elections in the years immediately ahead. McGurn wrote that, set against the British foreign secretary's assertion that he never actually promised that elections would be held in 1988, the secretary sounds like a divorce lawyer whose client suddenly decided he does not want to give his wife the house. In short, London and the Hong Kong governor are blamed for knuckling under to pressure from Beijing on a vital issue affecting the territory's future, because the Basic Law governing Hong Kong after 1997 will be in place by 1991. The great fear in Hong Kong is that the Chinese will see to it that the local legislature is powerless.

McGurn wrote: "The Hong Kong outlined in that (1984) accord would be similar to the Hong Kong of today, with the added benefit of representative government, and to that extend the British Foreign Secretary was right when he said that the accord was a 'good deal.' But the meeting at Yalta in February 1945 between Roosevelt and Churchill to discuss the post-war shape of Germany and the size of reparations it should pay, was a good deal, too, with its promises of elections and so forth; the trouble was, no one quite got Eastern Europe spelled out in that agreement and the signs are that we're not going to get the Hong Kong promised in the Joint Declaration of 1984."

No one yet knows whether the Chinese will do their best to make a go of taking back Hong Kong with a minimum of interference, a triumph that would boost not only Hong Kong's financial credibility throughout the world, but might even affect the thinking in Taiwan toward Beijing. Nor do we know whether Beijing bureaucrats are capable of running a city-state whose population by 1997 will be near six million, with complexities and problems unlike those anywhere else in the world. The Communist Party has had its people in Hong Kong since Mao took over in the People's Republic. If its local Cantonese representatives are given any credibility by their Han (northern Chinese) overlords in Beijing, then chances are good that the "homecoming" could be relatively comfortable.

The Xinhua News Agency (NCNA) of the People's Republic is a lot more than it appears to be, certainly more than just a news agency, according to the *South China Morning Post*. In a long study of the colony's communists, it found that since 1949, the NCNA has been Beijing's official representative in Hong Kong, serving as de facto consulate and main channel for news and propaganda. Not only is it Beijing's "mission" to the territory, it is also China's shadow government of Hong Kong. Although it has no diplomatic standing, the NCNA serves as the official contact point between mainland-based commercial and government interests, the Hong Kong government, and the overseas diplomatic community. The ballpark figure for its number of employees is more than 1,000.

NCNA employees are reluctant to speak on the record about their work and refuse all interviews, adding to the shadowy atmosphere surrounding the agency in its Queen's Road East offices. The offices supervise the activities of the Chinese Communist Party (CCP) in the colony. NCNA and CCP staffers are no longer easily identified by their Mao jackets. Today they dress like the rest of the population in fashionable, Western-style clothing. The main duty of all NCNA staffers is to present communism in its best light to the free-living, free-spending people around them. The NCNA now has branch offices in Kowloon and New Territories, and a parallel unit in Macau, which Portugal is handing over Hong Kong–style in 1999.

Han Chinese still outnumber Hong Kong locals in the pecking order of the CCP, probably because Beijing is leery of putting its political apparatus in the hands of the southern Cantonese, despite energetic efforts to recruit more of them into northern organizations. The urbane Chinese leader, Xu Jiatun, talks as easily to Hong Kong politicos as he does to those that matter in Beijing. He runs all communist organizations in Hong Kong and Macau and has done so since 1983. The official name of the CCP's operation in Hong Kong is the Hong Kong-Macau Work Committee (HMWC), which deals in counterintelligence, concentrating on the activities of the Kuomintang (pro-Taiwan groups). Xu Jiatun and his HMWC are themselves monitored by the Special Branch of the Royal Hong Kong Police. Xu Jiatun is so powerful now that he is regarded unofficially as the shadow governor of the colony.

To foreigners living in Hong Kong, there seems none of the heavy ominous undertones of communism one feels in cities such as East Berlin. The NCNA and the HMWC keep to the ground rules by not doing anything to interfere with the British administration—in contrast to the open confrontation of Cultural Revolution days. Most importantly, most Hong Kong Belongers are deeply mistrustful of communism.

The British colony that may, at worst, be turned into a Chinese communist colony in 1997, has been described as the most cosmopolitan place in the world. It consists of a string of beautiful islands and a peninsula from which rise 20 mountain peaks, some more than 1,000 feet above sea level. Two of those peaks rise to 2,700 feet. The colony has neither forest nor pasture land. Of Hong Kong's work force of 2.7 million, only 1.6% are in agriculture or fisheries. Of the remaining, 37.3% work in commercial services and 33.8% in construction.

Other statistics include: the life expectancy is 75, with 33% of deaths due to cancer, mostly of the pharynx; there is one physician for every 1,075 persons; there are 296,111 motorcycles and other vehicles; there are 840 miles (1,345 km) of roads; and there are slightly more than one million primary, secondary, and tertiary students.

At the noonday gun on Hong Kong Island, which is still fired daily, it seems that every one of the city's inhabitants is walking hard and straight at you, carrying ear-splitting transistor radios, pushing their way into jam-packed elevators without allowing passengers to disembark, and never saying "Thank you" or "I'm sorry." Although newspapers make much of the fact that free elections are being held back until 1991, the mood of the average person seems one of apathy and acceptance of the political facts of life. Recent local elections produced only a 30% turnout, perhaps because voters realize that their future will be decided for them. The British cannot and will not fight one billion Chinese on any issue.

There is a lot of money about—even after the crash of the world's stock exchanges in October 1987. The old, wrinkled *amahs* (nursemaids) still manage to pull out great rolls of "yellow" (HK$1,000 notes) at bank counters to play the stock market, while taxi boats, jetfoils, and high-speed ferries rush through the island corridors toward Macau and its round-the-clock gambling casino.

For investors, the low taxation rate is a great attraction: Many of these businesspeople are "overseas Chinese" (those who live abroad) on whose capital Hong Kong's prosperity has largely been built.

The initial impact on Hong Kong visitors is one of incredulity at the lavish display of expensive goods: designer gowns from Paris, Rome, New York, and Tokyo draped in huge store windows; luggage carrying price tags in the five digits; and new cars from Europe selling at more than HK$1 million—all within a few miles of where water buffalos wallow in mud pools.

As this is being written (late 1988), the takeover is slightly more than nine years away. Earlier, this would have been long enough for financial wizards to invest their money in, say, building construction and get their money back from the investment, plus a hefty profit; to invest the money again and then repeat the process twice more, with the capital getting fatter—all within 10 years. But not today. Old hands reckon there is time enough for only one further market surge (or fall) and just possibly a second; but the time frame and the aftermath of October 1987's stock panic leaves little room for maneuvering.

Business owners are putting in just enough money to keep the wheels turning fast enough to generate a profit. The value of plant, equipment, and domestic accommodation has been written down to nothing; antiques, china, and rugs have been sent abroad as investment in the future; and as much money as possible is being transferred (legally) into the currency of the country they have chosen as their future home—all in case of unbearable problems from living under a communist government. The present generation of children will have been educated abroad and have their residence and work permits in their adopted country to fall back on; so will subsequent generations. The final act of people with the foresight and finance to plan ahead will be to take their passports from the bottom drawer of their bedside cabinet and head for the airport, leaving only an empty shell of their former lives behind them. Everyone who can afford to do this today is preparing to do so.

As for the handful of Caucasian expatriates who choose to live here because they find it the most exciting, most beautiful place in the world, they will hang on—prepared, if forced, to leave on short notice. A number of expatriate men who have married Chinese women may have an easier adjustment to living under Chinese rule than others. But these men are the exceptions.

The expatriate community seems to rejuvenate itself every three years or so, when a new batch of people come out on three-year contracts.

With this society of expatriates, sometimes second-rate British, there also comes pomposity and snobbery. It is disturbing to hear and see expatriates from Europe behaving toward local people in a manner that would have been considered outrageous before World War II. This syndrome is brought on partly by their accommodations. Most firms who employ expatriates pay their employees more in rent allowances than they do in salaries, a point often lost on people who come from a modest suburban European home to a luxuriously furnished apartment, complete with servants, swimming pools, and tennis courts. The monthly rent is usually between the equivalent of U.S.$7,000 and U.S.$10,000 (unfurnished).

The bright side of the social scene is that the number of Asians one meets at dinner parties is increasing. Otherwise, such affairs tend to be cliquey: bankers dine with bankers, government workers with same-seniority government workers, and servicemen with other servicemen. Of course, there are a few splendid hostesses who manage to blend all of them successfully.

In public places, tourists will find themselves mostly with other tourists because "expats," as the expatriates call themselves, tend to find the prices too fierce. The young people who live with their families in the plushest accommodations do not necessarily have spending money to match. But they do have an edge, because the wage-earners work for people who prefer to see them channelled through approved relaxation outlets: They can eat and dance at clubs approved by their employers who pay for their membership in places such as the Hong Kong Club, which is as ugly and unwelcoming as an ice-rink cafeteria; the Royal Hong Kong Jockey Club, which has superb food; and the Country Club, where there is good Chinese food and tennis courts. The Americans have their own club, allowing only Americans to become members. The British clubs will take anyone, but even now there is only 10% Chinese membership in the British Hong Kong Club.

Very much down-market on the club list, but much more fun than the others, is the Foreign Correspondents Club, which actually enjoys having new faces at its bar. Almost anyone can enter for a short period, provided the person has some sort of connection with a member. The behavior there can swing from aloofness to the hurly-burly of a Wanchai bar.

Hong Kong, once derided as a cultural desert, is now awash with some of the world's best orchestras, singers, instrumentalists, and dancers. Unfortunately, this does not include pop stars, because they demand such huge sums of money up front that there is no auditorium large enough to house the gigantic audience needed to meet basic expenses. But any other Tokyo-bound artist of note will try and stop over in Hong Kong to play either at the City Hall or the Academy of Performing Arts. There are arts festivals, film festivals, and dance festivals every year; hotels run dinner-theater shows; and the big hongs (business houses) buy books of tickets to give out free to their employees. But invariably there is a noticeable number of empty seats, probably because the bankers and money-men who make it the exciting city that it is turn in early on weekdays. Somewhere there is a stock market open, or a crisis or economic upheaval that will directly affect the local textile, financial, electronic, banking, or rag-trade experts at some inconvenient Hong Kong time. They need their sleep.

Hong Kong has been called the most cosmopolitan, tolerant, and rewarding crossroads for trade, industry, and communications in the world, and so it is. But you have to shape up in quick time when you arrive if you want to survive. Failures are recycled quickly. The head of a trading company may have his desk crammed with party and dinner invitations from everyone who matters and then, when he has had his retirement party, to all intents and purposes he is dead, instantly forgotten. Some great merchants and traders, whose companies have been here since the 19th century, announced that they are moving headquarters elsewhere, and are rapidly moving out of living memories.

You cannot be poor and unsupported in Hong Kong for long, and there are only a handful of homeless people. Where do the poor go? No one really knows, but local sociologists bemoan the fact that young Chinese do not look after their old folk as they once did.

Hong Kong's first visitors were probably boat people of Malaysian-Oceanic origin; they left geometric-shaped graffiti that dates back some 5,000 years. More modern visitors, who continue to arrive, are Vietnamese, fleeing the biting poverty and repression of the Hanoi regime. Among the colony's own swelling Chinese population, there is little sympathy for people who cut into the availability of housing, hospital, and school allocations. Yet these people have been pretty well absorbed into the society. Between 1975 and 1988, 116,187 Vietnamese arrived and another 5,709 were born here. Today there are 9,773 in so-called "closed camps," which are really internment centers, on outlying islands.

But that is not what Hong Kong is about. Look at Cotton Tree Drive in Central at about 5 PM on a sweltering weekday (which is nine months of the year). You will see Rolls-Royces (more per capita than anywhere in the world), Mercedes, BMWs, Jaguars, Lamborghinis, and Maseratis going up the hill at about 21 miles per hour, air-conditioners tearing up their engines. Many live on The Peak, which, in a place where Face means everything, is the only place to live. They would do better in smaller, snappier French cars, but size is the thing.

This is a Texas-minded world—make your first Big One (million dollars) and do not think of retiring for a moment. Stay at the wicket or on the mound and have another go. When your wife complains of feeling frustrated and hemmed-in, put her on a Cathay Pacific flight for the beaches of Malaysia, Thailand, or the Philippines.

Food and Drink in Hong Kong and Macau

by Barry Girling

A food, travel, and entertainment columnist, Barry Girling has lived in Hong Kong since 1977.

If you are coming to Hong Kong for the first time, there are certain misconceptions that you must leave at home. First, Hong Kong doesn't just have some of the better Chinese food in the world; it has the best.

Such a statement may not find immediate recognition in Taiwan or the People's Republic of China, but the proof of the pudding is in the eating, as they say in the West, and those Taiwanese and mainland Chinese who can afford it come to Hong Kong to eat. It is historical fact that chefs were brought from Canton to Peking to serve in the Chinese emperors' kitchens, and that for many centuries the Cantonese were acknowledged as the Middle Kingdom's finest cooks.

There is an old Chinese maxim that tells listeners where to find the prettiest girls, where to get married, where to die, where to eat, and so forth; the answer to "where to eat" is Canton (now called Guangzhou in the approved official romanization of Chinese names).

Hong Kong's 5.5 million-plus population is 98% Chinese, and the vast majority of that number are Cantonese (that includes a significant group of Chiu Chow people, whose families originated around the port city of Swatow). Food is a subject of overriding importance to the Cantonese, and it can be claimed of them as it is of the French, that they live to eat rather than eat to live. Find out how true that statement is on a culinary tour of Hong Kong.

There's no such thing as a fortune cookie in a Hong Kong restaurant; it was the overseas Chinese who came up with that novelty. Chop suey was invented overseas, too. The exact origin is disputed: Some people say it began on the California gold fields; others give credit (or blame) to Australian gold miners.

The Cantonese made an art out of a necessity, and, during times of hardship, used every part of an animal, fish, or vegetable. Some dishes on a typical Hong Kong menu will sound strange, even unappetizing—goose webs, for example, or cockerels' testicles, cows' innards, snakes (in season), pigs' shanks, and other things that may not be served at McDonald's. But why not succumb to new taste experiences? Who scorns the French for eating snails and frogs, or the Japanese for eating raw fish, or the Scots for stuffing mince in a sheep's stomach lining?

Visit a daytime dim-sum palace. Served from before dawn to around 5 or 6 PM, the Cantonese daytime snacks of dim sum are miniature works of art. There are about 2,000 types in the Cantonese repertoire. Most dim-sum restaurants prepare 100 varieties daily. Generally served steaming in bamboo baskets, the buns, crepes, and cakes are among the world's finest hors d'oeuvres. Many are works of culinary engineering—such as a soup with prawns served in a translucent rice pastry shell, or a thousand-layer cake, or the ubiquitous spring roll.

There are hundreds of dim-sum restaurants. The Hong Kong Tourist Association (HKTA) publishes a comprehensive listing of some of the better ones that welcome tourists. The publication also provides color illustrations of the main dim-sum favorites. Many of the top-rated Chinese restaurants in hotels, and some of the better restaurants, provide (somewhat incongruously) elegant settings for lunchtime dim sum—with bilingual check sheets, waiter service, and private tables. Such class costs about HK$8 or more per basket. History-minded snackers will prefer, preferably in the company of Cantonese colleagues, to visit the culinary shrine of the **Luk Yu Teahouse** in Central (24 Stanley St.).

Luk Yu is more than a restaurant. It is one of Hong Kong's few historical monuments. It's fitting that a restaurant should be an unofficially preserved monument in this culinary capital of the world. It opened in the early 20th century as a wood-beamed, black-fanned, brass-edged place for Chinese gentlemen to partake of tea, dim sum, and gossip. When it was forced to relocate over a decade ago, everything was kept intact —marble-back chairs, floor spitoons, kettle warmers, brass coat hooks, lock-up liquor cabinets for regular patrons, and a Sikh doorman. Despite the modern air-conditioning, fans still decorate a plain ceiling that looks down on elaborately framed scrolls, carved-wood booth partitions, and colored glass panels. The ancient wood staircase still creaks as Hong Kong's gentlemen ascend to the upper floors to discuss the territory's government and business.

Modernity has brought the English language, bilingual menus (but not for the individually served dim sum items), and some good manners to Luk Yu. And so the adventurous tourist will seek out daytime dim-sum palaces where such modern affectations do not exist—as in the authentic teahouses of Mongkok, where local customers still "walk the bird" at dawn (the Chinese tradition—considered very "masculine"—of taking one's caged bird out for a morning stroll with its friends).

Birds are also to be eaten, of course. As far as the Cantonese are concerned, anything that "keeps its back to heaven" is fit for cooking. Only cannibals won't be satisfied in Hong Kong. Bird-tasting experiences in Hong Kong should include a feast of quails; smooth, salted chicken; sweet roasted chicken in lemon sauce; and minced pigeon served in lettuce leaf "bowls" (that are rolled up with a plum sauce "adhesive"). Pigeons in dozens of different forms can best be enjoyed in New Territories, around the new city of Shatin.

Fish can be enjoyed anywhere. Hong Kong is a major port with numerous fishing communities—something easily forgotten by the city-centered visitor. Go to the islands, to **Lamma** especially, for fine seafood feasts. Or take the bus and ferry trip to **Lyemun,** where you can choose your dinner from the massive fish tanks, haggle over its price, and take it into any restaurant for cooking and an al fresco feast.

At **Causeway Bay,** a small fleet of sampans turns dining out into a memorable experience. Your private floating restaurant table bobs past other craft selling shellfish, fresh fruit and vegetables, beer and spirits. There is even a floating Cantonese Opera minitroupe that can be hired to serenade your open-air floating meal.

The prime floating experience is, of course, the **Jumbo restaurant** at Aberdeen. It is moored to another floating home of seafood and gaudy multicolored carvings and murals that are a sight worth seeing. The Jumbo, a 2,000-seat three-decker, is a marvel of outrageous ostentatiousness.

It's time to note that there is no such thing as "Chinese" cooking in China. Every good "Chinese" cook has his (or sometimes her) own repertoire that will reflect his clan's origin. Most Hong Kong restaurants are Cantonese. Others concentrate on Pekingese or northern styles, Shanghai specialties, or the other regional styles of Szechuan or Chiu Chow cooking. There are a few spots that offer Hakka-style food, some Mongolian specialty restaurants (featuring hot pots), and even a Taiwanese cafe on Food Street.

Food Street, in Causeway Bay, is a good place for a first-timer to start discovering the variety of food available in Hong Kong. There are now two covered and fountained arcades of relatively well-managed restaurants to suit most tastes and budgets. All around them, in an area that's generally named after the "Daimaru" department store, are literally hundreds of other cafes and restaurants.

Other favored eating places are found in **Wanchai,** once the fictional home for "Suzie Wong" and now a struggling nightlife area that has run out of sailors. Restaurants have appeared instead, alongside the topless bars, hostess-filled nightclubs, and dance halls that are expensive ways to get a drink in Hong Kong.

In "old" **Tsimshatsui,** on both sides of Nathan Road, from the Peninsula Hotel up to the Jordan Road junction, there is another batch of good, long-established restaurants. And Tsimshatsui East has skyscrapers bursting with a wide variety of eating spots—from grand Cantonese restaurants to cheerful little cafes. There, as everywhere, you'll find not only Cantonese fare but Korean barbecues, Singaporean satays, Peking duck, Shanghainese breads and eel dishes, fine Western cuisine—and junk food, of course.

The **Harbour City** complex, along Canton Road, has many fine spots tucked into shopping arcades or courtyards. **Central,** once morguelike at night, is now a bustling dining district with a warren of trendy bistros and good Indian restaurants up the hillside lanes, on and off Wyndham Street and Lan Kwai Fong. All are much favored by resident expatriates.

Then there are the hotels, culinary competitors full of stylish salons—so stylish it's now hard to find a simple, old-fashioned coffee shop. Travel away from downtown districts and you find more temptations. Every housing estate and community center now boasts at least one brass-and-chrome home of good Cantonese cuisine, often as chic as it is wholesome.

Deciding what and where to eat can be a headache in Hong Kong. There is an embarrassment of riches. This guidebook's restaurant listings will help. Once in Hong Kong, buy the HKTA's *Visitor's Guide to Chinese Food in Hong Kong*. It costs HK$10 and is a useful introduction to Chinese regional cuisines, chopstick wielding, dim-sum selecting, and other topics that can confuse a novice.

Foodwise, it helps to think of China as a Europe with a difference. As in Europe, there are obvious culinary variations between the cold-wintered northern regions (the Pekingese/ Mongolian cuisine) and the temperate or semitropical southern climes (where Szechuan's chilied spiciness seems natural). The difference is that the various Chinese regions have been practicing cooking as a fine art for quite a few centuries longer than their European counterparts.

In simple terms, the Northern or Peking cuisine is designed to fill and warm—noodles, dumplings, and breads of various types are more evident than rice. Mongolian or Manchurian hot pots (a sort of fondue-cum-barbecue) are specialties, and firm flavors (garlic, ginger, leek, etc.) are popular. Desserts, of little interest to Cantonese, are heavy and sweet. Feasts have long been favored in the north, and not just by emperors composing week-long banquets with elaborate centerpieces such as Peking duck (a three-course marvel of skin slices, sautéed meat, a rich soup of duck bones, and Tien Tsin cabbage). Beggar's chicken, about which you'll hear varying legendary origins, is another culinary ceremony, in which a stuffed, seasoned, lotus-leaf-wrapped, and clay-baked bird releases heavenly aromas when its clay is cracked open.

Farther south, the Shanghai region (including Hangzhou) developed tastes similar to Peking's but with an oilier, sweeter style that favored preserved meats, fish, and vegetables. In Hong Kong, the Shanghainese cafes are generally just that—unostentatious cafes with massive "buffet" displays of preserved or fresh snacks that are popular with latenighters.

The phenomenal development of a middle class in Hong Kong in recent years has prompted the appearance of grander, glitzier restaurants, for Shanghainese and all other major regional cuisines. Those run by the Maxim's group are always reliable, moderately priced, and welcoming to visitors.

The territory's Chiu Chow restaurants also come alive late at night—especially in the Chiu Chow-populated areas of the Western District (on Hong Kong Island) or in parts of western Kowloon. As with Shanghainese and Cantonese cuisine, the Chiu Chow repertoire emphasizes its homeland's marine traditions, especially for shellfish. The exotic-sounding "bird's nest" is the great Chiu Chow delicacy. It's the refined, congealed saliva of nest-building swallows (mainly gathered from Gulf of Siam cliff-face nests). Although it may sound terrible, it is often exquisitely flavored. The dish is also deemed to be an aphrodisiac, as are many of China's most expensive luxury food items. That's why a visit to a Chinese department store should include a shocked glance at the "medicine" counter's natural foods. The prices of top-grade bird's nest, shark's fins, deer horns, ginseng roots, and other time-tested fortifications are staggering. The laws of supply and demand are very apparent on the price tags.

The roughest, simplest fare can appear to be that of the Szechuan region. At first tasting, the fiery peppercorned dishes, akin to both Thai and Indian cuisines, can be tongue-searing. After a while, when the taste buds have blossomed again, the subtleties of Szechuan spices will be apparent—particularly in the classic smoked duck specialty, where camphor wood chips and red tea leaves add magical tinges to a finely seasoned, day-long-marinated duck.

Other regional variations (such as those of Hunan or the Hakka people) are not as distinctive as the major regional cuisines and are rarely found in Hong Kong. But there are a host of alternates for any visitor who wants a taste of adventure.

Chinese-influenced Asian cuisines are well represented. Even before the exodus of ethnic Chinese from Vietnam, that nation's exciting blend of native, French, and Chinese cooking styles was popular in Hong Kong. Now there are many cafes and a few smart restaurants specializing in prawns on sugar cane, mint-leaved meals, Vietnamese-style (labeled "VN") salamis, omelets, and fondues. Look, too, for Burmese restaurants.

The most ubiquitous Asian cuisine is the multiethnic "Malaysian," a budget diner's culinary United Nations that includes native Malay, Indian, and Straits Chinese dishes, as well as "European" meals and the Sino-Malay culinary cross-culture of the *nonya* cooking (developed by Malay wives to satisfy Chinese spouses).

Indian restaurants are also popular, and not just with Hong Kong's population of immigrants from the subcontinent. Usually the Indian kitchens concentrate on the northern Moghul styles of cooking, with reliable tandoori dishes. Vegetarians also find pleasures at Indian cafes. Thailand has not been forgotten, and the territory sports more than 24 spicy Thai restaurants.

Northeast Asia is also well represented. Some observers claim that Hong Kong has some of the world's finest Japanese restaurants, which thrive on local seafood catches and still tempt big spenders with their imports of the highly prized Kobe or Matsukaya beef (marbled slices of fine flavor produced by beer-massaged and pampered steers). Smaller spenders welcome the many local Korean cafes, whose inexpensive *bulgogi* (barbecues) provide that country's distinctive, garlicky, marinated meats and the minibuffet of preserved kimchee selections.

Then there's Indonesia, which has given Hong Kong another host of inexpensive, nourishing cafes. From Europe, there is a culinary wonderland of fine French restaurants (mostly in the top hotels), British pubs, German wining-and-dining havens, deli delights, and a sprinkling of delightfully offbeat eating experiences—from Dutch-Flemish to Austrian, Spanish-Filipino, and Californian.

Although the Cantonese are the world's finest cooks, they are among the least polite waiters and waitresses in the world. The Cantonese are proud, some say arrogant, and their dialect has a belligerent tone and abruptness that translates poorly in English. Don't expect smiles or obsequiousness: Hong Kong isn't Bangkok or Manila. It's friendly in its own abrupt way, and it's certainly efficient, and if you meet smiles as well, count yourself lucky. And give the extra percentage on the tip that the pleasant waiter deserves.

Don't tip at local corner cafes or the few remaining roadside food stalls, since it's not expected. And wherever you eat, at the top or lower ends of the culinary scale, always check prices beforehand, especially for fresh fish, which is now a luxury in Hong Kong. "Seasonal" prices apply to many dishes and can be steep. And note that there are various categories of prized Chinese delicacies on menus—shark's fin, abalone, bird's nest, and bamboo fungus, for example—which can cost an emperor's ransom. Although few Hong Kong restaurants set out to rip off tourists (certainly not those that are sign-bearing members of the HKTA), waiters will of course try to "sell up."

Also, don't settle for the safe standbys for tourists. Sweet and sour pork, chop suey, and fried rice can be marvelous in Hong Kong. But the best dishes are off the menu, on table cards, written in Chinese, advertising seasonal specialties. Ask for translations, ask for interesting recommendations, try new items—show that you are adventurous and the captains will respond, giving you the respect and fine dishes you deserve.

A Shopper's Paradise

by Patricia Davis

A freelance writer based in Hong Kong, Trish Davis specializes in the arts and consumer affairs. Her shopping columns appear regularly and her background includes extensive experience with women's magazines and newspapers.

Whatever your reason for coming to Hong Kong, and whether or not you are a shopper by nature, it is very unlikely that you will leave the place without having bought *something*. Indeed, there's a roaring trade in bargain-priced luggage because so many visitors run out of space in the suitcases they arrived with. Even nonshoppers get tempted to part with their money—and some have admitted to actually enjoying the experience.

Although the thought of crowded streets, mind-boggling choices, and endless haggling can be daunting, there is no place more conducive to big-time spending than Hong Kong! The variety of goods is astonishing: everything from international designer products to intriguing treasures and handicrafts from all over Asia. Just as astonishing is the fantastic choice of places to shop, which range from sophisticated boutique-lined malls to open-air markets and shadowy alleyways.

There are several good reasons why Hong Kong is such an extraordinary shopping Mecca. The first is its status as a free port, whereby everything, other than alcohol, tobacco, perfumes, cosmetics, cars, and some petroleum products, comes in without import duty. The second is the fact that Hong Kong has a skilled and still relatively inexpensive labor force, so goods made here are considerably cheaper than they will be by the time they reach shop shelves anywhere else in the world. The third factor is the highly competitive nature of the retail business—the result of a local policy of free trade, which encourages everyone to try to undercut his neighbor. To this end, most shops, with the exception of those in the Western and Central districts, stay open until 10 PM. Shops are also humming on Sundays and on all holidays apart from Chinese New Year, which falls either in the last two weeks of January or during the first two of February, when everything closes for three days.

There's a saying among expatriate residents that nothing in Hong Kong is as you expect it, and it is certainly true where shopping is concerned! Hong Kong cannot be compared to any other international shopping center—Paris, Milan, London, or New York—and you will be disappointed if you try. The only practical comparisons worth making are those on your calculator.

So what's so different about Hong Kong? For a start, consider the geography of the place. It is very small, and very heavily populated. It has had to grow upward and downward rather than outward, which means that there are shops and small businesses in all sorts of unexpected places. You'll find a trendy fashion designer tucked away on the third floor of a scruffy alleyway building, a picture framer operating out of the basement of a lighting shop, a tailor snipping and stitching in the back room of a shoe shop. Many of the buildings will appear dingy and dirty, and you will be convinced that no self-respecting business can be carried on there. But it can and it is.

And these are the places where Hong Kong residents do much of their shopping. Also disconcerting for people who come expecting to find the streets lined with bargains, is the discovery that prices for the same goods vary from sky-high to rock-bottom within a 100-yard stretch of shops. But this is the land of free trade. And it is why shopping around and sticking to reputable establishments are prerequisites to any successful purchase, particularly if it is an expensive one.

By reputable establishments we mean ones that have been recommended by a friend who lives or shops regularly in Hong Kong, by this guide, or by the Hong Kong Tourist Association via its invaluable booklet *The Official Guide to Shopping, Eating Out and Services in Hong Kong,* or their leaflets on fur and *Factory Outlets in Hong Kong (Ready-to-Wear & Jewelry).* You have a better chance of getting a good buy if you are a friend of a valued customer, or if there is the risk of a complaint being lodged with the HKTA.

All shops bearing the HKTA's red junk logo in their window are supposed to provide good value for money, accurate representation of products sold, and prompt rectification of justified complaints, but if you have problems ring the HKTA at 5/244–191. For complaints about non-HKTA shops ring the Consumer Council (5/200–511).

The law of the jungle is alive and well in Hong Kong, so be prepared for lots of shoving and pushing on the sidewalks, little respect for taxi queues, a limited amount in the way of gallantry, and an overwhelming urge on the part of sales staff to sell you something, no matter what!

Contrary to popular belief, not everyone is English speaking. In the main tourist shopping areas you can probably count on most shop staff speaking some English—but do not assume that they understand all you say, even if they nod their heads confidently. Ridiculous things sometimes happen, as it did to the lady who inquired about the type of leather in which a bag was made and was presented with a tin of saddle soap! But don't get cross if communications get muddled. Displays of anger and raised voices do not impress the Chinese. In their eyes you will have lost respect and they will probably become less, rather than more, helpful.

Many of the taxi drivers' English is limited, too, and so it can make life easier if you get your destination written down in Chinese by the hotel concierge before you set off. Some taxis now carry a radio microphone that lets you speak to their headquarters where your instructions will be translated.

Once on the right road, however, shopping around and bargaining are your golden rules. The pressure from sales staff can sometimes be exasperating. If you are just browsing, make it very clear that is what you are doing. Don't be pushed into a big purchase. Make a note of the details of the item(s) and prices on the shop's business card so you know where to return. Always ask about discounts—sizable ones for multiple purchases. You should be able to get a discount just about everywhere except in Japanese department stores, the China product stores, and some of the larger boutiques which sell on a fixed price basis.

When other shops try to convince you that everything is fixed price, don't believe them. You should get at least 10%, and more likely 40%, from jewelers and furriers.

Equally, do not necessarily believe a salesman when he assures you that his price is his "very best" unless you have done enough shopping around to know that he is offering you a good deal. Never be bashful to ask for a discount. It is the accepted and expected way of conducting business all over Asia.

Your success in negotiating may be greater if the shop is not full. A salesman or woman is less likely to be beaten down if there is a large audience of other shoppers.

After checking out the prices in several different shops, you should get a good idea of what you should have to pay. Don't imagine that you will get the very best price (you won't know what it is, anyway); these are generally given only to local Chinese customers. Your best bet is to compare the price with what you might have to pay for such an item back home.

If you are planning to shop in markets, alleys, or market stalls, it's best not to go very dressed up, or to carry only large denomination notes or big-figure traveler's checks. This will not help your bargaining position, and will just serve to highlight the fact that you are a rich tourist able to pay at least three times the fair price!

When you are shopping in these places make sure you inspect the goods you buy very carefully. Many of them are "imperfects" that didn't make it through quality control; in other words, they are seconds. Look closely at lengths of fabric; they may have faults. When you buy clothing, inspect the actual item handed to you. You may have chosen it on the strength of a sample hanging up, but what you are given could be different. It may not be the same size, it could have more serious faults such as a broken zipper, loopy stitching, print out of register, stripes that don't match at the seams, or even a hole.

At the other end of the scale, if you are intending to shop for something important like jewelry or a fur coat, it can work in your favor to dress smartly. Sounds superficial, and it is. But it is amazing how much more seriously you are taken if you look the part.

If you do not know much about the commodity you are buying, do not hesitate to ask the salesperson to explain or show you the difference between, say, a HK$30,000 diamond and a HK$10,000 one of the same size, or the difference between the two mink coats that look similar to you but carry vastly different price tags. Any reputable dealer in these specialist items should be happy to show you what you are getting for the extra money, and how it compares to the less expensive item. The understanding of such factors can go a long way to helping you to make up your mind about which is really the better buy.

Having satisfied yourself that you really want the item and have struck the right price for it, it is time for the exchange of paper. A wad of cash, preferably, from you. (Although credit cards and traveler's checks are widely accepted, best prices are offered for cash purchases.) An appropriate guarantee and a fully-itemized receipt should be forthcoming from the shop for any major purchase. Such details as the model number and serial number of manufactured goods like cameras, audiovisual or electronic equipment, or the description of gems and precious metal content in jewelry and watches, should be noted down.

Check that your purchase is covered by the right kind of guarantee; local guarantees that are valid for 12 months in Hong Kong only, or local retailer guarantees, will not be much good to overseas visitors on a short shopping spree. Make sure you get a worldwide/international guarantee that carries the name or logo of the relevant sole agent in Hong Kong and that there is a service center in your home town or country. And if you are having something shipped home for you (many shops are geared up for this) make sure that the insurance covers not only loss, but also damage, in transit.

You may be reading this before leaving for Hong Kong, in which case you still have time to do a bit of advance homework. If furniture or carpets are on your shopping list, make a note of the measurements of the area into which it is supposed to fit. Likewise, if friends and relatives (and they start coming out of the woodwork when they hear you are off to Hong Kong) have asked you to pick up some bargain clothes for them, bring details of their measurements. Just a bit of forethought can prevent the frustration of not being sure if your purchase is the right size, and the disappointment of discovering you've brought home the wrong size. It is also worth checking out the prices of big items available at home, so you will know just how much of a savings you may or may not be making by buying in Hong Kong. Don't forget, too, that shipping costs and import duties may have to be added onto the price, and that the total may add up to nearly the same as what you'd pay at home, plus twice the hassle.

So much for the nuts and bolts. But forewarned is forearmed which, we hope, will make the whole experience of shopping in Hong Kong all the more fun. Because fun it certainly is. Whether you are drifting about in the comfort of the air-conditioned shopping malls, exploring the factory outlets of Hung Hom, or poking about in the alleys and back streets, you are getting a look at the life and guts of Hong Kong. It's as much a cultural experience as a shopping expedition. In a way, that can be the most unexpected bargain of your whole trip.

3 Essential Information

Arriving and Departing

Arrivals Efficiency is the word at the Hong Kong International Airport. Except for peak periods, you should locate your luggage and clear customs and immigration in less than 45 minutes.

There are free carts in the baggage area that you can wheel straight through to the exits marked Groups, Hotel Cars, Greeting Area, and Transportation Terminal (for taxis and buses into town). There are also airport porters available to help you, for HK$2 per piece of luggage.

The HKTA has an **Information Counter** just outside the customs hall where you can pick up free visitor publications and make inquiries. The **Hong Kong Hotels Association (HKHA)** runs a reservations service there, too. Both desks are open daily from 8 AM to 10:30 PM. Banks and currency exchange counters are also in this area.

There is often a long line for taxis, so if you're staying at a hotel, it's best to follow the signs to the area where the hotel limousines wait. If you do take a taxi, expect to pay HK$20 to HK$25 for a Kowloon destination and up to HK$55 for a Hong Kong Island destination, inclusive of a HK$20 fee for the Cross-Harbour Tunnel.

A fast and efficient way to get to and from the airport is to use the **Airbus** (tel. 3/745–4466), which runs every 15 minutes from 7 AM to 11:20 PM. Route A1 (HK$5) runs through the Kowloon tourist area, serving the Ambassador, Empress, Grand, Holiday Inn Golden Mile, Hong Kong, Hyatt Regency, Imperial, International, Kowloon, Miramar, New World, Park, Peninsula, Regent, Shangri-La, and Sheraton hotels, plus the YMCA, Chungking Mansions, and the Star Ferry. Routes A2 and A3 (HK$7) go to Hong Kong Island. A2 serves the Harbour View International House, Furama, Hilton, Mandarin, and Victoria hotels. A3 serves the Causeway Bay hotels—Caravelle, Excelsior, Lee Gardens, and Park Lane Radisson.

Departures To get to the airport, you can either order a hotel car in advance, take a taxi, or take the efficient Airbus that stops at most hotels (*see* Arrivals). A hotel car costs HK$90 to HK$155 from Hong Kong Island, and HK$50 to HK$195 from Kowloon.

At the airport, the departure tax is HK$100 (HK$60 for children under 11). This is collected at the airline check-in counters, though some travel agents will collect it when you buy your tickets. No flight-boarding announcements are made, so check developments on the arrivals and departures boards.

Luggage Check There is a place to check your luggage in the departure hall. The charge is HK$15 per piece per day for the first four days, and HK$25 per day thereafter.

Phone Calls Overseas phone calls can be made from the **Cable and Wireless (C&W)** office in the departure or transit halls.

Important Addresses and Numbers

Tourist Information **Information centers** are just beyond customs at the Hong Kong International Airport; on the Star Ferry Concourse in Kowloon, at Shop G8, ground floor, Empire Centre (68 Mody Rd., Tsimshatsui East, Kowloon), and in the foyer of the HKTA's main office at the Connaught Centre, Central District, Hong Kong Island. These centers stock in-depth fact sheets on specific areas, and a free shopping guide. They also have a monthly official guidebook for HK$10, which is available for free at the hotels.

Consulates and Commissions **U.S. Consulate** (26 Garden Rd., Hong Kong Island, tel. 5/239–011).

U.K. Commission (Overseas Visa Section, Hong Kong Immigration Dept., Upper Basement, Mirror Tower, 61 Mody Road, Tsimshatsui East, Kowloon, tel. 3/733–3111).

Canadian Commission (Tower 1, Exchange Sq., 11th–14th Floors, Connaught Pl., Hong Kong Island, tel. 5/810–4321).

Emergencies **Police, fire,** or **ambulance** (tel. 999).

Royal Hong Kong Police Visitor Hot Line (tel. 5/277–177). English-speaking policemen wear a red shoulder tab.

Doctors Hotels have a list of accredited doctors and can arrange for a doctor to visit your hotel room. Otherwise, consult the nearest government hospital. Check the Government section of the telephone directory under Medicine and Health Department for a list. The main ones are the **Queen Mary Hospital,** the **Queen Elizabeth Hospital,** the **British Military Hospital,** the **Tang Shiu Kin Hospital,** and the **Princess Margaret Hospital.** The fee for an office consultation can run from HK$120 to HK$350.

Special Phone Numbers **General Post Office** (tel. 5/231–071).

Taxi Complaints (tel. 5/277–177).

Time and Weather (tel. 1152).

Staying in Touch

Telephones
Local Calls Hong Kong is divided into three area codes: 5 for Hong Kong Island, 3 for Kowloon, and 0 for New Territories. If you are dialing within an area, you do not need to use the code. Local calls are free. For pay phones, use a HK$1 coin.

Although there are a growing number of pay phones, the tradition is to pop into any store and ask to use the telephone. Many small stores keep their telephone on the counter facing the street, no doubt hoping your eyes will browse while your ear and mouth are occupied.

Local Information Dial 108 for directory assistance. The operators usually speak English, but be prepared to spell out names. If a number is constantly busy and you think it might be out of order, call 109 and the operator will check the line.

International Many hotels offer direct dial, as do many business centers, but always with a hefty surcharge. Call 013 for international inquiries and for assistance with direct dialing. Call 010 for operator-assisted calls to most countries, including the United States, Canada, and the United Kingdom. Dial 011 for international conference calls or outgoing collect calls.

Mail
Postal Rates Postcards and letters under 10 grams for North America or Europe cost HK$1.80, and HK$.90 for each additional gram. Aerograms are HK$1.40.

Receiving Mail The General Post Office is speedy and efficient, with deliveries twice daily, six days a week, and overnight delivery in the main business areas.

Travelers can receive mail at the **American Express** office (16–18 Queen's Rd. Central, Basement, New World Bldg., Central, tel. 5/843–1888) Monday through Friday 9 AM–5 PM.

Getting Around

There are probably more kinds of transportation in Hong Kong than anywhere else in the world. Hong Kong is a series of inter-linked islands, plus a chunk of the Chinese mainland. Ferries, a subway system, and tunnels connect Hong Kong Island with the Kowloon peninsula and the Outer Islands. There are also excellent bus services throughout Hong Kong Island, Kowloon, and New Territories, and a number of routes linking the two sides of the harbor. On Hong Kong Island, there are two kinds of trams, a street-level tram running across the north shore of the island, and the Peak Tram, which is a funicular railway traveling up Victoria Peak, the mountain that dominates the central part of the island. Helpful in using this system effectively is the leaflet *Places of Public Interest by Public Transport,* published by the HKTA.

Walking is the easiest and most rewarding way to explore the built-up districts of Hong Kong Island and Kowloon. For trips around the island, into New Territories, and to the smaller, more remote islands you will need to travel by a combination of taxi, bus, tram, underground Mass Transit Railway (MTR), and various ferries. The harbor, that living, breathing focus of Hong Kong's energies, can be fully appreciated only by boat— on the Star Ferry, by organized tour on a *junk* (a type of Chinese boat), or aboard a two-masted brigantine.

By Subway The **Mass Transit Railway** (MTR) is a splendid, air-conditioned subway that links Hong Kong Island to the shopping area of Tsimshatsui and outward to parts of New Territories. Trains are frequent, safe, and easy to use (there are only three lines). Station entrances are marked with a simple line symbol resembling a man with arms and legs outstretched. There are clearly marked ticket machines inside the station that accept exact change. Change is available at the HK$1 and HK$2 machines or at the Hang Seng Bank counters, also inside the stations. The ticket machines issue plastic tickets with a magnetic strip through them. Tickets are the size of credit cards and give you access to the system through an electronic gate. Fares range from HK$2.50 to HK$6 and there is a special **Tourist Ticket** for HK$15, which can save you money.

By Taxi Taxis are easy to spot in Hong Kong because they are usually red and have a roof-sign saying "TAXI" that lights up when the taxi is available. They are obliged by law to have working meters. Fares in the urban areas start at HK$5.50 and go up by HK$.70 per 0.25 kilometer. There is a surcharge of HK$2 per large piece of baggage and a HK$20 surcharge for crossing the harbor through Cross-Harbour Tunnel. The Aberdeen and Lion Rock tunnels carry surcharges of HK$3. These surcharges are shown on a small sign on the dashboard. Most people give a small tip, either by leaving the odd change or from HK$0.50 to HK$1 for a large fare. Taxis are usually reliable in

Hong Kong, but if you have a complaint—about overcharging, for example—there is a special hot line (tel. 5/277-177). Be sure to have the taxi license number, which is usually displayed somewhere on the dashboard.

It is difficult to find taxis from 4 to 7 PM. Apart from these times, and on rainy days, there is seldom a shortage of taxis. If a taxi does not stop for you, check to see if you're in a no-stopping zone, identified by a yellow line along the curb of the main road. Most taxi drivers speak some English, but to avoid problems, get someone at your hotel to write out your destination in Chinese.

Outside the urban areas, in New Territories, taxis are mainly green and gray. They cost less than urban red taxis, with fares starting at HK$4.50 for the first two kilometers (1.2 mi), then HK$.90 per 400 meters (roughly, 1/5 mi). The boundary areas dividing urban taxis from rural taxis are near the New Clearwater Bay Road; Sek Kong north of the Chinese University; Shum Cheng; and the "10-mile" stone on Castle Peak Road. Urban taxis may travel into rural zones, but rural taxis must not cross into the urban zones. There are no interchange facilities for these taxis, so you are advised not to try to reach the urban area using a green taxi.

Many taxis are radio-controlled. When you call for one, you should expect to pay both for your ride and for the pick-up.

By Minibus Also known as Public Light Buses, these 14-seat yellow vehicles with single red stripes rush all over Hong Kong. They are quicker and slightly more expensive than ordinary buses, and stop almost anywhere on request. Their destination is written on the front, but the English-language characters are small. Wave the minibus down when you see the one you want. Since fares are adjusted throughout the journey, you could pay as little as HK$1 or as much as HK$5, according to time and place. Visitors who want to travel from Central to Causeway Bay for shopping should look for the minibus marked "Daimaru," the name of a big store in Causeway Bay.

By Maxicab These are the same as minibuses but have single green stripes and run fixed routes. They go from beside the car park at the Star Ferry, Hong Kong side, to Mid-levels and Ocean Park; and from HMS Tamar (just beyond City Hall at Star Ferry) they run to Victoria Peak. Fares begin at HK$3. The most popular route goes from Star Ferry Kowloon to Tsimshatsui East for HK$1.

By Tram All visitors should take a street tram, at least once. Take your camera and head for the upper deck. The trams run along Hong Kong Island's north shore from Kennedy Town in the west, all the way through Central, Wanchai, Causeway Bay, North Point, and Quarry Bay, ending in the former fishing village of Shaukeiwan. There is also a branch line that turns off in Wanchai toward Happy Valley, where horse races are held during the season. The destination is marked on the front and the fare is only HK$.60. Avoid rush hours.

By Peak Tram This funicular railway dates back to 1888 and rises from ground level to **Victoria Peak** (1,305 feet), offering a panoramic view of Hong Kong. Both residents and tourists use the tram, which has five stations. The fare is HK$6 one way or HK$10 round-trip. There are cafes and restaurants at the top. The tram runs daily from 7 AM to midnight, every 10–15 minutes. There is a free shuttle bus to and from the Star Ferry.

By Rickshaw Rickshaws are operated by a few old men who take tourists on a token ride and pose for pictures (for which they charge heavily). The scale of charges is supposed to be around HK$50 for a five-minute ride, but the rickshaw men are merciless. A posed snapshot costs from HK$10 to HK$20. Make sure the price is agreed upon before you take the photo, otherwise unpleasant scenes may follow.

By Train The **Kowloon-Canton Railway** (KCR) has 10 commuter stops on its 22-mile (35-km) journey through urban Kowloon and the new cities of Shatin and Taipo, on its way to the Chinese border. The main station is at Hung Hom, Kowloon, where you can catch the express trains to China. Fares range from HK$2.70 to HK$10.40. The crossover point with the MTR is at Kowloon Tong Station (tel. 0/606–9606).

By Ferry The **Star Ferry** is one of Hong Kong's most famous landmarks. These double-bowed, green-and-white vessels cross the harbor between Central on Hong Kong Island and Tsimshatsui in Kowloon. The ferries cross every few minutes, hundreds of times daily, from 6:30 AM to 11:30 PM. The cost for the seven-minute ride is HK$.80, upper deck, and HK$.60, lower deck (children HK$.50). The Star Ferry also runs a service to Hung Hom between 7 AM and 7:20 PM at 10- to 20-minute intervals for HK$.90 (HK$.50 children).

The **Hong Kong and Yaumati ferries (HYF)** go to Hong Kong's beautiful outer islands. There are two- and three-deck ferries; the ones with three decks have an air-conditioned first-class section on the top deck, with access to the outside deck for magnificent views. The ferries go regularly to Lantau, Lamma, Cheung Chau, and Peng Chau islands. The HYF ferries leave from the Outlying Islands Pier, about a 10-minute walk west of the Star Ferry Pier on Hong Kong Island. Telephone for exact timetables (tel. 5/423–081), or get ferry schedules from the HKTA. Return fares vary from HK$9 to HK$24. Most trips take about an hour and are very scenic. The ferries are extremely crowded and noisy on weekends. If you have to go to the more distant parts of Hong Kong, you may find that a linking ferry service will enable you to beat the traffic. For example, there are high-speed **hover-ferries** from Central to Tsuen Wan and to North Point. The fares are HK$5 during peak hours, HK$3 off-peak. These trips take about 20 minutes per section, which is much faster than the trip by road.

By Helicopter Hong Kong's only helicopter service offers tours (*see* Tours) and limited sky-taxi service. They fly to Sekkong Airstrip in New Territories and to a few other places in the area. They also have two helicopter pads in Lantau, one at Ngong Ping by the Po Lin Monastery, and the other by the popular beach of Cheung Sha. Fee for the air taxi service is HK$2,970 for 30 minutes. Contact **Heliservices** (tel. 5/202–200). The helipad is on Harcourt Road, Hong Kong Island.

By Limousine Most of the best hotels have their own limousines. The Mandarin and The Peninsula hotels have chauffeur-driven Rolls-Royces for rent. You can also rent cars (*see* Rental Cars in Before You Go), but only a masochist would do so in Hong Kong. Cars with drivers can be arranged through your hotel.

By Foot If you're not defeated by the heat, it is pleasant to stroll around parts of Hong Kong. On Hong Kong Island, for example, you can enjoy a walk through the very traditional Western district, where life has not changed much over the years. If you are a very keen walker, you can go for a long stroll in New Territories or on Lantau Island. Contact the HKTA for maps.

Guided Tours

It is possible to travel the length and breadth of Hong Kong Island, Kowloon, New Territories, and the Outlying Islands using public transportation, and perhaps a taxi or two. Those whose time is limited, or who prefer to relax and leave the organization to professionals, can choose from a wide variety of tours. Unless otherwise stated, the tours listed here can be booked at major hotels.

Orientation Tours **Hong Kong Island.** The standard is a three- to four-hour tour of the island that departs from all the major hotels daily in the mornings and afternoons. Costs by coach vary from HK$80 to HK$90; by private car, with a maximum of four passengers, HK$400 to HK$450. Although routes vary, the following areas are generally covered: Victoria Peak, Wanchai, Aw Boon Haw Gardens, Repulse Bay and Deep Water Bay, Aberdeen, the University of Hong Kong, and Western and Central districts.

Kowloon and New Territories. This tour usually takes in sights as varied as Kwai Chung Container Terminal, the Castle Peak fishing village, a Taoist temple, the town of Yuen Long, the Chinese border at Lokmachau, and the Royal Hong Kong Golf Club at Fanling. The tour has morning and afternoon departures from all major hotels, lasts three to four hours, and costs HK$80 to HK$90 by coach and HK$400 and HK$450 by car. A slight variation is "The Land Between Tour," which lasts six hours and costs HK$180 (HK$140 children). It offers a glimpse of rural Hong Kong and takes in Tai Mo Shan, Hong Kong's tallest mountain; the fish breeding ponds; chicken farms; the Luen Wo Market in Fanling; and the Chinese border at Luk Keng. The return route passes Plover Cover Reservoir, Tolo Harbour (where you'll lunch on a terrace), and the racetrack at Shatin.

Harbor and Islands. Watertours of Hong Kong Ltd. and the **Seaview Harbour Tour Co. Ltd.** operate a variety of tours by junks and cruisers within the harbor, and to some of Hong Kong's 235 islands, including Lamma, Lantau, and Cheung Chau. Some of the tours offer a land-and-sea combination. They vary from a two-hour "Harbour Afternoon" tour (HK$95) to an 8½–hour "Grand Combined" tour by junk, cruiser, and coach (HK$325). A "Sunset Cruise" lasts four hours and costs HK$185.

General-Interest **Sung Dynasty Village.** This is a replica of a 1,000-year-old **Tours** southern Chinese village, where you can wander through old shops to sample the wares, witness a traditional Chinese wedding ceremony, and have your fortune told. The tour takes about three hours and includes lunch, dinner, or a snack. Prices range from HK$145 to HK$190. Departures are staggered throughout the day, beginning at 10 AM.

Ocean Park. Tours to this marineland, amusement park, and aviary cost from HK$155 to HK$170 (HK$130 children) and include all rides. You can purchase a City Bus Tour ticket from any MTR Station for HK$100 (HK$50 children). The ticket includes round-trip transportation in an open-top double-decker bus from the MTR Admiralty Station in Central.

Special-Interest Tours
Helicopter
Heliservices Hong Kong Limited (St. George's Bldg., 22nd Fl., Hong Kong Island, tel. 5/202–200) offers a choice of flight paths around the colony during daylight hours in a four-seat Bell 206B Jetranger. The least expensive is a 15-minute spin around Hong Kong Island for HK$1,485 for four passengers. The heliport is on Harcourt Road, Central.

Horse Racing
The **HKTA** (tel. 5/244–191) runs a tour to both Shatin and Happy Valley tracks during the September through May season that includes hotel pickups and a meal. The cost is about HK$220. You must bring your passport because this tour is for nonresidents only.

Photography
Star Ferry Photographic Cruises (tel. 3/669–878) are one-hour jaunts up and down the harbor, including a souvenir and drinks. The cost is HK$60 (HK$50 children).

Nightlife
Most night tours take you out on the water for a glimpse of reflected neon. They include the "Hong Kong Night Tour," which offers a choice of Chinese or Western dinner at either the **Jumbo** floating restaurant in Aberdeen or the **Peak Tower Restaurant** atop Victoria Peak. Dinner is followed by a visit to a Chinese nightclub. Costs vary from HK$285 to HK$365. The HKTA (tel. 5/244–191) runs a slightly different kind of night tour where you move at your own pace, paying participating establishments with coupons. Prices start at HK$150 for a few drinks.

Sports
The HKTA provides hotel pickups, a Western meal, and admission to the **Clearwater Bay Golf & Country Club,** where you can play golf, squash, or tennis, and enjoy the saunas and Jacuzzis. The price is HK$190 (HK$150 children), plus individual charges for sports activities.

Sailing
The **Hilton Hotel** (tel. 5/523–311, ext. 2009) operates pleasure cruises on its brigantine, *Wan Fu,* which can also be rented for private parties. Cruise costs vary from HK$130 to HK$360 per person, and include a barbecue dinner. Fees for renting the brigantine for private parties range from HK$950 to HK$1,100 per hour, with a minimum of four hours.

Trams
Tourist Enterprises (tel. 5/674–143) has a tour that features an hour's clanking on one of Hong Kong Island's private trams each evening from 6 PM. The tour also includes a stop at the Poor Man's Nightclub street market, and a grand dinner cruise or dinner in a leading hotel of your choice. Prices start at HK$285.

4 Exploring Hong Kong

Orientation

Hong Kong is one of the world's most compact, intense travel experiences. The population density in the city is almost overwhelming, and the atmosphere everywhere is vibrant with life, energy, and the frantic quest for money and personal achievement. Here is the very essence of Western capitalism, yet the heart of the place is truly Oriental. This blend *and* contrast are what make Hong Kong so fascinating.

There is so much to see and do here that it's easy to be lured away from a hectic business schedule or a rigid sightseeing routine and instead head down alleyways lined with shops selling everything from fine jewelry to sportswear and filled with the aroma of food stalls and some of the world's best Chinese restaurants. You won't find much ancient history here because Hong Kong has existed as a city for little more than 100 years. But there's a feeling of old China here, more so than in mainland China: The Chinese have been flocking to Hong Kong for decades, bringing with them their traditions as well as their energy and entrepreneurial spirit. Hong Kong has given full scope to that spirit, leaving it unhindered by political or social limitations.

The feeling of Hong Kong, what it is and why it exists, can be discovered only from the harbor. That body of water, chosen centuries ago by fishermen from China as a perfect shelter for the raging *tai'foos* ("big winds," the origin of the word "typhoon"), is still the territory's centerpiece.

In the 1970s, the Cross-Harbour Tunnel was built, linking Hong Kong Island, the financial, business, and government center of the colony, with the mainland. The MTR opened in the mid 1980s, helping to link the far-flung parts of the territory to each other and to Hong Kong Island. Before that, the populace depended on passenger and vehicular ferries, the latter painfully slow, with great line-ups at either end. Furthermore, Hong Kong was run as a dual economy, with branches of offices, delivery fleets, and other businesses on one side of the harbor duplicating facilities on the other side. There were even separate laws and charges covering buses, taxes, and electricity.

The sense of separation still remains, even though it now takes only a few minutes to drive through the tunnel (excluding the often long waiting times on either side to get into the tunnel), or less than 30 minutes to get from Hong Kong Central to the farthest point in the territory on the MTR. The Hong Kong business world long ago gave up the dual-economy system and streamlined operations. But in the minds of many people, going from one section of the territory to another still seems akin to traveling for hours instead of minutes.

"Let's have dinner in Kowloon," says a Kowloon-side resident to his Hong Kong friend, and the first thought in the Hong Konger's mind is, "All the way to Kowloon!" The reverse is also true. Invite your colleague to dinner at your home on the south side of the island, in Repulse Bay or Shouson Hill, and, despite the Aberdeen Tunnel that cuts traveling time to mere minutes, the first response is likely to be, "So far?" And so it is for Hong

Kongers or Kowlooners to venture to New Territories, or for mainliners to visit the islands.

Hong Kong Island Until 1841, the island that is now modern Hong Kong was home to a few fishermen and their families. Hong Kong, 30 square miles (78 sq km) in size, did not have a single natural water source, its vegetation was sparse, and its center was mountainous. Except for the natural harbor, all its geographical, historical, and demographic factors should have guaranteed Hong Kong permanent obscurity.

Hong Kong was officially ceded to Great Britain in 1841 at the end of the First Opium War with China. At that time it was hardly considered a valuable prize. The British military acknowledged its usefulness as an operational base or transshipping port, but was angry that it wasn't offered a port on the mainland of China. The British foreign minister called Hong Kong "that barren island," and Queen Victoria's consort, Prince Albert, publicly laughed at this "jewel" in the British Crown.

Hardly an auspicious beginning for the island that author Han Su-Yin was to describe a century later as the "deep roaring bustling eternal market . . . in which life and love and souls and blood and all things made and grown under the sun are bought and sold and smuggled and squandered."

Han's description is the impression one gets now when arriving on the island for the first time by Star Ferry. (One of the unfortunate results of progress is that many visitors now get their initial view of Hong Kong Island as they emerge from the cavernous Cross-Harbour Tunnel, or from the steps of the MTR, rather than from the legendary Star Ferry.)

It was only blocks away from the Star Ferry terminal that Captain Charles Elliott of Britain's Royal Navy first set foot on what he called "this barren rock." Today, "this barren rock" contains some of the world's most expensive real estate and a skyline to rival that of any of the world's major cities.

Exploring Hong Kong Island

Many of the British who set up their trading warehouses on Hong Kong Island were of Scottish ancestry. They were among the most nationalistic (or homesick) in the Victorian world, and so almost everything of importance was named after Queen Victoria. The central section was named Victoria City, the mountain peak was Victoria Peak, the military barracks, Victoria Barracks, and the prison, Victoria Prison. Later came Victoria College and Victoria Park.

Central Hong Kong is still officially named Victoria City, but today everyone calls it **Central.** The buildings here are both modern and ornate. They gleam in gold, silver, ivory, and ebony, reflecting a jewellike iridescence from the harbor. No one can fail to be overwhelmed by this first view of Hong Kong.

Central District is in the center of the north side of the island, and, because the island is small, the truly energetic could walk its circumference in a day. The extreme western end of the island is **Western District.** To the east of Central lie **Wanchai,** famed at one time for its nightlife, and **Causeway Bay,** which was once a middle-class Chinese community but is now primarily a business and tourist area filled with offices, hotels, restaurants, and shops.

Farther east is **Quarry Bay,** once solely a factory and tenement section and now also a middle-class housing area. Shaukiwan and Chaiwan, at the eastern end of Quarry Bay, were once very poor, but are now undergoing rapid urban development.

In the center of the island is the **Mid-Levels** area, which is almost entirely residential. It is worth a visit because it has some of the few remaining examples of Victorian apartment architecture left in Hong Kong. Here, too, is **Hong Kong University** and the **Botanical Gardens.**

High above Mid-Level is **Victoria Peak,** known simply as the Peak, jutting up 1,805 feet above sea level. Residents here take special pride in the positions to which they have, quite literally, risen. It is the most exclusive residential area on the island.

Aberdeen, on the southwest side of the island, has a busy fisherman's harbor and is where you will find the "floating garden" restaurants. Aberdeen also contains a factory area, Wong Chuk Hang, and the highway interchange for the Aberdeen Tunnel, which slices through the mountains and comes out at **Happy Valley.** In Happy Valley you will find the race track and two theme parks—**Ocean Park,** which is Asia's largest oceanarium, and **Water World.**

Leaving Aberdeen and heading east on a winding ocean-front highway, you will come to scenic **Deep Water Bay.** Farther east is **Repulse Bay,** another of Hong Kong's prestigious residential areas, and a very popular beach. Still following the winding road, you will come upon the tiny village of **Stanley,** with its open-air market; then **Big Wave Bay,** one of the territory's few surfing beaches; and then the pleasant village of **Shek-O,** another old settlement that today is a mix of village houses and baronial mansions.

Central and Western Districts

Numbers in the margin correspond with points of interest on the Central and Western Districts map.

① **Star Ferry** is the logical place to start your tour of Central District. Since 1898, the ferry terminal has been the gateway to the island for visitors and commuters crossing the harbor from Kowloon. In front of the terminal you will usually see a few red rickshaws. Once numbering in the thousands, these two-wheel, man-powered "taxis" are all but gone. Also in front of the terminal is one of the *Tote* (off-track betting offices). To the right, as you face inland, are the main **Post Office** and the tow-
② ering 66-story **Connaught Centre.** The Connaught, easy to spot with its many round windows, was completed in 1973 and was one of Central's first skyscrapers.

③ Farther to your right is the futuristic **Exchange Square,** with its gold- and silver-striped glass towers. This complex is home to the Hong Kong Stock Exchange, and contains some of the
④ most expensive rental space on the island. In front is **Blake Pier.** The open-air cafe at the far end is one of the best and least expensive spots from which to enjoy the panoramic view of the harbor while eating or drinking.

⑤ The **City Hall complex** (Central, between Edinburgh Pl. and

Connaught Rd.) faces out over Queen's Pier and the harbor. In addition to municipal offices, it contains a theater, concert hall, museum, exhibition and art galleries, and a library. Many of the events in the annual International Arts and Film Festival are held here.

A popular attraction in the City Hall complex is the **Hong Kong Museum of Art,** which contains a large collection of Chinese antiquities, including ceramics, bronzes, lacquerware, jade, and embroideries. The art collection includes thousands of paintings and works of calligraphy from the 17th century to the present. The museum has a gift shop. *City Hall complex, tel. 5/224–127. Admission free. Open Mon.–Wed. and Fri.–Sat. 10–6, Sun. and holidays 1–6; closed Thurs.*

❻ **HMS** *Tamar,* next to the City Hall Complex, is not a ship but the 28-story headquarters of the British Army and Royal Navy. The building gets its name from a ship once anchored in the harbor. The building and a small harbor are all that remain of the old naval dockyard that occupied the entire shore area, as far as Wanchai. Today, visiting warships often anchor offshore here, their crews coming ashore for nightlife and shopping, as sailors have always done in Hong Kong.

❼ **Statue Square** is a small oasis of green between Connaught Road Central and Chater Road. Filled with shaded walks and fountains, it is popular with office workers during lunch time. It is also a favorite gathering spot on weekends for hundreds of housemaids from the Philippines. The square is surrounded by some of the most important buildings in Hong Kong, and is above the **Central MTR Station,** one of the busiest subway stations in the world, handling about 1.5 million passengers daily.

A modern building bordering the square houses the **Hong Kong Club,** one of the last social bastions of the fading British colonial system. The club, as attractive as an ice-rink cafeteria, will accept anyone today, but even now there is only 10% Chinese membership. Next door is the **Legislative Council** building, with its domes and colonnades. It formerly housed the Supreme Court and is one of the few remaining grand Victorian buildings left in this area. Right now the Council has a largely consultative role, without any real power. How important this body will be once the British hand over power to China in 1997 remains to be seen. In front of the Council building is the **Cenotaph** monument to all who lost their lives in the two world wars.

The modern glass-and-steel-structure at the end of the square is the headquarters of the **Hongkong and Shanghai Bank.** Known simply as The Bank, this is the largest and most powerful financial institution in Hong Kong. It still issues local bank notes and has enormous influence in every field of investment. The building was designed to make a positive statement about the future of Hong Kong and its capitalistic system. To the left of the bank is the even taller headquarters of the **Bank of China,** designed to rival its neighbor in both aesthetic and financial force. Perhaps this is an indication that China plans to challenge capitalism on its own terms after 1997.

To the left of the Bank of China is the **Hilton Hotel** (Queen's Rd., Central), one of the earliest of the post-war luxury hotels and still one of the best in town. As is the custom with many Hong Kong hotels, the lobby is several stories above ground level, to allow space for the all-important shopping arcades.

Western and Central Districts

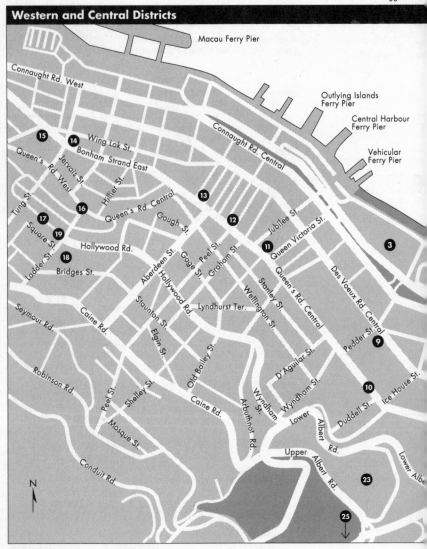

Macau Ferry Pier

Outlying Islands
Ferry Pier

Central Harbour
Ferry Pier

Vehicular
Ferry Pier

Connaught Rd. West

Connaught Rd. Central

Wing Lok St.

Bonham Strand East

Jervois St.

Hillier St.

Queen's Rd. West

Tung St.

Square St.

Ladder St.

Queen's Rd. Central

Gough St.

Hollywood Rd.

Bridges St.

Aberdeen St.

Hollywood Rd.

Gage St.

Peel St.

Graham St.

Jubilee St.

Queen Victoria St.

Queen's Rd. Central

Stanley St.

Wellington St.

Lyndhurst Ter.

Des Voeux Rd. Central

Seymour Rd.

Caine Rd.

Staunton St.

Elgin St.

Old Bailey St.

Pedder St.

Robinson Rd.

Peel St.

Shelley St.

Caine Rd.

Mosque St.

Arbuthnot Rd.

Wyndham St.

Wyndham St.

D'Aguilar St.

Duddell St.

Ice House St.

Lower Albert Rd.

Upper Albert Rd.

Conduit Rd.

N

Blake Pier, **4**

Bonham Strand East
and West, **15**

Central Market, **11**

Chater Garden, **8**

City Hall Complex, **5**

Connaught Centre, **2**

Exchange Square, **3**

Hilton Hotel, **20**

HMS Tamar, **6**

Hollywood Road, **17**

Landmark, The, **9**

Lascar Row/
Cat Street, **19**

Li Yuen Street East
and West, **10**

Man Mo Temple, **18**

Man Wa Lane, **14**

Museum of Tea Ware, **21**

Peak Tram, **24**

Queen's Road West, **16**

St. John's Cathedral, **22**

Star Ferry, **1**

Statue Square, **7**

Victoria Peak, **25**

Wing On Street, **12**

Wing Sing Street, **13**

Zoological and
Botanical Gardens, **23**

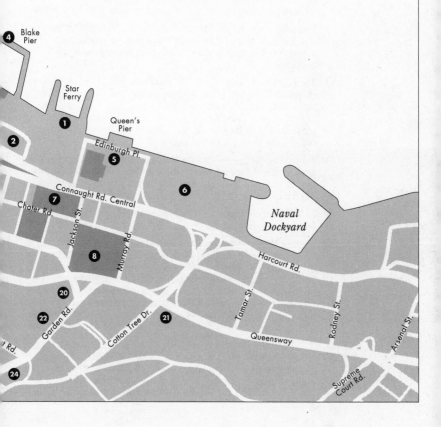

0 _____ 330 yards
0 _____ 300 meters

Victoria Harbour

Blake Pier

Star Ferry

Queen's Pier

Edinburgh Pl.

Connaught Rd. Central

Chater Rd.

Jackson St.

Murray Rd.

Naval Dockyard

Harcourt Rd.

Garden Rd.

Cotton Tree Dr.

Tamar St.

Rodney St.

Arsenal St.

Queensway

Supreme Court Rd.

Rd.

8 In front of the Hilton is a small park, **Chater Garden** (Chater and Jackson Rds.), former home of the Hong Kong Cricket Club. A favorite local pastime was watching the cricket players enjoying the game at a leisurely pace, oblivious to the traffic noise and bustle. The club has now moved to new grounds outside the city center, chased away by the high price of real estate. Conservationists won their battle against developers to preserve the park, to the delight of all who come to sit and relax in this small, green oasis.

On the west side of Statue Square is the **Mandarin Oriental Hotel** (5 Connaught Rd.), one of the finest hotels in the world. The mezzanine coffee lounge is a pleasant place to stop for a drink.

Head west and follow the tracks of the rattling old trams that pass in front of the Hong Kong Bank. This will take you to **Des Voeux Road,** which is lined with elegant shops and tall office buildings.

9 **The Landmark** (Des Voeux Rd. and Pedder St.) is an impressive shopping complex, with atrium, cafes, and hundreds of top-name shops equal in quality to anything New York or London has to offer. Concerts, cultural shows, and other events are presented here free of charge—one of the few experiences in Hong Kong without a price tag on it.

Follow Pedder Street, beside The Landmark, and turn west on **Queen's Road Central,** one of the main shopping arteries. Narrow lanes on either side are filled with tiny shops and stalls filled with goods.

10 **Li Yuen Street East and West,** for example, are bargain alleys for clothing, shoes, costume jewelry, woolens, and handbags.

11 **Central Market** (Queen's Rd. Central and Queen Victoria St.) is the city's largest public food market. More than 300 stalls offer every type of food—fish on the first floor, meat on the second, fruits and vegetables on the third. Opposite the market is **China Products** department store, which offers reasonably priced Chinese goods, from household items to antiques, handicrafts, luggage, and souvenirs. Next to Central Market is **Jubilee Street,** filled with food stalls offering bowls of noodles, rice dishes, and a wide variety of snacks.

12 **Wing On Street** (off Queen's Rd. Central) a small side street, better known as **Cloth Alley,** is worth exploring because of its stalls overflowing with fabrics and sewing accessories. If you buy here, bargain like mad, as you would in any open-air market area in Hong Kong.

13 On **Wing Sing Street** (off Queen's Rd. Central) you will find every type of egg on sale—tiny quail eggs, large goose eggs, and preserved eggs, known as 1,000-year-old eggs, which are actually only a few months old and treated with a pungent mixture of lime, wood-ash, and tea leaves. Eggs preserved in salt are also sold here, their shells black from a charcoal coating. The next alley to the west is **Wing Lok Street,** lined with many traditional Chinese shops selling everything from rattan goods to medicines.

14 Queen's Road Central now forks to the left, but you should continue straight ahead to Bonham Strand East. **Man Wa Lane** is a tiny street (off Bonham Strand East) where you'll find carvers of *chops* (engraved seals). You can have your initials engraved in roman letters or Chinese characters on plastic, ivory, or jade. It takes about an hour to engrave a chop, which you can pick up later or on the following day.

⑮ Bonham Strand East and West is an area left relatively untouched by the modern world. The streets are lined with traditional shops, many open-fronted. Among the most interesting ones are those selling live snakes, both for food and medicinal use. The snakes, from pythons to cobras, are imported from China and kept in cages outside the shops. Here you can sample a bowl of snake soup or an invigorating snakegall wine. The main season for the snake trade is October through February.

Bonham Strand West is famous for traditional Chinese medicines and herbal remedies. Many of the old shops have their original facades and are lined with shelves of jars and drawers containing hundreds of strange-smelling ingredients, such as wood barks and insects, all meant to be dried and ground up, infused in hot water or tea, or taken as powders or pills. Some of the more innocuous remedies are made from ginseng, said to be good for virility and prolonging life.

At the western end of Bonham Strand West is **Des Voeux Road West**—you'll recognize it by the tram tracks. On the left side of the street as you continue west, you will find all kinds of shops selling preserved foods such as dried and salted fish, black mushrooms, and vegetables. This is a good area for lunchtime *dim sum* (hot snacks).

If you want to see street barbers at work, turn left and walk up **Sutherland Street.**

⑯ Queen's Road West is filled with embroidery shops selling richly brocaded wedding clothes and all types of embroidered linens, clothing, and household goods. Also along this street are shops where colorful items are made and sold for burning at Chinese funerals. Houses, cars, furniture, and TV sets—all made of paper or bamboo—are among the items necessary to ensure the departed a good life in the hereafter.

⑰ Funerals are also the theme for some shops along **Hollywood Road.** Here you will find traditional Chinese coffins and more of the elaborate ceremonial items needed for a funeral. Farther along you will find shops selling different grades of rice, displayed in brass-banded wooded tubs. The rice is sold by the *catty* (about 1¼ lb). Look to the left for a sign saying "Possession Street." This was the place where Captain Charles Elliott of the British Royal Navy stepped ashore in 1841 and claimed Hong Kong for the British Empire. It is interesting to note how far today's harbor is from this area, which was once on the water's edge—the result of a century of massive land reclamation.

Farther east along Hollywood Road are many antiques, curio, and junk shops, as well as shops selling every type of Asian art and handicraft. Some items are genuinely old, but most are made to look old and passed off as antiques. Porcelain, embroidered robes, paintings, screens, snuff bottles, and wood and ivory carvings are among the many items that can be found here in profusion. Bargain hard if you want a good price.

⑱ Man Mo Temple is also on Hollywood Road, in the midst of the antiques and curio shops. It is one of Hong Kong's oldest and most important temples and is dedicated to Man, the god of literature, and Mo, the god of war. The statue of Man is dressed in green and holds a writing brush. Mo is dressed in red and holds a sword. To their left is a shrine to Pao Kung, god of justice, whose face is painted black. To the right is Shing Wong, god of the city. Coils of incense hang from the roof beams, filling the air with a heavy fragrance. The temple bell, cast in Canton in 1847, and the drum next to it are sounded to attract the attention of the gods when a prayer is being offered. If you want to check your fortune, stand in front of the altar, take one of the small bamboo cylinders available there, and shake it until one of the sticks falls out. The number on the stick corresponds to a particular fortune. But there's a catch—the English translation is in a book on sale in the temple.

⑲ To reach **Upper Lascar Row/Cat Street** from the temple, walk down the steps of **Ladder Street.** In the days before wheeled traffic, most of the steep, small lanes on the hillside were filled with steps. **Cat Street** (actually Upper Lascar Road) is a vast flea market. You won't find Ming vases here or anything else of real monetary value, but perhaps you'll come across an old Mao badge or an old teakettle or pot.

More worthwhile for the antiques collector is the section of shops and stalls known as **Cat Street Galleries,** adjacent to the flea market. The complex has four stories of galleries offering every type of art and handicraft, some old, most new. *38 Lok Ku Rd., tel. 5/431-609. Open Mon.–Sat. 9–6, Sun. 11–5.*

Continue downhill and you will return to **Queen's Road Central.** Along this section are shops selling many different kinds of tea and traditional Chinese art supplies, including writing brushes, paper, and ink. Here, too, you can buy fans or have a calligrapher write a good luck message for you on an item you purchase.

Heading back along Queen's Road Central, toward Central Market, you will see a number of street markets in the stepped lanes to your right. On the left is the ornate facade of the **Eu Yan Sang Medical Hall** where traditional Chinese medicines are sold. You can browse for hours throughout this area, past market stalls and shops selling strange and wonderful goods, streets filled with the aroma of exotic foods, and lined with ornate old buildings that seem to be begging to be explored.

From Central to the Peak

⑳ The **Hilton Hotel** (Queen's Rd. Central) is where you start this tour, which will eventually take you to the Peak, towering above the harbor and the city. But don't worry, you don't have to walk all the way.

Queen's Road Central was once the seafront, and site of the old military parade grounds. Most of the important colonial buildings of the Victorian era were within easy reach of this area. Walking around this part of Central is a bit tricky because of a series of elevated motorways. However, there are pedestrian tunnels and overpasses. With a little patience and a good map, you should not have too much trouble finding your way about on foot.

㉑ **The Museum of Tea Ware in Flagstaff House** is easy to reach by walking through the tunnel under Cotton Tree Drive. Built in

1845, Flagstaff House is one of the city's oldest buildings and once the official residence of the commander of the British forces. Since 1984 it has housed the Museum of Tea Ware. The museum displays include everything connected with the art of serving tea, from the 7th century onward. *Cotton Tree Dr., tel. 5/299–390. Admission free. Open 10–5. Closed Wed.*

㉒ **St. John's Cathedral,** completed in 1849 and a good example of Victorian-Gothic architecture, is the official Anglican cathedral. *Garden Rd., just above the Hilton. Open daily 10–8.*

Government House, a handsome white building up the hill from the cathedral, is the official residence of the governor. It was built in 1891 (Upper Albert Rd.).

㉓ A visit to **The Zoological and Botanical Gardens** is a delightful way to escape the city's traffic and crowds. In the early morning, people come here to practice t'ai chi ch'uan (the ancient art of shadow boxing). The quiet pathways are lined with semi-tropical trees, shrubs, and flowers. The collection of animals in the zoo is small, although there are some exotic ones, such as leopards and jaguars. There is also an aviary with more than 300 species of birds, including flocks of cranes and pink-and-white flamingos. *Upper Albert Rd., opposite Government House. Admission free. Open daily 6:30–7.*

㉔ Lower Peak Tram Terminus is where you will find **Peak Tram,** the steepest funicular railway in the world. It passes five intermediate stations en route to the upper terminal, 1,805 feet above sea level, and was opened in 1880 to transport people to the top of Victoria Peak, which is the highest hill overlooking Hong Kong Harbour. Before the tram, the only way to get to the top was to walk or take a bumpy ride up the steep steps in a sedan chair. The tram has two 72-seat cars that are hauled up the hill by cables attached to electric motors. *Between Garden Rd. and Cotton Tree Dr. Fare: HK$6 one way, HK$10 round-trip. Open daily 7 AM–midnight. Trams run every 10–15 min.*

㉕ The Chinese name for **Victoria Peak** is *Tai Ping Shan* (Mountain of Great Peace). It might also be called Mountain of Great Views, for the panorama is breathtaking. On a clear day you can see across the islands to the People's Republic of China. The area is a popular picnic spot and filled with beautiful walking paths that circle the peak.

The **Peak Tower Building,** completed in 1972, contains a restaurant, coffee shop, gift shops, and a post office. Just below the summit is a lookout pavilion which was once part of a former governor's residence. The original gardens and country walks remain and are open to the public.

As an alternative to taking the Peak Tram down the hillside, you can catch a no. 15 bus or a cab to Central. This will take you on a trip as exciting and beautiful as the one on the tram through the steep roads of the residential areas of Mid-Levels.

Wanchai

Those who expect to discover the raunchy world of the old Wanchai may be disappointed. Wanchai still has its nocturnal charms (*see* Nightlife), but the "Wanch" of Richard Mason's novel, *The World of Suzie Wong*, seems a bit faded now. Wanchai has always been a magnet for sailors on shore leave, and was especially popular with military men on leave during the Vietnam War. Today it's a bit more touristy and expensive, but you can still find topless bars, sailors from all nations, and military patrols (MPs) on the streets when a fleet is in town.

The Luk Kwok Hotel, better known as the Suzie Wong Hotel, is gone, but you can still wander about **Lockhart Road** made famous by the novel. It's filled with seedy bars and plenty of restaurants, British pubs, and tailors' shops.

Wanchai was once one of the five "wan," or areas that the British set aside for Chinese residences. Today, in addition to the old section with its bars and massage parlors, it is a mixture of office buildings, restaurants, apartment buildings, and shops. A good point to start a circular walking tour is at the junction of Queensway Road and Queen's Road East. This is a 10-minute ride from Central by tram or on the no. 5 bus. Get off just past the Marriott Hotel.

Numbers in the margin correspond with points of interest on the Wanchai, Causeway, Happy Valley, and North Point map.

❶ Queen's Road East is a busy shopping street. Heading east you pass rice and food shops and stores selling rattan and traditional furniture, paper lanterns, and materials for Chinese calligraphy. Further along, on the right, is the **Hung Shing Temple.** You can see its altar from the street and smell the scent of smoldering *joss* (Chinese idol) sticks.

❷ Hopewell Centre (Queen's Rd. East and Ship St.) is 66-stories high and was Hong Kong's tallest structure until the Bank of China building was completed. There is a revolving restaurant at the top, with superb views. Even if you don't plan to eat here, it's worth a visit just to ride the exterior "glass-bullet" elevator. Continuing along Queen's Road East, you will find, on your right, the **Wanchai Post Office,** one of Hong Kong's very few protected historical landmark buildings, with wonderful old, carved-wood counters. Turn left on **Wanchai Road,** a busy market area selling a variety of foods as well as clothing and household goods. It's a good place for browsing, especially along the narrow side alleyways. To the left are several small lanes leading to **Johnston Road,** where you'll see the tram lines again. There are a number of traditional shops here, including some selling household pets. Turn left on Johnston Road, and follow the edge of **Southern Playground,** a popular meeting place, especially for those looking for a game of cards or Chinese checkers.

Luard Road, with its cross streets—Hennessy, Lockhart, and Jaffee roads—is in the heart of Old Wanchai. At night this area is alive with multicolored neon signs and a lively trade at the bars, pubs, massage parlors, and restaurants. Hennessy Road, which roughly follows the line of the original harbor frontage, is one of the better shopping streets and another good place for browsing. For more good shopping, walk east on Hennessy Road to Fleming Road. Turn north, crossing Harbour Road, to the **China Resources** department store (26 Harbour Rd.).

❸ The nearby **Causeway Centre** building houses the **Museum of Chinese Historical Relics.** The collection covers 1,000 years of Chinese history and culture, with all types of art and crafts on display. You can rent a tape cassette for your own guided tour, and purchase replicas of some of the objects on exhibit.

28 Harbour Rd., tel. 5/742–692. Admission free. Open daily 9–6.

To the east of Causeway Centre is the **Wanchai Sports Grounds** (Harbour and Tonnachy roads), opened in 1979 to provide world-class facilities for competitive sports. It has a soccer field, running track, swimming pool, and an indoor games hall. Walking back (west) along Harbour Road, you will pass the **Hong Kong Convention and Exhibition Centre,** now under construction. When completed, it will be one of the largest in Asia.

❹ ❺ The **Arts Centre** and the **Academy for Performing Arts** are two separate buildings adjacent to each other and at the heart of Hong Kong's cultural activities. They have excellent facilities for both exhibitions and the performing arts. Throughout the year there is a busy program of activities, details of which you can obtain from the local press or at the ticket reservations office. The Academy for Performing Arts was financed with money donated by the Royal Hong Kong Jockey Club out of its profits from horse racing. Both the Academy and the Arts Centre have excellent restaurants. One of the interesting galleries in the Arts Centre is the **Pao Sui Loong Galleries,** which has no permanent collection but hosts international and local exhibitions throughout the year. *2 Harbour Rd. Academy, tel. 5/823–1500; Arts Centre, tel. 5/280–626; Pao Sui Loong: 4th–5th floors, Arts Centre Bldg., tel. 5/823–0200. Admission free. Open daily 10–8.*

From here you can taxi back to your hotel, catch the MTR at Admiralty Station, or continue walking along the harborfront to Wanchai Ferry Pier for a ferry back to Kowloon. East of the **❻** pier is the **Cargo Handling Basin** (Hung Hing Rd. near Wanchai Stadium), where you can watch the unloading of boats bringing cargo ashore from ships anchored in the harbor.

Causeway Bay, Happy Valley, and North Point

Causeway Bay is one of Hong Kong's best shopping areas. It also has a wide range of restaurants and a few sightseeing attractions. Much of the district can be easily reached from Central by the tram, which runs along Hennessy Road, or by the MTR to Causeway Bay Station. If you come by taxi, a good starting point is the Excelsior Hotel, which overlooks the harbor.

The **Excelsior Hotel** and **Noonday Gun** are a fun part of any tour of Causeway Bay. ". . . In Hong Kong they strike a gong and fire a noonday gun," wrote Noel Coward in his song, "Mad Dogs and Englishmen." They still fire that gun, exactly at noon each day, in a small enclosure overlooking the Yacht Club Basin and Typhoon Shelter, opposite the Excelsior Hotel and the World Trade Centre. The tradition was started by Jardines, the great *hong* (trading company) that gave James Clavell inspiration for his novels *Taipan* and *Noble House.* Jardines would fire a salute each time one of its ships arrived safely in the harbor. It is said that this angered the local governor, who ordered the company to use a gun instead of a cannon, and as a noon-time signal. The gun itself, with brasswork polished bright, is a three-pounder Hotchkiss, dating from 1901.

❼ On weekends, from spring through fall, it is pleasant to have coffee or lunch in the first floor coffee shop of the **Excelsior Hotel** (Gloucester Rd., Causeway), which overlooks the Yacht

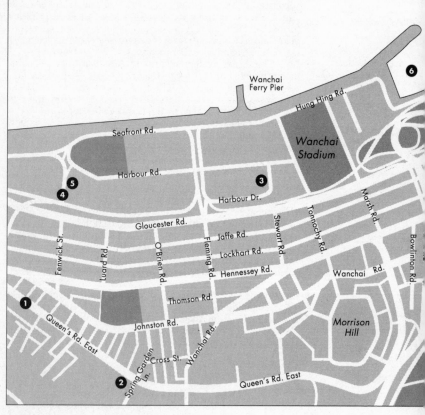

Wanchai, Causeway Bay, Happy Valley, and North Point

0 | 330 yards
0 | 300 meters

Wanchai
Ferry Pier

Hung Hing Rd.

Seafront Rd.

*Wanchai
Stadium*

Harbour Rd.

Harbour Dr.

Gloucester Rd.

Jaffe Rd.

Lockhart Rd.

Hennessey Rd.

Fenwick St.

Luard Rd.

O'Brien Rd.

Fleming Rd.

Stewart Rd.

Tonnochy Rd.

Marsh Rd.

Wanchai Rd.

Bowrington Rd.

Thomson Rd.

Johnston Rd.

Queen's Rd. East

Spring Garden Ln.

Cross St.

Wanchai Rd.

*Morrison
Hill*

Queen's Rd. East

Academy for
Performing Arts, **5**
Aw Boon Haw (Tiger
Balm) Gardens, **13**
Cargo Handling
Basin, **6**
Causeway Centre, **3**

Excelsior Hotel, **7**
Food Street, **9**
Hopewell Centre, **2**
Kwun Yum Temple, **12**
Queen's Road East, **1**
The Arts Centre, **4**
Tin Han Temple, **11**
Typhoon Shelter, **8**
Victoria Peak, **10**

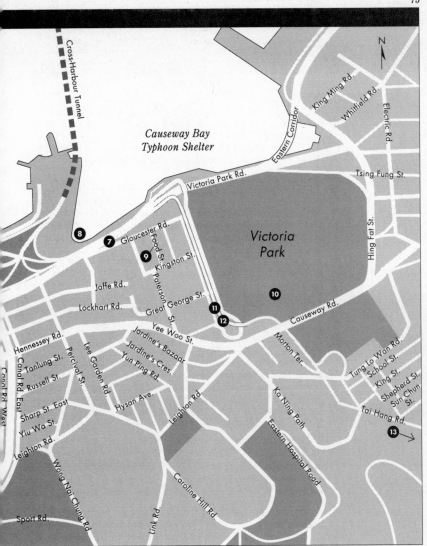

Club, and watch the yachts racing in the harbor. Every two years, at Easter time, this is the starting point for the South China Sea Race to Manila, in the Philippines. The next race will be held in 1990.

8 At the eastern end of **Typhoon Shelter** is a mass of tightly packed *sampans*, living quarters for a community of people who work in the harbor.

For a much better meal, explore the 25 or so restaurants on
9 **Food Street** (between Gloucester Rd. and Kingston St.). This is a small covered alley near the Excelsior Hotel, where virtually every type of cuisine is available, both Asian and Western. Most restaurants here are reasonably priced, with waiters who speak English.

10 **Victoria Park,** reached by passing under the elevated highway at the end of Gloucester Road, offers a delightful escape from the crowds and traffic, and the concrete canyons of the city. Beautifully landscaped with trees, shrubs, flowers, and lawns, it offers recreational facilities for swimming, bowling, tennis, and roller skating. There is even a go-cart track. The Lantern Festival is held here in mid-autumn, with the trees a mass of colored lights. Just before Chinese New Year, the park features a huge flower market. In the early morning, the park is filled with people practicing t'ai chi, which is fascinating to watch. At other times, the park can be a pleasant place to sit in the sun, stroll, or jog.

After relaxing in Victoria Park, you may be ready for more shopping. If so, you'll find plenty to keep you busy in Causeway Bay. The large Japanese department stores, **Sogo, Daimaru,** and **Matsuzakaya,** all have branches on or near **Great George Street,** off the end of Hennessy Road. This is a good area for buying photographic or electronic equipment—provided you bargain hard. Off Yee Woo Street is **Jardines Crescent,** an area packed with clothing stalls.

Tin Han and Kwun Yum Temples are two small Chinese temples
11 on the far (east) side of Victoria Park. **Tin Han Temple** is on a street of the same name off Causeway Road, behind Park Cinema. It is dedicated to the goddess of the sea, and is notable for its decorative roof and old stone walls. Walk south along Tung Lo Wan Road, a busy street of commercial shops, to where the road turns west, and you will find Lin Fa King Street West.
12 Turn left here and you will come to the **Kwun Yum Temple,** dedicated to the goddess of mercy. A temple has stood on this site for 200 years, but this one is in a heavily renovated building and is mostly new, dating from 1986. Constructed on top of a huge boulder, it has a high ceiling and gallery. The temple is very popular with local devotees and is open daily 7–6.

Left of Tung Lo Wan Road is **Jones Street,** which has some fine old traditional Chinese houses. From here continue uphill on Tai Hang Road (a 15-minute walk or a brief taxi or No. 11 bus
13 ride) to **Aw Boon Haw (Tiger Balm) Gardens.** Built in 1935 with profits from sales of a popular menthol balm, the gardens were the pet project of two Chinese brothers, who also built their mansion here. Eight acres of hillside are covered with grottos and pavilions filled with garishly painted statues and models of Chinese gods, mythical animals, and scenes depicting fables and moralistic stories. It's a sort of Oriental Disneyland, and great fun to explore, especially for children. But be

forewarned, some of the scenes of Taoist and Buddhist mythology are decidedly gruesome. There is also an ornate pagoda, seven stories high, containing Buddhist relics and the ashes of monks and nuns. *Tai Hang Rd., Happy Valley. Admission: to gardens free. Open daily 10–4.*

The area east of Victoria Park offers very little for the first-time visitor. **North Point** and **Quarry Bay** are both undeniably the "real" Hong Kong. But this means tenements and factories. From Causeway Bay you can take the tram for a couple of miles through this area, which is perhaps the best way to get the flavor of the environment. **Shau Kei Wan** has two noteworthy sights. One is the ferry service to Kowloon's **Lei Yue Mun Village,** with its fishing restaurants. The other is **Tai Koo Shing,** a massive city-within-a-city. Some years ago this was barren, reclaimed land. Today, it's a middle-class housing estate. The shopping center, **Cityplaza,** has an ice-skating rink, gardens, restaurants, and hundreds of shops. The village is virtually self-sufficient in everything except home-grown food.

The South Side

Numbers in the margin correspond with points of interest on the Hong Kong Island map.

The easiest way to tour the south is on an organized bus tour, lasting about four hours, but this will show you only a few highlights. If you have time, take a city bus or taxi from Central, and stop at the following points of interest along the way.

❶ Starting in Central and passing through Western, the first major point of interest will be **Hong Kong University.** Established in 1911, it has about 6,000 undergraduate and 1,700 post-graduate students. Most of its buildings are spread along Bonham Road. In this area you will also find the **Fung Ping Shan Museum,** founded in 1953. It contains an excellent collection of Chinese antiquities, especially ceramics and bronzes dating from 3,000 BC. There are also some fine paintings, lacquerware, and carvings in jade, stone, and wood. *94 Bonham Rd. Admission free. Open Mon.–Sat. 9:30–6.*

Continuing around the western end of the island, you come to **Pok Fu Lam** and **Why Fu Estate** overlooking **Lamma Island.** These are two huge housing developments, complete with shops, recreational facilities, and banks. They are typical of Hong Kong's approach to mass housing. From here you ride downhill to Aberdeen, an area deserving exploration.

❷ **Aberdeen,** named after an English lord, not the Scottish city, got its start as a refuge for pirates some 200 years ago. After World War II, Aberdeen became fairly commercial as the *Tanka* (boat people) attracted tourists to their floating restaurants. Today, these people continue to live on houseboats and are as picturesque to the occasional visitor as their economic conditions are depressing. Some visitors regret the fact that many of these boat people are turning to factory work, but drab as that work may be, it's a definite improvement over their old way of life. The government is offering the young boat people an education geared to the needs of a fishing community.

You can still see much of traditional Aberdeen, such as the **Aberdeen Cemetery** (Aberdeen Main Rd.), with its enormous

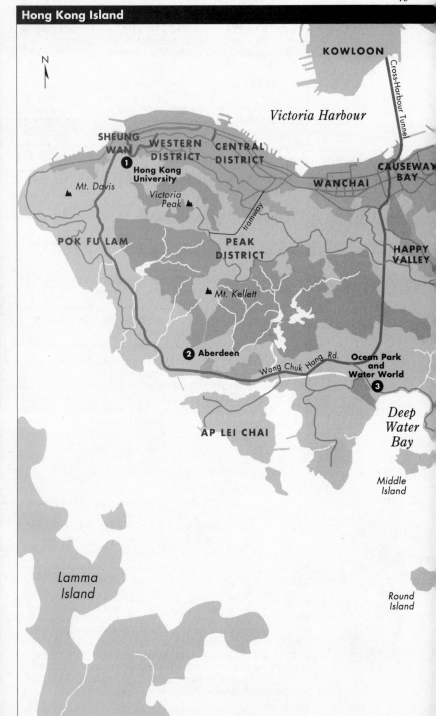

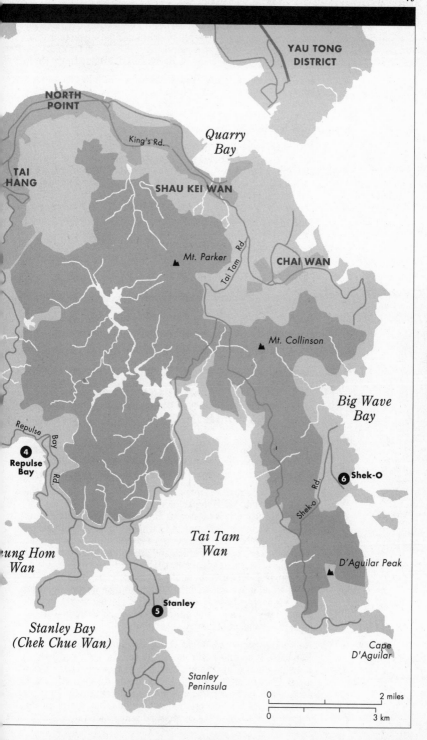

YAU TONG DISTRICT

NORTH POINT

King's Rd.

Quarry Bay

TAI HANG

SHAU KEI WAN

Mt. Parker

Tai Tam Rd.

CHAI WAN

Mt. Collinson

Big Wave Bay

Repulse Bay

Bay Rd.

4 **Repulse Bay**

6 Shek-O

Shek-o Rd.

Tai Tam Wan

ung Hom Wan

D'Aguilar Peak

5 **Stanley**

Stanley Bay (Chek Chue Wan)

Stanley Peninsula

Cape D'Aguilar

0   2 miles
0   3 km

gravestones and its glorious view. Along Aberdeen's side streets you can find outdoor barbers at work and many dim sum restaurants. In the harbor, along with the floating restaurants, are some 3,000 junks and sampans. You will undoubtedly be asked to board one of these boats for a ride through the harbor.

Also in Aberdeen is the **Tin Hau Temple,** which has an ancient bell and drum that are still used to open and close the temple. Although rather shabby, this shrine to the goddess of the sea is very colorful during the Tin Hau Festival in April and May when hundreds of boats converge along the shore.

Aberdeen's most interesting section is **Aplichau Island,** which can be reached by bridge or sampan. The island has a boat-building yard where junks are constructed, as well as some yachts and sampans. Almost all the boats are built without formal plans. From the bridge you can get a superb view of the harbor and its countless number of junks (you'll have to walk back to take a photo, since vehicles are not allowed to stop on the bridge).

❸ East of Aberdeen are **Ocean Park** and **Water World,** two theme parks managed by the Royal Hong Kong Jockey Club. Ocean Park is on 170 acres of land overlooking the sea and is one of the world's largest oceanariums, attracting thousands of visitors daily. On the "lowland" site are gardens, parks, and a children's zoo. A cable car, providing spectacular views of the entire south coast, takes you to the "headland" side and to Ocean Theatre, the world's largest marine mammal theater, with seats for 4,000 people. Here, too, is one of the world's largest roller coasters and various other rides. The adjacent, 65-acre Water World is an aquatic fun park with slides, rapids, pools, and a wave cove. *Wong Chuk Hang Rd., tel. 5/532–2244 or 5/550–947. Ocean Park admission (all inclusive): HK$95 adults, HK$45 children. Open daily. Water World: tel. 5/555–234 or 5/555–222. Admission: HK$45/HK$30 adults, HK$20/$15 children. Open May–Oct.*

Deep Water Bay (Island Rd.) is just to the east of the theme parks. This was the site of the film *Love Is a Many-Splendored Thing.* Its beauty and deep coves are still many-splendored.

❹ The waterside road continues to **Repulse Bay,** named after the British warship HMS *Repulse* (not, as some local wags say, after the pollution of its waters). The famed Repulse Bay Hotel was demolished in 1982, but the **Repulse Bay Verandah Restaurant and Bamboo Bar,** replicas of the restaurant and bar in the old hotel, were opened in 1986 and are run by the same people who operated the original hotel. The hotel gained notoriety in December 1941 when invading Japanese clambered over the hills behind it and entered its gardens, which were being used as headquarters by the British. After a brief battle, the British surrendered. Today, the hillside behind the hotel features a huge development of luxury apartments.

❺ Another reminder of World War II is **Stanley Bay** (Wong Ma Kak Rd.). It became notorious as the home of the largest Hong Kong prisoner-of-war camps run by the Japanese. Today, Stanley is known for its superb beaches and its market, where designer fashions are sold at wholesale prices. Hong Kong has dozens of shops offering similar bargains, but it's more fun shopping for them in the countrified atmosphere around Stanley. You can also find ceramics, paintings, and secondhand books.

6 **Shek-O,** the easternmost village on the south side of the island, is filled with old houses, great mansions, a superb golf course and club, a few simple restaurants, a pretty beach, and fine views. Leave the little town square and take the curving path across a footbridge to the "island" of **Tai Tau Chau,** which is really a great rock with a lookout for scanning the South China Sea. Little more than a century ago, this open water was ruled by pirates.

From Shek-O, the round-island route continues back to the north, to the housing and industrial estate of **Chai Wan** (Chai Wan Rd.). From here you have a choice of a fast journey back to Central on the MTR, or a slow ride to Central on the two-decker tram that crosses the entire south side of the island, via Quarry Bay, North Point, and Causeway Bay.

Exploring Kowloon

Numbers in the margin correspond with points of interest on the Kowloon map.

Kowloon is a peninsula on mainland China, directly across Victoria Harbour from Central. Legend has it that Kowloon was named by a Chinese emperor who fled here during the Sung Dynasty (960–1279). He counted eight hills on the peninsula and called them the Eight Dragons—so the account goes—but a servant reminded him that an emperor is also considered a dragon, and so the emperor called the region *Gau-lung* (nine dragons), which became Kow-loon in English.

Kowloon is where most of Hong Kong's hotels are located. In the Old Tsimshatsui district is the Victorian-era clock tower of the old Kowloon-Canton Railway station, the YMCA, the Peninsula Hotel, and the bustling Nathan Road area. The new Tsimshatsui district is on land reclaimed from the harbor and contains many luxury hotels and shopping centers, the Space Museum, and a waterfront esplanade running through the even newer Tsimshatsui East district. It is here that you will find the new railroad station.

In Victorian times, people would take the Star Ferry from Hong Kong Island to Kowloon and stay overnight at the still-elegant Peninsula Hotel, which was located next door to the railroad station. The next morning they boarded the Kowloon-Canton Railway trains for Peking, Moscow, London, and other Western cities.

Today visitors can take a taxi through the Cross-Harbour Tunnel from Causeway Bay or Central to Kowloon, or ride the MTR from Central to Kowloon in minutes. The Star Ferry, however, is still unquestionably the most exciting way to cross the harbor.

1 **Star Ferry Pier** is a convenient starting place for any tour of Kowloon. Here you will also find the bus terminal, with traffic going to all parts of Kowloon and New Territories. On your left, as you face the bus station, is **Ocean Terminal,** where luxury cruise ships berth. Inside this terminal and in the adjacent **Ocean Centre** are miles of air-conditioned shopping arcades filled with hundreds of shops.

Bird Market, **13**
Kansu Street
Jade Market, **10**
Kowloon Park, **8**
Nathan Road, **7**
Peninsula Hotel, **2**
Regent Hotel, **5**
Space Museum, **4**
Star Ferry Pier, **1**
Sung Dynasty
Village, **14**
Temple Street, **9**
Tin Hau Temple, **11**
Tsim Sha Tsui
Cultural Centre, **3**
Tsim Sha Tsui East, **6**
Yaomatei Typhoon
Shelter, **12**

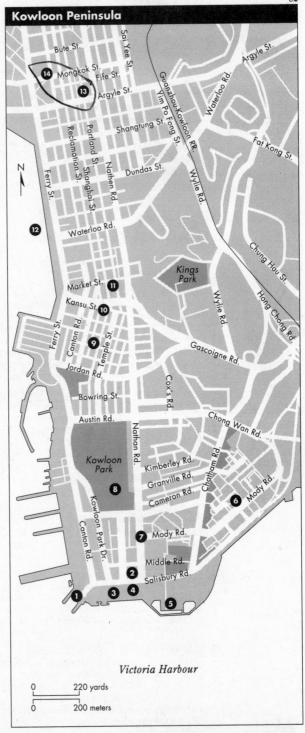

Kowloon Peninsula

Bute St.
Sai Yee St.
Mongkok St.
Fife St.
Argyle St.
Argyle St.
Waterloo Rd.
Fat Kong St.
Guanzhou Kowloon RR.
Yim Po Fong St.
Shangtung St.
Reclamation St.
Portland St.
Shanghai St.
Nathan Rd.
Dundas St.
Wylie Rd.
Ferry St.
N
Waterloo Rd.
Kings Park
Wylie Rd.
Chung Hau St.
Hong Chong Rd.
Market St.
Kansu St.
Ferry St.
Canton Rd.
Temple St.
Jordan Rd.
Gascoigne Rd.
Cox's Rd.
Bowring St.
Austin Rd.
Chong Wan Rd.
Kowloon Park
Nathan Rd.
Kimberley Rd.
Granville Rd.
Cameron Rd.
Chatham Rd.
Mody Rd.
Kowloon Park Dr.
Mody Rd.
Canton Rd.
Middle Rd.
Salisbury Rd.

Victoria Harbour

0   220 yards
0   200 meters

To the right of the Star Ferry is the **Victoria Clock Tower,** all that is left of the Kowloon-Canton Railway Station, which once stood on this site. The new station, for travel within China, is a mile (1.6 km) to the east.

Head east along **Salisbury Road,** and immediately on your left is **Star House,** where you'll find one of the best branches of the **China Arts and Crafts** department stores. Crossing Canton Road, you'll see a tree-covered hill to your left, headquarters of the **Marine Police** (Canton and Salisbury Rds.). On the far corner (Peking Rd. and Kowloon Park Dr.) is a branch of **Welfare Handicrafts,** which sells souvenir goods made in Hong Kong prisons. Taking the underpass across Kowloon Park Drive, you will come to the **YMCA** (41 Salisbury Rd.), one of Kowloon's oldest institutional buildings. The "Y" has an excellent bookshop specializing in travel guides and books on Asia, and an inexpensive coffee shop.

2 The next block on the left contains the superb **Peninsula Hotel** (Salisbury Rd.). Outside are its fleet of Rolls-Royce taxis, and doormen in white uniforms. Be certain to enter the ornate lobby and enjoy an afternoon tea here at some point during your stay. Return to the Clock Tower and follow Salisbury Road past

3 the **Tsim Sha Tsui Cultural Centre** which is under construction When it opens in 1989, the center will have theaters, concert halls, museums, and libraries.

4 The dome-shaped **Space Museum** houses one of the most advanced planetariums in Asia. It contains a **Hall of Solar Science, Exhibition Halls,** and a **Space Theatre** with shows on the night sky and space travel. Only some shows are in English. *10 Salisbury Rd., tel. 3/721–2361. Space Theater: Admission HK$15 adults, HK$10 children. Open Mon. and Wed.–Sun.; 7 shows daily, weekdays beginning at 2:30; 8 shows Sat., beginning at 1:30; 10 shows Sun., beginning at 11:30. Closed Tues. Exhibition Hall and Hall of Solar Science: Admission free. Open Mon. and Wed.–Fri. 2–9:30, Sat. 1–9:30, Sun.; and holidays 10:30–9:30. Closed Tues.*

5 Among Hong Kong's finest luxury hotels is the **Regent** (Salisbury Rd.). Its lobby has windows offering panoramic views of the harbor—a good place for a drink at sunset.

6 **Tsim sha tsui East** is part of the land reclamation that has transformed the entire district into a galaxy of luxury hotels, restaurants, and entertainment and shopping complexes.

7 **Nathan Road,** the "Golden Mile" runs north for several miles, and is filled with hotels and shops of every description. To the left and right are mazes of narrow streets lined with additional shops crammed with every possible type of merchandise.

8 Just off Nathan Road is **Kowloon Park.** The former site of Whitfield Military Barracks is today a restful, green oasis featuring a **Chinese Garden** with lotus pond, streams, a lake, and an aviary with a colorful selection of rare birds. On the south end of the park, near Haiphong Road entrance, is the **Jamai Masjid and Islamic Centre.** This is Hong Kong's main mosque, built in 1984. It has four minarets, decorative arches, and a marble dome.

The **Hong Kong Museum of History** is temporarily housed in two former barracks in the park. Its collection covers local history, archaeology, ethnography, and natural history, with both permanent and changing exhibitions. The museum's photographs of old Hong Kong are of particular interest. *Haiphong Rd., tel. 3/671–124. Admission free. Open Sat.–Thurs. 10–6, Sun. 1–6. Closed Fri.*

Continue north on Nathan Road three blocks to Jordan Road, make a left and another left onto Temple Street. The tiny streets to your right are ideal for wandering and people-watching. There is too much here to be described in detail, but ⑨ the highlight of this shopping area is **Temple Street,** which becomes an **open-air market** in the evening filled with street doctors offering cures for almost any complaint, fortune tellers, and, on most nights, Chinese opera. The best time to visit is 8–11 PM.

Shanghai Street and **Canton Road** are also worth a visit for their colorful shops and stalls selling everything from herbal remedies to jade and ivory. **Ning Po Street** specializes in shops selling paper kites and colorful paper and bamboo models of worldly possessions that are burned at Chinese funerals.

⑩ North of this maze of streets is the **Kansu Street Jade Market.** You'll get there by following Temple Street to Kansu Street and turning left. The daily jade market carries everything from ordinary pendants to precious carvings. If you don't know much about jade, take along someone who does, or you may well pay a lot more than you should. The best time to visit is from 10 to noon.

⑪ **Tin Hau Temple** (Market St., one block north of Kansu St.), is a colorful sight, with its curved tile roofs designed to deter evil spirits. One of Kowloon's oldest temples, it is filled with incense and crowds of worshipers. You'll probably be encouraged to have a try with the fortune sticks.

⑫ **The Yaomatei Typhoon Shelter,** opposite Ferry Street, is home to a colorful floating community living on the packed sampans and fishing junks. It is best explored by one of the small boats that ply the harbor. The fishermen and their families still follow their traditional way of life, departing from here each day and returning to unload their catch at local markets.

⑬ Return to Nathan Road, walk north eight blocks to Argyle Street, and turn left. You can hear the **Bird Market** (Hong Lok St., behind Mong Kok MTR Station) long before you see it. Though the area is only two blocks long, it is packed with hundreds of caged birds for sale, all singing and chirping at one time. Song birds have always been prized by the Chinese.

⑭ To go back in history hundreds of years, visit **Sung Dynasty Village,** northwest of Kowloon city. Take the MTR at Mong Kok station and go five stops north to Mei Foo station. From here it is a short walk along Lai Wan and Mei Lai roads. The village recreates the life of a Sung village 1,000 years ago. There are faithful replicas of the houses, shops, restaurants, and temples of the period. You can watch men work at ancient crafts, and see people dressed in costumes of the time. The easiest way to see the village is to take an organized tour, which can be arranged through your hotel tour desk. You can also visit on your own. *Lai-Chi-Kok Amusement Park, tel. 3/741–5111. Admission: HK$35 adults, HK$15 children. Open Sat.–Sun. and holidays, 12:30–5.*

Exploring New Territories

The visitor who has taken the trouble to explore Hong Kong and Kowloon should go one step farther and spend at least a day in **New Territories**. Here you will not only look across the border into the People's Republic of China, you will also be able to enjoy broad vistas of forested mountainsides and visit some of the many ancient temples that fill the area.

Only about 15 miles (25 km) separate Kowloon's waterfront from the People's Republic of China. New Territories is often referred to as "the land between," because it is the area between Kowloon and the Chinese border. It is called New Territories because it was the last area of land claimed by the British in extending their Hong Kong colony. A day's touring around New Territories will show you yet another face of Hong Kong, a rural one, with small villages, and peasants working in their rice fields and market gardens. You will be surprised at how remote and undeveloped some parts of New Territories are, at the miles of land without a single building, at the forests, and at the hilltops free of high-rise, or even low-rise, buildings. The easiest way to see the region is by taking a six-hour "Land Between" tour organized by the HKTA. *Tel. 5/244–191. Departs Queen's Pier, Central, at 8:30 AM, Holiday Inn Golden Mile at 9 AM, and Holiday Inn Harbour View at 9:10 AM. Cost: HK$180 adults, HK$140 children. Weekdays only.*

You can also rent a self-drive car or a chauffeur-driven car for a day, or take the Kowloon-Canton Railway from Kowloon to the Lo Wu Station on the Chinese border. There are nine stations en route, and you can get off at any one of them. The Kowloon-Canton Railway Corporation provides a leaflet outlining main attractions in the areas near the railroad stations. You can pick one up at the railroad station or any HKTA office. *For information, tel. 0/606–9606. First-class fare to Sheung Shui, the stop before the border: HK$10.40.*

Below is a brief description of the highlights of a New Territories tour, circling clockwise out of Kowloon.

Chuk Lam Sim is one of Hong Kong's most impressive monasteries. The name means "The Bamboo Forest Monastery." It has three large statues of Buddha; on festival days it is packed with worshipers. Visitors going to the monastery may want to join "The Land Between Tour" organized by the Hong Kong Tourist Association (*see* Tourist Information above).

Ching Chung Koon Taoist Temple is located near the town of Tuen Mun. This huge temple has room after room of altars, all filled with the heady scent of incense burning in bronze holders. On one side of the main entrance is a cast-iron bell with a circumference of about five feet. All large monasteries in ancient China had such bells, which were rung at daybreak to wake the monks and nuns who would go out into the rice fields and work all day. On the opposite side of the entrance is a huge drum that was used to call the workers back in the evenings. Inside are rooms with walls of small pictures of the departed. Their relatives pay the temple to have these photos displayed, so they can see them as they pray. The temple also includes a retirement home, built from donations, which provides a quiet and serene atmosphere for the elderly. The grounds are beautiful, with plants and flowers, hundreds of dwarf shrubs, ornamental fish ponds, and pagodas.

Tuen Mun has a population of 200,000 and is one of Hong Kong's "new towns"—independent, small cities created to take the spillover of population from the crowded areas of Kowloon and Hong Kong Island. They provide both industrial areas and living accommodations for the workers and their families. Other new towns are Tsuen Wan, Yuen Long, Shatin, Taipo, Fanling, and Junk Bay. By 1990 the seven towns are expected to house three million people, or 41% of Hong Kong's projected population of 7.3 million.

Min Fat Buddhist Monastery, located on Castle Peak Road near Tuen Mun, is a popular place for a vegetarian lunch. The monastery itself is ornate, with large, carved-stone animals guarding the front. Farther on is Yuen Long, completely redeveloped as an industrial and residential complex.

Lau Fau Shan is a village famous for its fish market. Here you will find people selling freshly caught fish and shellfish, as well as dried fish and salted fish. Select what you want, pay for it, take it to one of the many restaurants, and have it cooked to order. This is the oyster capital of Hong Kong, but don't eat them raw.

Kam Tin Walled Village, a regular stop on most tours, was built in the 1600s as a fortified village belonging to the Tang clan. The original walls are intact, with guardhouses on the four corners and arrow slits for fighting off attackers. The image of antiquity is somewhat spoiled now by the modern homes and their TV antennas looming over the ancient fortifications. Directly inside the main gate is a narrow street lined with shops selling souvenirs and mass-produced oil paintings.

Next stop is the town of **Lok Ma Chau,** where the big attraction is the view. You can stand on a hill and look down on vast fields and the Shenzhen River winding through them. Across the river, barely a mile (1.6 km) away, is the People's Republic of China. Unless you plan a tour into China, this is as close as you will get. Elderly "models" here demand HK$1 before you can photograph them.

Fanling is a town that combines the serene atmosphere of the Royal Hong Kong Golf Club with the chaos of rapid growth. The nearby **Luen Wo Market** is a traditional Chinese market, well worth visiting.

Taipo means shopping place in Chinese and every visitor here discovers that the town more than lives up to its name. Located in the heart of the region's breadbasket, Taipo has long been a trading and meeting place for local farmers and fishermen. It is now being developed, with new housing and highways everywhere you look.

South of Taipo is the **Chinese University.** The **Art Gallery,** located in the university's **Institute of Chinese Studies** building, is well worth a visit. It has large exhibits of paintings and calligraphy from the Ming period to modern times. There are also important collections of bronze seals, carved jade flowers, and ceramics from South China. *Tel. 0/695–2218. Admission free. Open Mon.–Sat. 10–4:30, Sun. and holidays 12:30–4:30.*

Across from the campus is the popular **Yucca de Lac Restaurant** which has outdoor dining facilities. About a 15-minute walk from the University is the starting point for a ferry tour of **Tolo Harbour** and the **Sai Kung Peninsula.** *Call the Hong Kong and Youmati Ferry Co. for ferry schedule, tel. 5/423–081.*

Whether you enter **Shatin** by road or rail, you will be amazed to find this metropolis in the middle of New Territories. Another of the "new towns," Shatin underwent a population explosion that took it from a town of 30,000 to one of almost 225,000 in less than 10 years. It is home to the **Shatin Racecourse,** Hong Kong's second largest. Nearby is the huge **Jubilee Sports Centre,** a vast complex of tracks and training fields designed to give Hong Kong's athletes space to train under professional, full-time coaches for international competition. Shatin is also home of **New Town Plaza,** the most extensive shopping complex in New Territories.

You'll need to climb some 500 steps to reach the **Temple of Ten Thousand Buddhas,** nestled among the foothills of Shatin, but a visit is worth every step. Inside the main temple are nearly 13,000 gilded clay statues of Buddha, all virtually identical. They were made by Shanghai craftsmen and donated by worshipers. From this perch you can see the famous **Amah Rock.** Amah means "nurse" in Chinese, and the rock, which resembles a woman with a child on her back, is popular with female worshipers. To the west of the temple is **Tai Mo Shan,** Hong Kong's highest peak, rising 3,230 feet above sea level.

The **Sai Kung Peninsula** consists mostly of park land. Clearwater Bay Road, past Kai Tak Airport, will take you into forested areas, and land that is only partially developed, with Spanish-style villas overlooking the sea.

Exploring the Outer Islands

Looking out the airplane window on the approach to Kai Tak Airport on a fine day, you will see clusters of small islands dotting the South China Sea. Fishing fleets trawl slowly through the blue waters. Tiny *sampans* (flat-bottom boats) scamper from one outcrop to another, ignoring the junks, ocean liners, and cargo ships steaming in and out of Hong Kong Harbour. Look closer and you will see sandy coves, long strands of fine yellow sand massaged by gentle surf, and countless tiny village settlements clinging to rocky bays and small sand bars.

These outer islands are the "Other Hong Kong," that unspoiled natural beauty that is as much a part of Hong Kong as Kowloon's crowded tenements or Hong Kong Island's concrete canyons. But most visitors miss the opportunity to see this side of the territory.

In addition to Hong Kong Island and the mainland sections of Kowloon and New Territories, there are 235 islands under the control of the British—at least until 1997. The largest, Lantau, is bigger than Hong Kong Island; the smallest is just a few square feet of rock. Most of them are uninhabited. Others are gradually being developed, but at nowhere near the density of the main urban areas.

Visiting the outer islands is a wonderfully escapist experience after the people, noise, traffic, and frantic activity of the city.

Try to go on a weekday; on weekends, Hong Kongers flock to them and pack the ferries.

You can reach the islands by scheduled ferry services operated by the Hong Kong and Yaumati Ferry Company (HYFC). The ferries are easy to recognize by the large HYF letters painted on their funnels. *Leave from the Outlying Districts Services Pier and Government Pier, Central. Tel. 5/423–081 for schedule. Round-trip fare: HK$9–$22.*

The biggest of the islands, **Lantau,** covers 55 square miles and is almost twice the size of Hong Kong Island. However, Lantau's population is less than 17,000, compared with Hong Kong Island's 1.5 million. Lantau is well worth a full day's visit, even two. The ferry will take you to **Silvermine Bay,** which is being developed as a commuter's suburb of Hong Kong Island.

Safe, sandy beaches, such as those of **Cheung Sha,** stretch along southern Lantau's shoreline. The island's private bus services link the main ferry town, **Mui Wo** in Silvermine Bay, with **Tung Chung,** which has a Sung Dynasty fort, and **Tai O,** the capital of Lantau. Tai O, once an ancient fishing village, is divided into two parts connected by a rope-drawn ferry. In the mountainous interior of the island you will find a tea plantation with a horseback riding camp, and a Buddhist monastery. The monastery, **Precious Lotus Monastery,** is near **Ngong Ping** and has one of the world's largest statues of Buddha. The statue, on Lantau Peak, 3,000 feet above sea level, has a red flashing light for warning aircraft. The monastery, gaudy and exuberantly commercial, is famous for its vegetarian meals served in the temple refectory, as well as for the giant Buddha.

The visitor with historical interests will find many surprises on Lantau. The imperial hold on the islands of the South China Sea was tenuous, but at one time Lantau was the temporary home for an emperor of the Sung Dynasty. That was in 1277, when 10-year-old Emperor Ti Cheng and his small retinue set up camp just behind modern Silvermine Bay's beaches. They were fleeing the Mongol forces of Kublai Khan. The young emperor died on Lantau. The Sung Dynasty was crushed the following year, leaving no traces of the island's brief moment of imperial glory.

There are traces, however, of Sung Dynasty communities of the 13th century, including their kilns and burial sites. Many excavations on the island show evidence of even earlier settlements, some dating back to Neolithic times.

For quiet and solitude, visit the **Trappist Monastery** on Eastern Lantau, and drink the fresh milk produced by a small dairy herd owned by the monks. You can spend the night in simple accommodations, but you must make reservations well in advance. Although the monastery can be reached from Silvermine Bay, it's best to go there via Peng Chau Island, a small community en route to Silvermine Bay (*see* Peng Chau Island below).

Visitors may also stay overnight at a tea plantation or at the Precious Lotus Monastery. The HKTA has an information sheet on these and other accommodations available on Lantau.

For a gentle two-hour trip into what rural China must have been like in past centuries wander across **Lamma Island,** which faces the fishing port of Aberdeen on Hong Kong Island's south side. Farmers, shielded from the sun by black-fringed straw hats, grow vegetables, while fishermen gather shellfish, much as their ancestors did before them. Ignore the power station and cement factory and seek out the small bays along narrow paths that offer changing views of the ocean and of Hong Kong Island.

Allow time to stop for a meal at either of Lamma's two ferry villages: **Sok Kwu Wan** and **Yung Shue Wan.** In both villages, lines of friendly, open-air harborside restaurants, some with amazingly diverse wine lists, offer feasts of freshness that put many restaurants on Hong Kong Island to shame.

Dining out is a major joy on **Cheung Chau Island,** which lies south of Lantau. Almost every Western visitor's favorite Hong Kong island, it has dozens of good, open-air cafes on either side of its crowded sand bar township—both on the **Praya Promenade** along the waterfront and overlooking the main public beach on **Tung Wan.**

Cheung Chau is Hong Kong's most crowded outlying island, with 30,000 or more people, most of them living on the sand bar that connects the dumbbell-shaped island's two hilly tips. It has a Mediterranean flavor to it that has attracted artists and writers from around the world, some of whom have created an expatriate's artist's colony here. The entry into Cheung Chau's harbor, through lines of gaily bannered fishing boats, is an exhilarating experience. Also colorful is the island's annual springtime Bun Festival, one of Hong Kong's most popular community galas. There is also history on Cheung Chau— pirate caves, ancient rock carvings, and a 200-year-old temple built to protect the islanders from the twin dangers of plagues and pirates.

Throughout the year, small sampans provide ferry service from Hong Kong Island to beaches on Cheung Chau—beaches that are virtually deserted and have beautiful, clear water.

With the opening of the island's first hotel, **Cheung Chau Warwick Hotel** on Tung Wan Beach, it is now possible to stay on the island in reasonable comfort.

The tiniest of Hong Kong's four major islands, **Peng Chau** was once home for a few farmers, fishermen, and a fireworks factory. Although the factory is now closed and the villagers have built three-story weekend retreats for Hong Kong's city folks, the community feeling remains.

Stand on the Peng Chau ferry quay and watch the *kaido* (ferryboat) for Lantau's Trappist monastery sputter toward dark green hills. Choose your fresh shellfish from baskets held aloft by local fishermen bobbing in boats below the quay, and take it back to a cafe to be cooked. Then breathe in that stirring ambience of Hong Kong's islands—a mix of salt air, shrimp paste, and dried fish, combined with a strong dose of local pride and a sense of independence that has been lost or never found in urban Hong Kong.

Major Sights and Attractions

Museums and libraries, parks, and beaches are listed separately below.

Hong Kong Island

Central District **Cat Street.** Once the center of Hong Kong's underworld, this is now one of the island's prime shopping areas.

Hollywood Road. Here, between Arbuthnot Road and its junction with Lyndhurst Terrace, is the most important street for antiques and flea-market merchandise. Each step of nearby **Ladder Street** is filled with hawkers.

Hongkong and Shanghai Banking Corporation Building. Hong Kong's largest bank has its headquarters in this glass-and-steel structure with towers and modular walls—an example of high-tech at its best.

The Landmark (Pedder Street and Des Voeux Road). This is one of the Territory's best shopping centers, home of some of the classiest boutiques in town. There is free entertainment daily.

Legislative Council Building (Chater and Jackson Rds.). This is one of the few historic buildings in Central that is still standing (though vibrations from the drills during construction of the subway nearly caused it to collapse). It was built in 1910 and once housed the Supreme Court.

Mandarin Oriental Hotel. Located at the end of the Star Ferry pedestrian underpass, the hotel is frequently mentioned as one of the world's finest hotels. It is a splendid place for people-watching, particularly in the **Captain's Bar,** where billion-dollar deals are negotiated over brandy.

Man Mo Temple (Hollywood Rd.). Hong Kong's oldest temple dates back to the 1840s.

Peak Tram Terminal (Garden Rd., behind the Hilton Hotel). Built in 1888, this is the starting point for trips up the funicular railway to the top of 1,805-foot Victoria Peak. From here you'll enjoy breathtaking views of Hong Kong Harbour, the outer islands, and sometimes even the Chinese border.

Poor Man's Nightclub. Located next to Macau Ferry Pier, this is one of the two best night markets. It's open from about 6:30 PM–1 AM.

Star Ferry Terminal. This is the starting point for one of the world's most famous harbor ferry rides. The journey takes only about 10 minutes, but is unforgettable.

St. John's Cathedral. The official Anglican church, completed in 1849, still shows off its early Victorian-Gothic elegance. Open daily 10–8. Sunday services are open to the public.

Wing On Street. This is the main street for cloth and clothing. Others are Li Yuen Street East and Li Yuen Street West, which run between Queen's Road Central and Des Voeux Road.

**Wanchai/
Causeway Bay**

Causeway Bay. This is a top shopping area with big Japanese and Chinese department stores, street hawkers, and lots of little shops. Prices are cheaper than in Central.

Food Street. This street in Causeway Bay boasts some three dozen restaurants serving everything from abalone to zabaglione.

Kwan Ti Temple (Queen's Rd. East area). The temple is filled with mirrors left by people who have prayed for cures.

Noonday Gun. Tourists come here every day, opposite the Excelsior Hotel, to hear the famous gun go off.

Victoria Park. This great park has been built entirely from land reclaimed from the sea. Open 14 hours a day, it is filled with people practicing t'ai chi at dawn, as well as joggers, tennis players, and strollers.

Wanchai Post Office (Queen's Road East area) is one of the few surviving and preserved historical buildings in Hong Kong.

Happy Valley

Happy Valley Race Course. This is one of two race tracks in Hong Kong. Though built in 1841, it is continually being modernized and includes a huge outdoor video screen for close-ups, slow motion, and instant replays.

Aw Boon Haw (Tiger Balm) Gardens. A veritable Disneyland of gardens and Chinese mythology spread over eight acres.

**Mid-Levels, Upper
Western, Peak**

Hong Kong Zoological and Botanical Gardens. Opened in 1871, the gardens have a superb aviary, a fair zoo, and, of course, fine plants and flowers. In the morning the 12.5-acre site is filled with people practicing t'ai chi.

Hong Kong University. You'll find good examples of Victorian-Colonial architecture here, and an excellent museum and library.

The Peak. Visitors enjoy a scenic tram ride from the Botanical Gardens to Victoria Peak.

South Side

Aberdeen. This is one of the two oldest settlements on Hong Kong Island, and still a spectacular waterfront, with some 5,000 people living in sampans and fishing boats. Although Aberdeen is becoming more industrialized, it still presents a colorful sight. The famous floating restaurants are open until midnight, but they are not the best place to sample Cantonese food, nor are they known for their courtesy.

Ocean Park and Water World. This is one of the most popular family outing places in Hong Kong. The 170-acre park is divided into two sections linked by a cablecar. One section has parks and playgrounds; the other, the *Ocean Theatre*, with performing dolphins and a killer whale, a wave cove and an aquarium, plus an amusement park and a walk-through aviary. The adjacent 65-acre Water World is an aquatic fun park with slides, rapids, and pools. *Open May–October.*

Stanley. This was the largest town on the island in 1841, when the British arrived. Today it is a fairly posh residential town. The **Tin Hau Temple** is venerable, for Hong Kong; the market has good bargains in rattan, clothing, porcelain, and bric-a-brac.

Kowloon

Tsimshatsui **Ocean Centre/Ocean Terminal/Harbour City.** Even in this city of shopping centers, the two "Oceans" and their "Harbour" are the biggest. You can buy everything from emerald-laden abacuses to gold-encrusted zircons through miles of air-conditioned comfort. A luxury liner may be parked right by the second floor of Ocean Terminal. Take a stroll along the veranda for some unparalleled views across the harbor.

Peninsula Hotel. Once rated b the *Wall Street Journal* as one of the "10 most exciting hotel lobbies in Asia," this huge colonnaded lobby still has charm, grandeur, celebrities (though with the opening of the Regent Hotel, no longer a monopoly on them), string quartets playing music, and a British "high tea." Rest your shopping feet in style.

Space Museum. Just opposite The Peninsula, the Space Museum has a fine planetarium, a hall of solar sciences, and good exhibitions.

New World Centre. Another huge shopping center, adjacent to New World and Regent hotels. Seemingly a baffling maze, you can find everything you want, from bookshops to a kosher delicatessen.

Tsimshatsui East. Five years ago, Tsimshatsui East was just a few wharves, empty lots, even a quarry or two. Today, the area houses four first-class hotels, a dozen shopping centers, and restaurants. The latter run the gamut from pizzas to Peking duck.

Nathan Road. The so-called "Golden Mile," runs up through Kowloon to Boundary Street and New Territories. While the shopping is excellent on the main road, the best specialty shops are in the streets and alleys running at right angles to the main thoroughfare.

Yaumatei and **Bird Market, Hong Lok Street.** Here are teahouses and shops
Northern Kowloon filled with all kinds of birds, singing, playing on tables, even being taken for walks.

Kansu and Reclamation streets. Here's where you'll find the **Jade Market**—curbs and pavements virtually carpeted with jade bangles, pendants, and stones. Most of the jade is exceptionally inexpensive, but you must bargain hard and know what you're doing or you're liable to end up with fakes. The colors of the jade stones, in every shade of green imaginable, are magnificent. *The market is open daily from 10 to 3:30, arrive early for the best buys.*

Lei Yue Mun. This old fishing village, once the haunt of pirates, sits at the eastern end of Kowloon. You choose your fare (live fish) from the markets and the restaurants cook it for a nominal price.

Shanghai Street. All the streets in this area are fascinating, day and night. During the daytime, search around Shanghai Street, Temple Street, and Public Square Street for old wine shops, market stalls, and street barbers. On Battery Street, you see nothing but shops selling goods made from paper. Public Square Street has little lanes filled with fortune tellers. The Tin Hau Temple is old and dazzling.

Sung Dynasty Village. This miniature village recreates life during the Sung Dynasty (A.D. 960 to 1279). It has interesting architecture, costumes (the people who work in the village dress in Sung fashions), restaurants, street performances, and a wax museum.

New Territories

Kam Tin Walled Villages. On the western side of New Territories are the villages of **Kai Hing Wai, Wing Lung Wai,** and **Shui Tau.** They are all some 500 years old and known collectively as the Kam Tin Walled Villages. All are interesting, though Kai Hing Wai is very tourist-oriented. **Hung Shing Temple** is in Shui tau Village, a 30-minute walk from Kai Hing Wai Village.

Museums and Libraries

Museums

Most museums in Hong Kong specialize in the arts and crafts of China. A few collections, however, stress the colony's history and cultural traditions.

Hong Kong Island **Fung Ping Shan Museum.** Run by the University of Hong Kong, the museum has the world's largest collection of Nestorial crosses of the Yuan Dynasty (1279–1644). It also has superb pieces from pre-Christian periods: ritual vessels, decorative mirrors, and painted pottery. This museum is a bit out of the way, but a must for lovers of Chinese art. *University of Hong Kong, 94 Bonham Rd., Western District, tel. 5/859–2114. Admission free. Open Mon.–Sat. 9:30–6.*

Hong Kong Museum of Art. An excellent collection of Chinese art and antiquities, including fine ceramics, quality paintings, drawings, and a pictorial record of Sino-British relations. Interesting temporary exhibitions usually change monthly. *City Hall, High Block, 10th–11th floors, Connaught Rd. Central, tel. 5/224–127. Admission free. Open Mon.–Wed. and Fri.–Sat. 10–6; Sun. 1–6. Closed Thurs. and major holidays.*

Museum of Chinese Historical Relics. Ancient Chinese relics are on display. *Causeway Centre, 28 Harbour Rd., Wanchai, tel. 5/832–0411. Admission free. Open daily 10–6. Closed Jan. 1, and Chinese New Year, Oct. 1.*

Museum of Tea Ware. Built in 1845, this is the oldest Western-style building in Hong Kong. The museum opened in 1984 and has displays of tea ware, including Yi Xing tea ware, the most famous tea sets from Jiangsu Province, China. There are also slide shows and exhibitions on tea planting and harvesting. This is a branch of the Hong Kong Museum of Art, located in Flagstaff House. *Victoria Barracks, Cotton Tree Dr., Queensway, tel. 5/299–390. Admission free. Open 10–5. Closed Wed.*

Kowloon **Hong Kong Museum of History.** This is the most comprehensive museum in the colony, with permanent and temporary displays on local history and traditions, archaeology, and arts and crafts. It also houses a large photographic collection that traces Hong Kong's history. *Haiphong Rd., Kowloon Park, Tsimshatsui, tel. 3/671–124. Admission free. Open Mon.–Thurs. and Sat. 10–6, Sun. 1–6. Closed Fri. and bank holidays.*

Hong Kong Space Museum. The main **Exhibition Hall** has several exhibits at one time, and the **Hall of Solar Sciences** has a solar telescope that permits visitors a close look at the sun. The museum also has a planetarium show that explores the night skies and space travel. A few shows are in English, most are in Cantonese. A simultaneous translation service is available, through headphones attached to special seats. *Salisbury Rd., Tsimshatsui, opposite Peninsula Hotel, tel. 3/721-2361. Space Theatre show: Admission: HK$15 adults, HK$10 children (those under 6 not admitted). Exhibition Hall: Admission free. Open Mon. and Wed.–Fri. 2–9:30, Sat. 1–9:30, Sun. 10:30–9:30. Closed Tues. For times of Space Theatre shows, tel. 3/721-2361.*

Lei Cheung Uk Museum. This is actually a burial vault from the late Han Dynasty (AD 25–220), discovered in 1955. The four barrel-vaulted brick chambers form a cross around a domed vault. The funerary objects are typical of the tombs of this era. *Tonkin St., Lei Cheng Uk Resettlement Estate, Shamshuipo, tel. 3/862-863. Admission: HK10¢. Open Mon.–Sat. 10–1 and 2–6, Sun. 1–6.*

Sung Dynasty Wax Museum. A visit here is included in the guided tour of the Sung Dynasty Village. The museum depicts life in the Sung Dynasty (960–1279), one of the great periods in Chinese history. *11 Kau Wa Heng, Laichikok, tel. 3/741-5111. Group tours daily, 10, 12:30, 3, and 5:30; individuals can tour weekends and public holidays 12:30–5.*

New Territories **Chinese University.** The Arts Gallery of the Institute of Chinese Studies displays the work of Cantonese artists from the last 300 years along with bronze seals, pre-Christian stone rubbings, and jade flower carvings. *Shatin, tel. 0/695-2218. Admission free. Open Mon.–Sat. 10–4:30, Sun. 12:30–4:30. Closed on major holidays.*

Libraries

Hong Kong Island **City Hall Libraries** has three libraries of general interest: the fifth-floor **Reference Library,** which has over 400,000 volumes, half in English, half in Chinese, plus microfilm collections of rare books from the Peking National Library, and back-dated Hong Kong newspapers; the **Children's Library,** fourth floor; and the **General Reading Library,** third floor. Only residents are allowed to check out books. Take your passport; the museum is meticulous about checking identification. *City Hall High Block, near Star Ferry, Hong Kong Island, tel. 5/262-747. Open Mon.–Thurs. 10–7, Friday 10–9, Sat. 10–5, and Sun. 10–1.*

United States Information Service (USIA) Library. This is the place to go for current and backdate American magazines and books. Microfilm editions of *The New York Times* are also available. Only residents can check out materials. *1st floor, United Centre, Queensway Rd., Queensway, next to Admiralty Center MTR Station, tel. 5/299-661. Open weekdays 10–6.*

Parks

About 40% of Hong Kong's tiny land mass is given over to 21 country parks on Hong Kong Island, Lantau Island, and New Territories. These areas are very popular with Hong Kong residents, especially on weekends and holidays, so try to go on a weekday. Maps and publications on the flora and fauna of Hong Kong are available at the Government Publications Office in the General Post Office building (Connaught Pl., by the Star Ferry, on the Hong Kong Island side).

New Territories

The **MacLehose Trail,** named after a former governor, stretches 60 miles (100 km) and links eight of the area's most beautiful parks. The trail starts at **Pak Tam Chung** on the Saikung Peninsula and is split into 10 sections, ranging from three to nine miles (5–16 km), each graded according to difficulty. Most parts of the trail can easily be reached by public transportation. From **Pak Tam Chung to Long Ke** is a seven-mile (11-km) hike. At Long Ke you can either return on a circular route (about 11 mi or 18 km), or continue along the coast until you reach **Pak Tam Au**—15 miles (24 km) of hard walking. The scenery is magnificent, with dramatic coastline and sweeping landscapes, and views all the way to China. *No. 5 bus from Star Ferry to Choi Hung; change to No. 92, which takes you to Sai Kung; pick up no. 94 to Pak Tam Chung; take first section of the trail to Long Ke.*

You can also stay on the bus past Pak Tam Chung and start the trail at **Pak Tam Au.** The rough four-mile (6.5 km) walk **to Kei Ling Ha** offers breathtaking views of the entire Sai Kung Peninsula. The path takes you uphill, through a forest and past some beautiful tree nurseries, to an area with a stunning glimpse of the entire peninsula, as well as High Island, and Ma On Shan Mountain, 2,100 feet above sea level. The walk downhill will take you to Kei Ling Ha Road where you can catch a bus for Tsimshatsui, Kowloon. *No. 94 bus from Choi Hung to Pak Tam Au. Return trip: no. 99 bus from Kei Ling Ha Rd. to Tsimshatsui.*

The **Shing Mun Reservoir,** on the western side of New Territories, is also a popular walking and picnic spot. The trail around the reservoir is easy and pleasant, with many picnic areas along the way. *Mass Transit Railway (MTR) to Tsuen Wan; change to no. 32A bus and get off at Cheung Shan Housing Estate; trail crosses main road and leads to reservoir. Return trip: no. 32B bus from Cheung Shan Housing Estate to Tsuen Wan Ferry Pier; hoverferry back to Central, Hong Kong Island Hoverferry fare: HK$5 (HK$3 off-peak hrs).*

Hong Kong Island

Tai Tam Country Park spreads around the magnificent Tai Tam Reservoir, near Tai Tam Bay on the south side of the island. *Take bus no. 2 or no. 20 from Central, in front of Connaught Centre or Star Ferry Pier, or outside City Hall; get off at Shaukiwan terminal, walk a short distance to the main road, and catch No. 14 bus to the reservoir. Alternate route: no. 6 or no. 260 bus from Central to Stanley; transfer to no. 14 to the reservoir.*

If you want beautiful, manicured gardens instead of nature trails, head for the **Zoological and Botanical Gardens** in Central (across from Governor's Residence, Upper Albert and Garden roads). The gardens are small but beautifully laid out, and the zoo has a small but very fine collection of animals, including jaguars, and an aviary with cranes and flamingos.

Another beautiful city park is **Victoria Park** in Causeway Bay (Victoria Park Rd.), which holds fairs and other events throughout the year.

Beaches

Few tourists think of Hong Kong as a place for swimming or sunbathing. Yet Hong Kong has hundreds of beaches, mostly unused, and most with clear water and clean sand. About 30 of them are "gazetted"—cleaned and maintained by the government, with services that include lifeguards, floats, and swimming-zone safety markers. Almost all the beaches can be reached by public transportation, but knowing which bus to catch and where to get off can be difficult. Most bus drivers have neither the time nor the ability to give instructions in English. If you want to try the double-decker buses, call the HKTA (tel. 3/722–5555) and ask for the bus route to a certain beach. Otherwise, use the MTR and then a taxi, or take a taxi all the way. Beaches on outlying islands are reached by HYF ferry from Central and are often a short walk from the pier.

Many beaches listed below were closed at press time because of severe pollution. Check with the HKTA before taking the plunge.

If the red flag is hoisted at a beach, stay out of the water; it indicates pollution or an approaching storm. The red flag is often flying at Big Wave Bay (on Hong Kong Island, south side) because of the rough surf. Check with the HKTA or listen to announcements on radio or TV before heading out there.

Hong Kong Island

Repulse Bay is Hong Kong's answer to Coney Island. It has changing rooms, showers, toilets, swimming rafts, swimming-safety zone markers, and playgrounds. There are also several Chinese restaurants, and kiosks serving light refreshments. The beach has an interesting building at one end resembling a Chinese temple, with large statues of Tin Hau, goddess of the sea, and Kwun Yum, goddess of mercy. Small rowboats are available for rent at the beach. *Take bus no. 6, 61, 260, or 262 from Central. All drivers on this route speak English and can tell you when to get off. Fare: HK$5 or less.*

At **Deep Water Bay** the action starts at dawn every morning, winter and summer, when members of the "Polar Bear Club" go for a dip. The beach is packed in summer, when there are lifeguards, swimming rafts, and safety-zone markers, plus a police reporting center. Barbecue pits, showers, and restrooms are open year-round. *20 min from Central by taxi or take no. 7 bus to Aberdeen and change for no. 73, which passes the beach en route to Stanley.*

Middle Bay is about a mile (1.6 km) from Repulse Bay. Because the beach has few public facilities, it is relatively quiet and rarely crowded, except on Sundays, when it is a haven for pleasure boats. *Take the bus from Central to Repulse Bay, exit one stop after Repulse Bay beach, and walk down South Bay Rd. for about 1 mi (1.6 km); or take a taxi from Central.*

South Bay is a bigger edition of Middle Bay. Far from the noise and traffic of the main beaches, it is quiet and rarely crowded, except on Sundays. There are kiosks with light refreshments, barbecue pits, swimming rafts, changing rooms, showers, and toilets. *Take a bus from Central to Repulse Bay, exit one stop past the beach, walk down South Bay Rd. past Middle Bay for 1.5 mi (2.4 km); or take a taxi from Central to Repulse Bay.*

Chung Hom Kok is a short but nice beach between towering cliffs; it has kiosks with light refreshments, barbecue pits, swimming rafts, changing rooms, showers, and toilets. *Take a taxi or bus no. 262 from Central.*

Stanley Main, a wide sweep of beach, is popular with the Hobie Cat crowd, and has a Kent Windsurfing Centre where you can rent equipment or take lessons. It also has a refreshment kiosk, swimming raft, changing rooms, showers, and toilets. *Take a taxi from Central, or bus no. 6 or 260.*

St. Stephen's, about one mile (1.6 km) from Stanley Village, has lifeguards, a refreshment kiosk, barbecue pits, swimming raft, changing rooms, showers, and toilets. *Take a taxi from Central via Stanley Village; or take a bus to Stanley Main Beach and then walk or take a taxi.*

Turtle Cove, isolated but picturesque, has lifeguards and rafts in summer, plus barbecue pits, a kiosk, changing rooms, showers, and toilets. *Take a taxi from Central or a bus to Stanley Main Beach.*

Shek O is almost Mediterranean in aspect. A fine, wide beach with nearby shops and restaurants, it has kiosks, barbecue pits, lifeguards, swimming rafts, playgrounds, changing rooms, showers, and toilets. This is one of the few beaches directly accessible by bus. *Take bus no. 2 from Central to the end of the line in Shau Kei Wan, then bus no. 9 to the end of the line.*

Big Wave Bay, Hong Kong's only surfing beach, often lives up to its name and is frequently closed for swimming because of high surf. When the red flag goes up, signaling dangerous waves, get out of the water. The beach has kiosks, barbecue pits, a playground, changing rooms, showers, and toilets. *Take no. 9 bus to the end of the line at Shek O, then walk for about 20 min.*

Lido is popular with schoolchildren on outings. It has rafts, tents for rent, barbecue pits, a kiosk, changing rooms, showers, and toilets. *MTR to Tsuen Wan, then bus no. 34B.*

Hoi Mei is a gem of a beach, with white sand and gently lapping waves, ideal for young children. It has shower and bathroom facilities, but no swimming rafts, playgrounds, or tents.

New Territories

New Cafeteria has no cafeteria, but it does have a decent beach, with a kiosk serving light refreshments, and with barbecue pits, changing rooms, showers, and toilets. *MTR to Tsuen Wan, then bus no. 52 or 53 from Tsuen Wan.*

Kadoorie is a tiny beach, but it has most of the standard amenities. The small sandy strip is guarded by ancient cannons. *MTR to Tsuen Wan, then bus no. 52.*

Silverstrand is the most popular beach on Sai Kung Peninsula and is always crowded on summer weekends. Although a little rocky in spots, it has good, soft sand and all the facilities, including changing rooms, showers, and toilets. *MTR to Choi Hung, then bus no. 92 or taxi.*

Tai Au Mun, also on the Sai Kung Peninsula, has two beaches, both on the edge of Clearwater Bay and accessible by footpaths from Tai Au Mun Village. They have all the usual facilities. *MTR to Choi Hung, then bus no. 91 to the end of the line; or take a taxi.*

Camper's, near the Sai Kung Peninsula, is a lovely beach, but can be reached only by sampan from Pak Sha Wan Village on Hiram's Highway. *Take MTR to Choi Hung, then bus no. 92 to Pak Sha Wan, then a sampan.*

Kiu Tsui and Hap Mun are on an island that can be reached only by small boat or sampan from Sai Kung Town. Both beaches have most of the amenities. *Take the MTR to Choi Hung, then bus no. 92 to Sai Kung, and walk to the waterfront to pick up a boat.*

Pak Sha Chau is a gem of a beach with brilliant golden sand located on a grassy island near Sai Kung Town. Amenities include barbecue pits and toilets. It can be reached only by sampan. *Take MTR to Choi Hung, then bus no. 92 to Sai Kung.*

At **Sha Ha** the water is sometimes dirty; but because it is rather shallow far out from shore, it's ideal for beginning windsurfers. You can take lessons or rent a board at the Kent Windsurfing Centre. Facilities include refreshment stands, a coffee shop, and a Chinese restaurant in the adjacent Surf Hotel. *Take MTR to Choi Hung, then bus no. 92 to the end of the line at Sai Kung, and walk or take a taxi for 1 mi (1.6 km).*

Outer Islands

Hung Shing Yeh on Lamma Island is very popular with local young people. There are no swimming rafts, but there are tents to rent, and showers, toilets, changing rooms, barbecue pits, and a kiosk. *Take the ferry from Central to Yung Shue Wan and then walk over a low hill.*

Lo So Sing, also on Lamma Island, is a good beach, but to get there requires a rather strenuous hike over hills or along the rocky shore from Yung Shue Wan. Facilities include a kiosk, barbecue pits, swimming rafts, changing rooms, showers, and toilets. *Take a ferry from Central to Sok Wan and then walk for 20–30 min.*

Pui O, also on Lantau Island, is a tiny but popular beach around the headland from Silvermine Bay ferry pier. It has a kiosk, barbecue pits, changing rooms, showers, and toilets. *Take the ferry from Central to Silvermine Bay and walk.*

Cheung Sha is a very popular beach located only a short taxi or bus ride from Silvermine Bay ferry pier. It has a sandy beach one mile (1.6 km) long and is excellent for swimming. All the standard facilities are available. *Take the ferry from Central to Silvermine Bay. Buses meet the ferry every half-hour on weekdays; on Sun. and holidays buses leave when full.*

Tung Wan is the main beach on Lantau Island, and the wide sweep of golden sand is hardly visible on weekends because it's so crowded with sunbathers. At one end is the Warwick Hotel.

There are plenty of restaurants along the beach for refreshments, seafood, and shade. The standard amenities are available. *Take the ferry from Central to Silvermine Bay ferry pier and walk 5 min through the village to the beach.*

Kwun Yum Wan is not far from Tung Wan and is a popular spot with young people on summer weekends. It has all the amenities including showers, changing rooms, and toilets. *Take the ferry from Central to Silvermine Bay ferry pier. It's about a 30-min walk along narrow footpaths and over hills.*

Hong Kong for Free

Considering what a materialistic and profit-conscious place Hong Kong is, it's surprising how many activities are free. Many museums, for example, do not charge admission. Among the most interesting of these are the **Hong Kong Museum of History,** the **Museum of Art,** and the **Tea Ware Museum** in historic Flagstaff House. Among the best free sightseeing experiences are the garishly elaborate **Aw Boon Haw Gardens,** also known as "Tiger Balm" gardens because they belong to two brothers who invented the popular balm. The **Zoological and Botanical Gardens** are also free and well worth a visit.

Free entertainment, including concerts, Chinese opera excerpts, film, traditional dancing, and acrobatics is offered in shopping centers such as **Cityplaza, New World,** and **The Landmark.** These performances do not have regular schedules but are listed in the tourist newspapers given away at hotel front desks.

Perhaps the best free shows of all are the colorful **street markets,** where everything from vegetables to jade is sold. And in the midst of these you'll find Buddhist and Taoist **temples,** which do not charge admission.

Crossing the harbor on the **Star Ferry** and riding around Hong Kong Island on the two-decker tram are two musts for first-time visitors. The charge is minimal: the train from Central to Causeway Bay and beyond is only HK60¢. The Star Ferry charges only HK80¢ first class, HK60¢ second class.

What to See and Do with Children

Since most visitors seem intent on squeezing as much shopping or business as they can into a brief stay (the average visit is 3½ days), activities for children are usually ignored. Yet they needn't be.

For example, if you are going to shop in the Ocean Terminal–Ocean Centre–Ocean Galleries–Harbour City complex (**Tsimshatsui,** Kowloon), you can time your trip to coincide with the free cultural shows performed in the **New World Centre** under the auspices of the Hong Kong Tourist Association (HKTA). In addition, the **Landmark** (Central, Hong Kong) has its own schedule of daily events. If you take your children with you to **Cityplaza** in Taikoo Shing (Hong Kong Island), you will find roller-skating and ice-skating rinks, and the newly opened "World of Whimsy" with exciting rides and games.

The **Sung Dynasty Village,** with its acrobats and jugglers, is fun for kids (*see* Exploring Kowloon). Specific tour details are available at the HKTA. Next door is the **Laichikok Amusement Park.** It is not as fancy as the theme parks in the United States, but it can be a pleasant diversion. The park also has a small zoo —though there's an even better one at the **Botanical and Zoological Gardens,** Mid-Levels (Hong Kong Island).

Many museums, especially the **Space Museum** (Kowloon), have programs that appeal to children.

Two of the best places to take children are the **Ocean Park** and **Water World** theme parks (south side of Hong Kong Island). The Headland section of **Ocean Park,** reached by an exciting cable-car ride, has the **Ocean Theatre,** with performing dolphins and a killer whale; a wave cove, where you can watch seals, sea lions, penguins, and other marine animals frolic; and Atoll Reef, a giant aquarium filled with hundreds of fish, including sharks. Also in the Headland is the "Dragon," one of the world's longest roller coaster rides. The bottom section of the park has a Golden Pagoda with a display of various kinds of goldfish, a large-screen theater, and trained bird and animal shows. There is also a huge, walk-through aviary. **Water World** (open May–October) is a water play park adjacent to Ocean Park with swimming pools and water slides. *Ocean Park: tel. 5/550–947. Admission, including rides: HK$95 adults, HK$45 children. Open 10–6 daily. Water World: tel. 5/556–055. Admission: HK$45 adults, HK$30 children. Opening and closing times vary. Direct transport by Citybus from Admiralty MTR Station. Fare: HK$105 adults, HK$51 children.*

While you are on the south side of the island, you may want to visit the nearby beaches of **Deep Water Bay** or **Repulse Bay** (*see* Beaches) or the **Aberdeen Floating Restaurants** (*see* Dining). If the kids are old enough, head for **Stanley Village,** where they can go windsurfing while you visit the village's famous market.

Tennis, golf, squash, scuba diving, boating, water skiing, and many other sports are available in Hong Kong. If you have the time and money, look into the **Sports and Recreation Tour** offered by the Clearwater Golf and Country Club (*see* Sports).

The Royal Hong Kong Jockey Club has riding facilities for children and adults, with all levels of instruction, at its **Pokfulam Riding School.** *75 Pokfulam Reservoir Rd., Hong Kong Island, tel. 5/501–359. Cost: HK$150 for horses, HK$120 for ponies, for 45 min.*

A few Borneo Mountain ponies and horses are available at the **Lantau Tea Gardens.** Since these animals are not for beginners, your children will have to prove their equestrian skills before they may ride. *Lantau Island, tel. 5/985–5718.*

Off the Beaten Track

The **Tramways Depot,** unchanged since Victorian times, offers a contrast to the modern face of Hong Kong. The depot, open 24 hours a day, is off Hennessy Road in Causeway Bay. Walk up Canal Road East and you'll find the depot hidden between Sharp Street East and Russell Street. Across the street are open-front cafes for a coffee or lunch.

A place worth a visit but not open to the public is the **Royal Hong Kong Yacht Club** in Causeway Bay (off Hung Hing Rd., tel. 5/832–5972). Try to find a local resident who is a member, or who knows one. If you belong to a yacht club at home, you may have reciprocal guest privileges. Once inside you are surrounded by glass-fronted cabinets containing silver prize trophies and a delightfully old-fashioned bar with magnificent views of the harbor. The menu in the members' restaurant is excellent. On weekends the place hums with activity, especially when there are races being held, a common event from the spring through the fall.

For the freshest seafood, cooked to order, visit **Lei Yue Mun,** a village in Kowloon situated where the harbor narrows, east of the airport. You can make your selection in the market from tanks filled with live fish and shellfish, and then take it to a restaurant for preparation to your specifications. *Take the North Point Ferry or a ferry from the public ferry pier in Central to Kwun Tong. From here, take a taxi or bus along Lei Mun Rd.*

Visit the 1,600-year-old **Han Dynasty burial vault** at Lei Cheng Uk, in Sham Shui Po, Kowloon. It was discovered in 1955, during excavations for a huge housing estate that now surrounds it. *41 Tonkin St., Lei Cheng Uk Resettlement Estate. Take No. 2 bus from Kowloon Star Ferry terminal to Tonkin St. (10¢), or MTR to Chueng Sha Wan Station. Admission: HK10¢. Open Mon.–Wed. and Fri.–Sat. 10–1 and 2–6, Sun. 1–6. Closed Thurs.*

5 Shopping

Major Shopping Areas

Hong Kong Island
Western District

From the edge of Central to Kennedy Town (Sheung Wan MTR or Western Market tram stop) is **Western District,** one of the oldest and most typically Chinese areas of Hong Kong. Here you can find craftsmen making mah-jongg tiles, opera costumes, fans, and *chops* (seals carved in stone with engraved initials); Chinese medicine shops selling ginseng, snake musk, shark fins, and powdered lizards; rice shops and rattan furniture dealers; and cobblers, tinkers, and tailors. Here, too, you will find numerous alleyways filled with knickknacks and curios.

Also in Western, opposite Central Market, is the huge **Chinese Merchandise Emporium** (92–104 Queen's Rd. Central) with a vast display of goods made in China. Next to the Emporium, on Pottinger Street, are stalls selling every kind of button, bow, zipper, and sewing gadget. Cloth Alley, on Wing On Street, is nearby, and so is Wellington Street, where you'll find a variety of picture framers, mah-jongg makers, and small boutiques. Going west, don't miss Man Wa Lane, where you can buy your personal Chinese chop. In this area you will also find Western's two largest department stores: **Sincere** (173 Des Voeux Rd. Central) and **Wing On** (211 Des Voeux Rd. Central).

The streets behind Western Market are where you will really feel you're in a traditional Chinese world. Wing Lok Street and Bonham Strand West are excellent browsing areas, with their herbal shops and snake gall bladder wine shops (visit **She Wong Yuen,** 89–93 Bonham Strand, for a taste), and shops selling rice, tea, and Chinese medicines. Heading uphill, don't miss the stalls selling bric-a-brac on **Ladder Street,** which zigzags from Queen's Road in Central to Hollywood and Caine roads. For genuine antiques, **Hollywood Road** is the place. If you are in Western at night, try the **Night Market** by the Macau Ferry Pier.

Central District

The financial and business center of Hong Kong, **Central** offers an extraordinary mixture of boutiques, department stores, hotel shopping arcades, narrow lanes in which vendors sell copies of designer goods, and alleys full of inexpensive clothing.

Lane Crawford (50 Queen's Rd. Central), east of the Chinese Emporium, is Hong Kong's most luxurious department store. Other exclusive shops can be found in Central's major business and shopping complex, the **Landmark;** in the adjoining **Central Building,** in nearby **Prince's Building,** and in **Swire House.** The shopping arcades of the **Mandarin, Hilton,** and **Furama Inter-Continental** hotels also have luxury shops. A branch of **Chinese Arts & Crafts** (Shell House, 28 Queen's Rd., with entrance on Wyndham St.) is in this area. It has a small but excellent range of clothing, linens, silks, jewelry, and art objects.

The two most interesting alleys in Central for clothing and accessories are **Li Yuen streets East and West** (between Queen's Rd. and Des Voeux Rd.). **Wyndham** and **On Lan streets** have several good embroidery and linen shops, and **D'Aguilar Street** has interesting boutiques.

Wanchai District

More famous for its "Suzie Wong" nighttime meanderings than for daytime shopping, this district still has some interesting spots for the curious or adventurous shopper. Tattoos, for in-

Shopping

0 — 440 yards
0 — 400 meters

Victoria Harbour

Macau Ferry Pier

⑫ Connaught Rd. West ⑭ ⑮

Bonham Strand

Wing Lok St.

⑬ Connaught Rd. Central

SHEUNG WAN

⑪
⑩
Bridges St.

Aberdeen St.

Staunton St.

⑯

Caine Rd.

Wellington St.

Stanley St.

Queen's Rd. Central

Des Voeux Rd.

⑰ ⑱

CENTRAL

⑲ D'Aguilar St.
Wyndham St.

⑳ Central
㉑
Pedder St.

㉓ ㉔
㉒ Chater Rd.
㉕

㉖ ㉗
Garden Rd.
Cotton Tree Dr.

Distance from Kowloon to Hong Kong Island districts has been reduced.

Naval Dockyard

Harcourt Rd.

ADMIRALTY

Queen's Way

Admiralty, **27**
Central Building, **21**
China Products, **33**
Chinese Arts and Crafts, **2**
Chinese Merchandise Emporium, **17**

D'Aguilar Street, **19**
Daimaru, **32**
Eastern Dreams, **16**
Excelsior Hotel Shopping Centre, **31**
Furama Inter-Continental, **25**
Hollywood Road, **10**
Hong Kong Hilton, **26**

Isetan, **6**
Jade Market, **4**
Jardine's Bazaar, **35**
Johnston Road, **28**
Ladder Street, **11**
Landmark, The, **20**

Li Yuen Streets East and West, **18**
Mandarin Hotel, **23**
Mitsukashi, **30**
Mody Road, **7**
New World Shopping Centre, **8**
Night Market, **14**

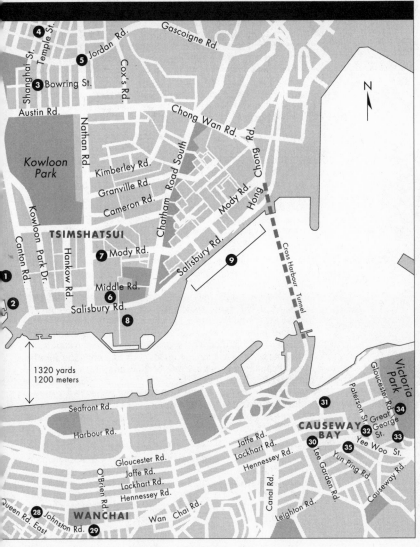

N

Temple St.
Shanghai St.
Jordan Rd.
Gascoigne Rd.
Bowring St.
Cox's Rd.
Austin Rd.
Chong Wan Rd.
Kowloon Park
Nathan Rd.
Kimberley Rd.
Granville Rd.
Cameron Rd.
Chong Rd.
Mody Rd.
Hong Chong Rd.
TSIMSHATSUI
Kowloon Park Dr.
Hankow Rd.
Mody Rd.
Salisbury Rd.
Canton Rd.
Middle Rd.
Salisbury Rd.
Cross Harbour Tunnel
1320 yards
1200 meters
Seafront Rd.
Victoria Park
Harbour Rd.
Gloucester Rd.
Paterson St.
Great George St.
CAUSEWAY BAY
Jaffe Rd.
Lockhart Rd.
Hennessey Rd.
Gloucester Rd.
Jaffe Rd.
Lockhart Rd.
Hennessey Rd.
O'Brien Rd.
Canal Rd.
Yee Woo St.
Lee Garden Rd.
Yun Ping Rd.
Causeway Rd.
Leighton Rd.
Queen Rd. East
Johnston Rd.
WANCHAI
Wan Chai Rd.

Ocean Terminal-
Ocean Centre-
Harbour City-
Hong Kong Hotel, **1**
Park Lane Hotel, **34**
Poor Man's Nightclub, **12**
Prince's Building, **22**
Shun Tak Centre, **15**

Spring Garden
Lane, **29**
Swire House, **24**
Temple Street, **3**
Tsimshatsui East, **9**
Wing Lok Street, **13**
Yue Hwa, **5**

stance, are available on **Jaffe Road,** and traditional Chinese bamboo bird cages on **Johnston Road.** Wandering through the lanes between Johnston Street and Queen's Road East, with their vegetable and fruit markets, you can find dozens of stalls selling buttons and bows, and inexpensive clothes. In tiny **Spring Garden Lane,** you will also find several small factory outlets. **Queen's Road East** (near its junction with Queensway) is famous for shops that make blackwood and rosewood furniture and camphorwood chests. There are more furniture shops on **Wanchai Road,** off Queen's Road East.

Happy Valley   This area, known to locals for its horse-racing track, is also a good place to shop for shoes. Follow Wong Nai Chung Road around the eastern edge of the race course to Leighton Road. At the intersection of these two roads you will find several shops that make shoes, boots, and handbags to order, at reasonable prices. The nearby **Leighton Centre** (77 Leighton Rd., between Matheson Rd. and Percival St.) has several fashionable boutiques, toy shops, and accessory shops. But prices are higher here than they are in the boutiques of nearby Causeway Bay, Hong Kong Island's largest shopping area.

Causeway Bay   Four large Japanese department stores dominate Causeway Bay: **Mitsukoshi** (corner Hennessy and Lee Garden Rds.), **Sogo** (545–555 Hennessy Rd., East Point Centre), **Daimaru** (corner Great George and Patterson Sts.), and **Matsuzakaya** (2–20 Patterson St.). The main branch of the **China Products** chain (31 Yee Wo St., next to Victoria Park) is here, and a branch of **Lane Crawford** is in nearby Windsor House (311 Gloucester Rd.). **Hennessy Road** is filled with shops selling jewelry, watches, hi-fis, cameras, and electronic goods. Surrounding the nearby Lee Gardens Hotel are hundreds of small boutiques and tailors. **Lockhart Road,** parallel to Hennessy Road, has some good shoe shops; the nearby **Excelsior Hotel Shopping Centre** features a wide range of art, gift, and souvenir shops. Don't miss **Jardine's Bazaar** (Jardine's Bazaar Rd.), with its bustling stalls and shops filled with inexpensive clothing.

Eastern District   This area, which includes North Point, Quarry Bay, and Shaukiwan, is more of a residential and restaurant area than an exciting shopping area. Although there are a few large department stores along King's Road, the best shopping is found farther east on King's Road in the huge shopping complexes of **Cityplaza I & II** (at Taikooshing MTR), which houses Hong Kong's largest department store, **UNY.**

Stanley Village   The best and most popular shopping area on the south side of the island is **Stanley Market,** a mecca for bargain hunters, particularly those looking for sportswear and casual clothing. It's also a good place to shop for handicrafts, gifts, curios, and linens. The area around Main Street has a trendy, artsy ambience. On the way to Stanley Market, stop at Repulse Bay, which has a shopping arcade filled with boutiques. Nearby, on Beach Road, is the **Lido Bazaar,** a series of stalls selling souvenirs, curios, jewelry, and clothing.

Kowloon   Known for its "Golden Mile" of shopping along Nathan Road, *Tsimshatsui* Tsimshatsui is justifiably popular with tourists because of its *District* hundreds of hi-fi, camera, jewelry, cosmetic, fashion, and souvenir shops. Also investigate the streets east of Nathan Road, such as **Granville Road,** with its clothing factory outlets, and its embroidery and porcelain shops; and **Mody Road,** with its souvenir-shop alleys. In Tsimshatsui you'll also find three large and well-stocked branches of **Chinese Arts & Crafts,** the Japanese **Isetan** department store (in the shopping arcade of the Sheraton Hotel), the multistory maze of the **New World Shopping Centre,** and the vast, air-conditioned shopping complex of **Ocean Terminal-Ocean Centre-Harbour City-Hong Kong Hotel** (next to Star Ferry). The new **Tsimshatsui East** area provides a host of other air-conditioned shopping complexes.

There are two good Chinese stores near the Jordan MTR station (where Jordan and Nathan Rds. meet): **Chinese Arts & Crafts** and **Yue Hwa Chinese Products Emporium.** Nathan Road leads to the Shamshuipo area. Here you'll find the **Golden Shopping Centre** (Fuk Wah St.), filled with Hong Kong-made computer goods.

Hung Hom, the center of Hong Kong's jewelry and textile-manufacturing industries, offers a tremendous choice in designer and factory-outlet bargains. **Man Yue Street** (Kaiser Estate) is where many of the outlets are clustered.

Shopping Centers

Hong Kong Island   **Admiralty.** This complex (MTR Admiralty Station) features a large selection of shops clustered in three shopping centers: *Queensway Plaza, United Centre,* and *Admiralty Centre.* An air-conditioned walkway connects them to the Hilton Hotel in Central. Queensway Plaza features a branch of the expensive Japanese *Matsuzukaya* department stores. In the Admiralty Centre you will find optical shops and men's tailors.

Cityplaza I & II. This is one of Hong Kong's newest shopping centers (above Taikooshing MTR Station, Quarry Bay), popular with families because of its ice- and roller-skating rinks, bowling alley, and weekly cultural shows. Many shops feature children's clothing, with labels such as Les Enfants, Crocodile, Peter Pan, and Crystal. There are also plenty of toy shops, and fashion shops for men and women.

The Landmark. One of Central's most prestigious shopping sites, The Landmark (Des Vouex Rd. and Pedder St., above Central MTR Station) is filled with boutiques and galleries. It's a multistory complex featuring names such as Celine, Loewe, D'Urban, Gucci, Joyce Boutique, and Hermès of Paris. There are also art galleries and fine jewelry shops. The information board on the mezzanine near the top of the escalators will help you find a specific boutique or gallery. A pedestrian bridge links The Landmark with shopping arcades at the *Swire House, Connaught Centre,* and *Central Building.* The shopping arcades of the *Prince's Building* (behind the Mandarin Hotel on Des Voeux Rd.) are also packed with name-brand shops.

Shun Tak Centre. The MTR stops at Sheung Wan Street, where you'll find yourself at the Shun Tak Centre Shopping Arcade (at Macau Ferry Terminal). Here there is also a good choice of boutiques featuring clothing, handbags, toys, and novelties.

Kowloon   **New World Shopping Centre.** Another harborfront shopping center is the New World Shopping Centre (next to the New World Hotel). This boasts four floors of fashion and leather boutiques, jewelry shops, restaurants, optical shops, tailors, hi-fi stores, arts and crafts shops, and the Japanese *Tokyu Department*

Store. The *Regent Hotel Shopping Arcade*, featuring mostly designer boutiques, can be reached through the center.

Ocean Terminal-Ocean Centre-Hong Kong Hotel-Harbour City. Located next to the Star Ferry Terminal, it is one of the largest shopping complexes in the world; if you can't find it here, it probably doesn't exist. Harbour City alone is Asia's largest shopping, office, and residential complex, with about 140 clothing shops, 36 shoe shops, 31 jewelry and watch stores, and 46 restaurants. It is connected by moving sidewalk to Ocean Terminal and Ocean Centre, which lead into the Hong Kong Hotel Shopping Arcade. Harbour City has Hong Kong's largest *Dodwell Department Store* (Shop 231, Ocean Galleries), which sells goods from Great Britain.

Tsimshatsui East. From the Kowloon Star Ferry you can take a mini-bus to Tsimshatsui East, an area of hotels, shops, and offices east of Chatham Road. There are 15 different shopping plazas clustered in this area, including *Wing On Plaza, Tsimshatsui Centre, Empire Centre, Houston Centre, South Seas Centre,* and *Energy Plaza*. Prices are reasonable and the atmosphere is lively.

Department Stores

Chinese The various Chinese-product stores give shoppers some of the most unusual and spectacular buys in Hong Kong—and often at better prices than in China. Whether you are looking for pearls, gold, jade, silk jackets, fur hats, Chinese stationery, or just a pair of chopsticks, you cannot go wrong with these stores. Most are open seven days a week but tend to be very crowded on Saturdays, Sunday sale days, and weekday lunchtimes. These shopkeepers are expert at packing, shipping, and mailing goods abroad, but are not so talented in the finer arts of pleasant service.

Chinese Arts & Crafts is a chain that's particularly good for silk-embroidered clothing, jewelry, carpets, and art objects, but prices may be a bit higher than at other stores. *Star House, 24 Queen's Rd. Central; New World Shopping Centre; Silvercord Bldg., opposite Harbour City Tsimshatsui; and 233 Nathan Rd., Tsimshatsui.*

China Products Company offers an excellent selection of goods, including household items. *19–31 Yee Wo St., next to Victoria Park, Causeway Bay; 488 Hennessy Rd., Causeway Bay; and 73 Argyle St., Kowloon.*

China Resources Artland Centre (26 Harbour Rd., Wanchai) is an enormous, two-story store, where you can find anything from vast cloisonné urns to antiques, linens, jewelry, rosewood furniture, handmade curios, Christmas tree decorations, and carpets.

Chinese Merchandise Emporium (92–104 Queen's Rd., Central) serves a bustling local clientele. The fabric, toy, and stationery departments are particularly good here. **Yue Hwa Chinese Products Emporium** (301–309 Nathan Rd., Yaumatei and 54–64 Nathan Rd., Tsimshatsui) features a broad selection of Chinese goods and has a popular medicine counter. **Chung Kiu Chinese Products Emporium** (17 Hankow Rd. and 530 Nathan Rd., Tsimshatsui) specializes in arts and crafts but also has a good selection of traditional Chinese clothing and fine silk lingerie. The **Taiwan Man Sang Product** stores (777 Nathan Rd., Kowloon) stock goods from the People's Republic of China.

Japanese Japanese department stores are very popular in Hong Kong. Several located in Causeway Bay include: **Daimaru** and **Matsuzukaya** (both on Peterson St.), **Mitsukoshi** and **Sogo** (both on Hennessy Rd.), and **UNY** (Cityplaza II, Taikoo Sing, Quarry Bay). On the Kowloon side, **Iseten** (Sheraton Hotel, 20 Nathan Rd.) is smaller but equally popular. Opposite, in the New World Shopping Centre, is **Tokyu Department Store.**

Western Of the department stores that stock large selections of Western goods at fixed prices, the oldest and largest chains are **Wing On** (9 branches), **Sincere** (173 Des Voeux Rd., Central and 83 Argyle St., Kowloon), and **Shui Hing** (23 Nathan St., Tsimshatsui). **Lane Crawford** is the most prestigious department store of all, with prices to match. Special sales here can be exhausting because everyone pushes and shoves to find bargains. The main store (50 Queen's Rd., Central) is the best. Branches are in Windsor House, Causeway, Hong Kong; and Manson House, Nathan Rd., in Kowloon.

The **Dragon Seed** chain has two department stores (39 Queen's Rd., Central; 226 Granville Rd., Kowloon). The one in Central has a wide range of classic European clothing and shoes, and a full floor of novelty gift items. The Kowloon store has clothes, furniture, and interior design products.

Some of these department stores hold Sunday sales, and all hold seasonal sales. But stay clear of these unless you have stamina.

Markets, Bazaars, and Alleys

These give you some of the best of Hong Kong shopping—good bargains, exciting atmosphere, and a fascinating setting. The once-famous Cat Street, the curio haunt in Upper Lascar Row, running behind the Central and Western districts, has fallen to office development. But there are still plenty of other alleys and streets filled with bazaars. Some of the best are listed here.

Cloth Alley (Wing On St., west of Central Market). This alley has fantastic bargains in all kinds of fabrics.

Jade Market (Kansu St., off Nathan Rd., Tsimshatsui). Jade in every form, color, shape, and size is on display in the Jade Market. This is *the* place for jade. The market is full of traders carrying out intriguing deals and keen-witted sellers trying to lure tourists. Some trinkets are reasonably priced, but unless you know a lot about jade, don't be tempted into buying expensive items.

Jardine's Bazaar. Located on Causeway Bay, this area merges a fruit and vegetable market with a tightly packed cluster of clothing stalls. The shops behind them sell attractively priced clothing and sportswear.

Kowloon City Market (No. 1 or 1A bus from Star Ferry in Kowloon, and get off opposite the airport). This market near the airport is a favorite with local bargain hunters because of its huge array of clothes, porcelain, household goods, and electrical gadgets.

Li Yuen Streets East and West (between Queen's and Des Voeux Central Rds.). This area offers some of the best bargains in fashions, with or without famous brand names. Many of the shops also feature trendy jewelry and accessories. You can also find traditional Chinese quilted jackets. Bags of every variety, many in designer styles, are particularly good buys here. Watch out for pickpockets in these crowded lanes.

Lido Bazaar (Beach Rd., Repulse Bay). This bazaar is a series of small stalls selling souvenirs, costume jewelry, bags, belts, and some clothing.

Poor Man's Nightclub (in front of the China Ferry Terminal and the Shun Tak Centre). This small market operates at night and is so called because of stalls of inexpensive food available here. Its popularity has diminished due to the many building sites nearby, but it is still worth a visit if you are after jeans, sequined sweaters, "designer" watches, or beaded bags. It is a fun place, but avoid eating at the food stalls.

Stanley Village Market (take the no. 6 or 260 bus from Central). This is a popular haunt for Western residents and tourists looking for designer fashions, jeans, T-shirts, and sportswear, all at factory prices and in Western sizes. **Stanley's Selection** (11B New St.) usually has a good choice of sportswear, as does **Fashion Shop** (53 Stanley Style House), which is always piled high with jeans. Also interesting are the shops selling curios and household items from throughout Asia. **Manor House Collection** (17 Main St.) has a large choice of lacquerware, Korean chests, and Thai carvings. **Ah Kam Arts & Crafts** (160 Main St.) stocks mostly Chinese products, such as rosewood boxes, porcelain dolls, and traditional tea baskets. **Oriental Corner** (125A Stanley Main St., directly behind Main St.) has Chinese wedding boxes and other carved items. Stanley Village Market is also a good place to buy linen. There are four linen shops here, and they are all worth exploring. The market is at its most enjoyable on weekdays when it's less crowded.

Temple Street. In Kowloon (near the Jordan MTR Station), this is another nighttime marketplace, filled with a colorful collection of clothes, handbags, electrical goods, gadgets, and all sorts of household items. By the light of lamps strung up between stalls, hawkers try to catch the eye of shoppers by flinging clothes up from their stalls; Cantonese opera competes with pop music, and there's a constant chatter of hawkers' cries and shoppers' bargaining. The market stretches for almost a mile (1.6 km) and is one of Hong Kong's liveliest nighttime shopping experiences.

Specialty Stores

Antiques Bargains and discoveries are much harder to find these days than they were a few years ago. If you want to be sure of your purchase, patronize shops such as **Charlotte Horstmann and Gerald Godfrey** (Ocean Terminal, Tsimshatsui; and a nearby warehouse in Harbour City), **Eileen Kershaw** (Peninsula Hotel, Tsimshatsui), **Lattices** (38 Hollywood Rd., Central), **Zitan** (43–55 Wyndham St., Central), **Gallery 69** (123 Edinburgh Tower and Landmark, both in Central), or **Lane Crawford** (50 Queen's Rd., Central).

For shoppers with more curiosity than cash, Hollywood Road is a fun place to visit. The street, running from Central to Western, is undeniably the best place for poking about in shops and stalls selling antiques from many Asian countries. Treasures are hidden away among a jumble of old family curio shops, sidewalk junk stalls, slick new display windows, and dilapidated warehouses.

Eastern Dreams (corner of Lyndhurst Terr. and Hollywood Rd.) has two floors of antique and reproduction furniture, screens, and curios. **Yue Po Chai Antique Co.** (132–136 Hollywood Rd. and 8–10 Upper Lascar Row, Central) is one of Hollywood Road's oldest, and has a vast and varied stock. **Schoeni Fine Arts** (27 Hollywood Rd. and 3rd floor Hong Kong Hotel, Tsimishatsui), sells Japanese, Chinese, and Thai antiques and specializes in Chinese silverware, such as opium boxes. **Kim's Gallery** (5 Hollywood Rd., Central) is stuffed full of antique and reproduction Korean chests.

In the Cat Street area, once famous for its thieves' market of secondhand stolen goods, there is now almost nothing of interest for antiques hunters. However, **Cat Street Galleries** (38 Lok Ku Rd., Sheung Wan, Western) has a collection of dealers, all under one roof. You'll find them tucked away among the highrise office buildings that are the result of the area's redevelopment.

In the unlikely event that you cannot find anything to interest you on Hollywood Road, there are several other fascinating but contemporary emporiums worth investigating. **Amazing Grace Elephant Co.** (242 Ocean Terminal, Ocean Centre; Excelsior Hotel, Cityplaza; and Landmark) has a wide range of Asian antiques, curios, and gifts at reasonable prices. The **Banyan Tree** (Shop 214, Prince's Building, Central; 304 World Finance Centre; and Ocean Galleries, Harbour City, Tsimshatsui) also has a huge choice of things Asian, both old and new. **Treasures of China** (312 Ocean Galleries, Harbour City, Tsimshatsui) stocks art and antiques from most of the dynasties.

If you know what you are after, keep an eye out for auction announcements in the classified section of the *South China Morning Post.* **Lammert Brothers** (9th floor, Malahon Centre, 10–12 Stanley St., Central) holds regular carpet and antiques sales. **Victoria Auctioneers** (Century Sq., D'Aguilar St., Central) has sales of a more general nature.

Much more up-market, with prices to match, is **The Asian Collector Gallery** (19–27 Wyndham St., Central), a highly regarded gallery specializing in Japanese prints, old maps and engravings, and 19th-century China-trade paintings. It also runs an "Art for Offices" service. For antique embroidered pieces, try **Teresa Coleman** (7th floor, Seabird House, 22–28 Wyndham St., Central). For Japanese art, mostly prints and lithographs, look in at **Sumi Arts Ltd.** (3A Wyndham St., Central) and **Koto Arts** (1/F, Arts Centre, 2 Harbour Rd., Wanchai), which often has ceramics, fans, and other attractive items.

It may be worth having your artwork framed in Hong Kong, because prices are much lower than in Europe and the United States. Shops in Central that do excellent work include **Man Fong** (41 Wellington St.), **Wah Cheong** (7 Wellington St.), and **Kinming Glass & Frames Co.** (13 Lyndhurst Terr.).

If you are interested in seeing the latest developments in the East-meets-West art of local painters, visit **Alvin Gallery** (51 Wyndham St., Central); **The Arts Centre** (2 Harbour Rd., Wanchai), which often has exhibitions with works for sale; or the **Hong Kong Museum of Art** (City Hall High Block, Connaught Rd., Central).

Cameras/Lenses/ Binoculars Many of Hong Kong's thousands of camera shops are clustered on the Lock Road-lower Nathan Road area of Tsimshatsui, in the back streets of Central, and Hennessy Road at Causeway Bay. Two well-known and knowledgeable dealers are **Williams Photo Supply** (Prince's Bldg. and Furama Inter-Continental Hotel, Central) and **Photo Scientific Appliances** (6 Stanley St., Central). If you are interested in buying a number of different items in the shop (most also stock binoculars, calculators, radios, and other electronic gadgets), you should be able to bargain for a good discount.

If in doubt about where to shop for such items, stick to the HKTA member shops. Pick up its *Official Guide to Shopping, Eating Out & Services* at any of its information centers and authorized dealers. All reputable dealers should give you a one-year, worldwide guarantee. Unauthorized dealers, who obtain their camera gear legally from sources other than the official agent, may not provide a proper guarantee—although you may pick up better bargains in these outlets.

Carpets and Rugs Regular imports from China, Iran, India, Pakistan, Afghanistan, and Kashmir make carpets and rugs a very good buy in Hong Kong. There are also plenty of carpets made locally. Though prices have increased in recent years, carpets are still cheaper in Hong Kong than they are in Europe and the United States. For Chinese carpets, branches of **China Product** and **Chinese Arts & Crafts** shops give the best selection and price range. For locally made carpets, **Tai Ping Carpets** (Shop 110, G/F, Hutchinson House, 10 Harcourt Rd., Central) is highly regarded, especially for custom-made rugs and wall-to-wall carpets. The store takes four to six weeks to make specially ordered carpets; customers can specify color, thickness, and even the direction of the weave. There is a showroom on the ground floor of Hutchinson House. Tai Ping's occasional sales are well worth attending. Check the classified section of the *South China Morning Post* for dates. **Peking Carpets** (79 Wong Nei Chung Rd., Happy Valley) and **Sammy Lee & Wang's Co.** (Windsor Mansions, 29 Chatham Rd., Kowloon) both carry good selections.

In Upper Wyndham Street, Central, you will find several shops selling Persian, Turkish, Indian, Pakistani, Tibetan, and Afghan rugs—though don't expect miraculously low prices. **Oriental Carpet Trading** (42 Wyndham St.), **Mir Oriental Carpets** (71 Wyndham St.), **Tribal Arts & Crafts** (41 Wyndham St.), and **Tribal Rugs Ltd.** (Unit 66, 2/F at Admiralty Centre, Central) are all reputable dealers.

Ceramics Fine English porcelain dinner, tea, and coffee sets are popular buys in Hong Kong and are best found at **Craig's** (St. George's Bldg., 2 Ice House St., Central; Shop 342 in Ocean Centre, Tsimshatsui). Royal Worcester and Royal Crown Derby are among the fine china stocked at Craig's. **Rosenthal** (Prince's Bldg., in Central; Ocean Terminal, Kowloon), **Wedgewood**

(Landmark), and **Dragon Seed** (Ruttonjee Centre, Duddell St., Central) are other shops selling top-quality porcelain.

For a full range of ceramic Chinese tableware, visit the various **China Products** stores. They also offer fantastic bargains and attractive designs on vases, bowls, and table lamps. Inexpensive buys can also be found in the shops along Queen's Road East in Wanchai, in the streets of Tsimshatsui, in the shopping centers of Tsimshatsui East and Ocean Terminal/Centre, and in such street markets as **Kowloon City Market.**

Factory outlets are also a good source. Two of the most popular, offering good bargains, are **Overjoy Porcelain** (1st floor, 10–18 Chun Pin St., Kwai Chung, New Territories) and **Ah Chow Porcelain** (Block B, 7th floor, 1&2 Hong Kong Industrial Bldg., Cheung Sha Wan Rd., Lai Chi Kok.) For Overjoy Porcelain, take MTR to Kwai Hing Station, then a taxi. For Ah Chow, take MTR to Lai Chi Kok Station and follow exit signs to Leighton Textile Building/Tung Chau West.

For antique ceramic items, visit **Yue Po Chai Antique Co.** (132–136 Hollywood Rd., next to Man Mo Temple). For good reproductions, try **Sheung Yu Ceramic Arts** showroom (South Seas Centre, Tsimshatsui East). For unusual and very beautiful reproductions of Chinese vases and bowls, try **Mei Ping** (Wilson House, 19–27 Wyndham St., Central). Ceramic elephant stools from Vietnam make delightful table bases, stools, or decorative items, and can be found at **Amazing Grace Elephant Co.** (Excelsior Shopping Centre, Causeway Bay; Cityplaza, Quarry Bay; Ocean Terminal/Ocean Centre, Tsimshatsui; and Landmark).

Children's Clothing There are plenty of stores in Hong Kong that sell Western-style, ready-to-wear children's clothing. Among the best are **G2000** (Queen's Rd., Central, and New World Centre, Tsimshatsui), **Paul Stefano** (Shop 51, in the basement of the New World Centre, Tsimshatsui), and **Cacharel** (Landmark, Central). For traditional English-style smocks and rompers, go to **Baba's** (Mainslit Bldg., 42 Stanley and Potter Sts.), or **Even Chance** (Far Eastern Exchange Bldg., Wyndham St., Central). Another good place for smocks and rompers is Britain's **Mothercare** (Windsor House, 311 Gloucester Rd., Causeway Bay; Ocean Terminal, Tsimshatsui). You can also find fabulous, traditional Chinese-style clothing for tots in two clothing alleys in Central—Li Yuen streets East and West. Branches of the **Welfare Handicraft Shops** (G/F Connaught Centre, Central; Ocean Terminal; Salisbury Rd., Tsimshatsui) have interesting selections of Eastern and Western children's wear.

Computers and Peripheral Devices All of the big names—Apple, Sinclair, Osbourne, IBM, BBC/Acorn—sell in Hong Kong. If you are going to buy, make sure the machines will work on the voltage in your country—an IBM personal computer sold in Hong Kong will work on 220 volts, while the identical machine in the United States will work on 110 volts. Servicing is a major concern, too.

The real bargains in computers are the locally made versions of the most popular brands. But be forewarned: Even though the prices are lower than in Europe and the United States, you may have trouble getting your Hong Kong computer past customs on your return.

The Asia Computer Plaza (Silvercord, Canton Rd., Tsimshatsui) has 40,000 square feet devoted to everything connected with computers. Most big names have outlets here. There are also three shopping centers into which are crammed dozens of small computer shops. On Hong Kong Island, the most accessible are the **Ocean Shopping Arcade** (140 Wanchai Rd.) and the **Hong Kong Computer Centre** (54 Lockhart Rd., Wanchai). The **Golden Shopping Centre** (Shamshuipo, Kowloon) is more difficult to reach. Take the MTR to Shamshuipo Station, and use the Fuk Wah Street exit. The shopping center is across the street. You will find countless stalls here selling everything related to computers.

Electronic Gimmicks and Gadgets For those electronic devices that shoppers love to take home, the **Special Interest Electronic Co.** (Hutchison House, 10 Harcourt Rd., Central) has hundreds of strange and not-so-strange items.

Factory Outlets For the best buys in designer clothes, visit some of the factory outlets and pick up high-fashion (almost indiscernibly damaged seconds or overruns) at a fraction of the normal price. One of the best areas for silks is Man Yue Street in Hung Hom, Kowloon (take a taxi to Kaiser Estate, Phase I, II, and III). Here are factories such as **Camberley, Four Seasons, Vica Moda,** and **Bendini,** all of which produce for the fashion houses of Europe and the United States.

Furniture and Furnishings Home decor has boomed tremendously in Hong Kong in recent years, and manufacturers of furniture and home furnishings have been quick to expand their activities. **Design Selection** (39 Wyndham St., Central) has a good choice of Indian fabrics. **Interiors** (38 D'Aguilar St., Central) and **Furniture Boutique** (3 Tin Hau Temple Rd., Causeway Bay) stock imported and locally made goods. **The Banyan Tree** (Prince's Bldg., Central; World Finance Centre and Harbour City, Tsimshatsui) sells ready-made or made-to-order rattan furniture and some antique Chinese, Korean, and Filipino pieces. Queen's Road East, in Wanchai, has several furniture shops specializing in rattan.

Rosewood furniture is a very popular buy in Hong Kong. Queen's Road East, in Wanchai, the great furniture retail and manufacturing area, offers everything from full rosewood dining sets in Ming style to furniture in French, English, or Chinese styles. Custom-made orders are accepted in most shops on this street. **Choy Lee Co. Ltd** (1 Queen's Rd. East) is the best known. Other Rosewood furniture dealers, such as **Cathay Arts** (Shop 5, 31F at Ocean Centre), can also be found in the Ocean Terminal complex at Tsimshatsui.

There are a number of old-style shops specializing in the rich-looking blackwood furniture (chairs, chests, and couches made in Southern China at the turn of the century). These are in the Western end of Hollywood Road, near Man Mo Temple. Queen's Road East and nearby Wanchai Road are also good sources for camphorwood chests, as is Canton Road in Kowloon.

Luk's Furniture (25/F Gee Chang Hong Centre, Wong Chuk Hang Rd., Aberdeen) is a bit off the beaten path, but offers a huge range of rosewood and lacquer furniture at warehouse prices. It also will make to order.

Reproductions are common, so "antique" furniture should be inspected carefully. Some points to look for include: a mature sheen on the wood, slight gaps at the joints that have resulted from natural drying, signs of former restorations, and signs of gradual wear, especially at leg bottoms.

Blackwood, like rosewood and teak, must be properly dried, seasoned, and aged to prevent future cracking in climates that are less humid than Hong Kong's.

Furs It seems bizarre that Hong Kong, with its tropical climate, should host so many fur shops. But furs are a good buy here, with high-quality skins, meticulous tailoring, excellent hand-finishing, and competitive prices. Some of the largest and most popular shops are **Siberian Fur Store** (21 Chatham Rd., Tsimshatsui, and 29 Des Voeux Rd. Central); **Stylette Models** (L2–38B New World Shopping Centre, Tsimshatsui; the Excelsior Hotel at Causeway Bay), and **Jindo Fur Salon** (World Finance Centre, Harbour City, Tsimshatsui), which offers a wide range at factory prices.

Handicrafts and Curios The traditional crafts of China include a fascinating range of items: lanterns, temple rubbings, screen paintings, paper cuttings, seal engravings, and wooden birds. The HKTA publishes a useful pamphlet, *Arts and Crafts and Museums*, listing places where you can buy these specialty items; it is available at all HKTA information centers.

The Welfare Handicrafts Shop (Connaught Center, Central) stocks a good collection of inexpensive Chinese handicrafts for both adults and children. All profits go to charity. For contemporary gifts, T-shirts, dolls, posters, and hats try **Startram (HK) Ltd.** (Star House, by Kowloon Star Ferry; Regal Meridien Hotel, Tsimshatsui; and Peak Tower, on the Hong Kong side). Small and inexpensive curios from other parts of Asia are on sale at **Amazing Grace Elephant Co.** (Ocean Terminal and Ocean Centre, Tsimshatsui; Excelsior Hotel, at Causeway Bay; Cityplaza, Quarry Bay, Hong Kong Isl.; and Landmark, in Central).

Mountain Folkcraft (Shop 239B, 3/F, Ocean Terminal, Tsimshatsui; and 12 Wo On La., Central) offers a varied collection of fascinating curios. **The Forms Folkcrafts** (1/F, 37 Wyndham St., Central) is worth a visit if you like goods from China, Nepal, and Tibet. **Banyan Tree** (Harbour City and World Finance Bldg., Tsimshatsui; and Prince's Bldg., Central) features a slightly more pricey but attractive selection of items from different Asian countries. More can be found in **Tribal Arts & Crafts** (41 Wyndham St., Central). For Filipino goods, visit **Collecciones** (61 Wyndham St., Central); for Indonesian goods, **Vincent Sum Designs Ltd.** (54 Lyndhurst Terr., Central); for Thai crafts, **Thai Shop** (Silvercord, Haiphong and Candon Rds., Tsimshatsui).

Stanley Market is also worth visiting for ethnic goods. Some of the more interesting shops there are **Manor House Collections** (17 Main St.) and **Kam Arts and Crafts** (48–50 Main St.).

Hi-Fis, Stereos, Tape Recorders Hennessy Road in Causeway Bay has long been the mecca for finding hi-fi gear, although many small shops in Central's Queen Victoria and Stanley streets and in Tsimshatsui's Nathan Road offer a similar variety of goods. Be sure to compare prices before buying, as they can vary widely. Also make sure that guarantees are worldwide and applicable in your home town or country. It helps to know exactly what you want, since most shopkeepers don't have the room or inclination to give you a chance to test and compare sound systems. However, some major manufacturers do have individual showrooms where you can test the equipment before buying. The shopkeeper will be able to direct you. Another tip: Though most of the export gear sold in Hong Kong has fuses or dual wiring that can be used in any country, it pays to double check.

Ivory Ivory, like jade, is highly prized by the Chinese and comes in all forms, from entire elephant tusks to tiny toothpicks. **Schoeni Fine Arts** (27 Hollywood Rd., Central) sells antique ivory pieces. You will find collections in many other shops as well, particularly in the Hollywood Road antiques shops and in the arts and crafts shops of Wyndham and Wellington streets in Central. Beware of the old-looking yellow stain on some supposedly antique pieces. It is not necessarily an indication of age —unscrupulous dealers sometimes stain ivory deliberately. Also, look for a crisscross grain which distinguishes ivory from bone.

Most ivory sold in Hong Kong comes from the African elephant, which is not yet an endangered species. But as various restrictions have been placed on the importation of ivory items by most European countries and the United States, it is advisable to check with your home customs office or consulate in Hong Kong before buying. The shop where you buy your ivory should give you a *Certificate of Origin* issued by the Hong Kong Customs and Excise Department.

In Central there are several ivory factories. The best known are **Tsang King Kee Ivory Factory Ltd.,** (18–20 Wyndham St.), **Kwong Fat Cheung Ivory and Mahjong Factory** (27 Wellington St.), and **Tack Cheung Ivory Factory** (36 Wyndham St.).

Jewelry Jewelry is the most popular item among visitors to Hong Kong. It is not subject to any local tax or duty, so prices are normally much lower than they are in most other places of the world. Turnover is fast, competition fierce, and the selection fantastic. As one of the world's largest diamond-trading centers, Hong Kong offers these gems at prices that are at least 10% lower than world-market levels. Settings will also cost less here than in most Western capitals, but check your country's customs regulations, as some countries charge a great deal more for imported set jewelry than for unset gems.

If you are not a gemologist, shop only in reputable outlets— preferably one recommended by someone who lives in Hong Kong or listed in *The Official Guide to Shopping, Eating Out and Services in Hong Kong.* You might want to invest in a booklet, *Gems & Jewellery—in Hong Kong—A Buyer's Guide.* Hong Kong law requires all jewelers to indicate on every gold item displayed or offered for sale both the number of carats and the identity of the shop or manufacturer—make sure these marks are present. Also, check the current gold prices, which most stores will have displayed, against the price of the gold item that you are thinking of buying.

When buying diamonds, check the "Four C's": color, clarity, carat (size), and cut. *For information or advice on diamonds, call the Diamond Importers Association, Hong Kong Island, tel. 5/235–497.*

Pearls, another good buy, should be checked for color against a white background. Colors vary from white, silvery white, light pink, darker pink, to cream. Cultured pearls usually have a perfect round shape, semi-baroque pearls have slight imperfections, and baroque pearls are distinctly misshapen. Also check for luster, which is never found in synthetics. Freshwater pearls from China, which look like rough grains of rice, are inexpensive and look lovely in several twisted strands. For jewelry appraisals, contact **S.P.H. DeSilva** (Central Bldg., Pedder St., Central, tel. 5/220–639.)

Jade is Hong Kong's most famous stone. But beware. Although you will see "jade" trinkets and figurines everywhere in Hong Kong, the good jade is rare and expensive. Its quality is determined by the degree of translucency and by the evenness of color and texture.

Jade is not only green; it comes in shades of purple, orange, yellow, brown, white, and violet. The most expensive color is a deep, translucent emerald green. Be careful not to pay jade prices for green stones sold as "jade" (such as aventurine, bowenite, soapstone, serpentine, and Australian jade). Inexperienced shoppers are well advised to buy only from reputable shops. However, a visit to the **Jade Market** (Kansu St., Kowloon) is a must. Walking among the many dealers you will get an excellent idea of the range of jade's many colors, shapes, and forms.

If you are wary of spending your money on Kansu Street, visit **Jade House** (Regent Hotel Shopping Arcade) or **Jade Creations** (Lane Crawford House, Queen's Rd., Central; or Shop 110 in Ocean Terminal, Tsimshatsui). The more opulent, big-name, and reputable jewelers include **Kevin Jewellery** (Hilton Hotel); **Larry Jewelry** (Landmark and 33 Nathan Rd.); **Dickson Watch and Jewellery** (Peninsula and Holiday Inn Golden Mile hotels, Tsimshatsui); **De Silva's** (Central Bldg and Landmark); **Manchu Gems** (Shop 120D in Ocean Terminal); **Dabera** (Shop 2801 in Admiralty Centre); **King Fook** (various locations throughout Hong Kong); and **House of Shen** (Peninsula Hotel). **Chinese Arts & Crafts** (various locations throughout Hong Kong) has a wide collection of jade, pearls, and gold as well as porcelain, jewelry, and enamelware.

For pearls, try **The Pearl Gallery** (1/F New World Tower, Queen's Rd., Central) or **Amerex** (702 Tak Shing House, 20 Des Voeux Rd., Central). Famous international jewelers with shops in Hong Kong include **Van Cleef & Arpels** (Landmark, and Peninsula Hotel in Tsimshatsui); **Cartier** (Peninsula Hotel; Prince's Bldg. in Central), and **Ilias Lalaounis** (Regent Hotel lobby, in Tsimshatsui, and Landmark). For modern jewelry with an Oriental influence, take a look at the fabulous designs by **Kai Yin Lo** (Mandarin Hotel, Central).

Kung-Fu Supplies There are hundreds of kung-fu schools and supply shops in Hong Kong, especially in the areas of Mongkok, Yaumatei, and Wanchai, but often they are hidden away in back streets and up narrow stairways. The two most convenient places to buy your drum cymbal, leather boots, sword, whip, double dagger, studded wrist bracelet, Bruce Lee kempo gloves, and other kung-fu exotica are **Kung Fu Supplies Co.** (188 Johnson Rd., Wanchai) and **Shang Wu Kung Fu Appliance Centre** (322A Excelsior Hotel Shopping Arcade, Causeway Bay).

Leather From belts to bags, luggage to briefcases, leather items are high on the list for the Hong Kong shopper. The best and most expensive leather goods come from Europe, but locally made leather bags in designer styles go for a song on Li Yuen streets East and West, in Central, and in other shopping lanes. The leather-garment industry is a growing one, and although most of the production is for export, some good buys can be found in the factory outlets in Hung Hom, Kowloon.

For top-brand international products, visit department stores such as **Lane Crawford** (50 Queen's Rd., Central, is the best branch), **Wing On** (Des Voeux Rd., Central and in other locations), **Sincere** (Des Veoux Rd., Central), and **Cave Boutique** (two branches, 72 and 34 Stanley Main St., Stanley). Also visit the Japanese stores in Causeway Bay: **Daimaru, Mitsukoshi, Matsuzakaya,** and **Sogo**. All stock designer brands, such as Nina Ricci, Cartier, Lancel, II Bisonte, Comtesse, Guido Borelli, Caran d'Ache, Franco Pugi, and Christian Dior.

Linens, Silks, Embroideries Pure silk shantung, silk and gold brocade, silk velvet, silk damask, and printed, silk crepe de Chine are just some of the exquisite materials available in Hong Kong at reasonable prices. The best selections are in the **China Products Emporiums, Chinese Arts & Crafts,** and **Yue Hwa stores.** Ready-to-wear silk garments, from mandarin coats and cheongsams to negligees, dresses, blouses, and slacks are good buys at Chinese Arts & Crafts.

Irish linens, Swiss cotton, Thai silks, and Indian, Malay, and Indonesian fabrics are among the imported cloths available in Hong Kong. Many of them can be found on Wing On Lane in Central. **Vincent Sum Designs** (5A Lyndhurst Terr., Central) specializes in Indonesian batik. A small selection of Indonesian batik can also be found in **Mountain Folkcraft** (Ocean Terminal, Tsimshatsui; and 12 Wo On La., Central). Thai silks are about the same price in Hong Kong as they are in Bangkok. A large range of selections can be found in branches of **China Arts & Crafts** and in **V Thailand** (Sheraton Hotel in Tsimshatsui). Attractive fabrics from India are available from **Design Selection** (39 Windham St., Central) and **The Thailand Shop** (Silvercord, Canton Rd., Tsimshatsui).

The best buys from China are hand-embroidered and appliquéed linens and cottons. You can find a magnificent range of tablecloths, place mats, napkins, and handkerchiefs in the **China Products** and **Chinese Arts & Crafts** stores, and in linen shops in Stanley Market. Also, look in the various shops on Wyndham and On Lan streets in Central. The art of embroidery is said to have originated in Sawtow, a port city in China's Kwangtung Province. A shop named after this city, **Sawtow Drawn Work** (G2–3 Worldwide House, Central) sells some of the best examples of this delicate art form. When buying hand-embroidered items, be certain the edges are properly overcast and beware of machine-made versions being passed off as handmade.

Miscellaneous Chinese Gifts If you are really stuck for a gift idea, think Chinese. Some of the most unusual gifts are often the simplest. How about a pair of chopsticks, in black lacquer and finely painted? Or how about a Chinese chop, engraved with your friend's name in Chinese? These are available at shops throughout Hong Kong. For chop ideas, take a walk down **Man Wa Lane** in Central (opposite Wing On Dept. Store, 26 Des Voeux Rd.). For those who live in cold climates, wonderful *mien laps* (padded silk jackets) are sold in the alleys of Central or in the various shops featuring Chinese products. Another unusual item for rainy weather —or even as a decorative display—is a hand-painted Chinese umbrella, available very inexpensively at **Chinese Arts & Crafts** and **China Product** stores. Chinese tea, packed in colorful, traditional tins, can be picked up in the teahouses in Bonham Strand and Wing Lok Street in Western. A bit more expensive, but a novel idea, are the padded tea baskets with teapot and tea cups; or tiered bamboo food baskets, which make good sewing baskets. All can be found in China Product stores.

Optical Goods There are a vast number of optical shops in Hong Kong, and some surprising bargains, too. Soft contact lenses, hard lenses, and frames for glasses go for considerably less than in many other places. All the latest styles and best quality frames are available at leading optical shops at prices generally much lower than in Europe and the United States. **The Optical Shop** (branches throughout Hong Kong) is the fanciest and probably the most reliable store. Make sure you bring your own lens prescription, as local opticians are not always reliable.

Perfume and Cosmetics Although aromatic ointments were believed to have been used by the Egyptians over 5,000 years ago, it was Asia that made the major contributions to the art of perfumery. Today, Chinese perfumes are hardly a match for Western fragrances. Scented sandalwood soap is the one exception (the "Maxam" label in China-product stores is prettily packaged). For Western perfumes, the best buys are in department stores such as **Wing On** and **Sincere,** drugstores such as **Manning's** and **Watson's,** and branches of **Fanda Perfume Co. Ltd** (21 Lock Rd., Kowloon; World Wide House, Pedder St., Central; and 71 Des Voeux Rd., Central).

Shoes The place to buy shoes in Hong Kong is on **Wong Nai Chung Road,** in Happy Valley, next to the race course. Here you will find many shoe shops selling inexpensive, locally made shoes and Japanese-made shoes. Shoes from Europe are available occasionally, but most are brought in solely for the purpose of copying. If you have small feet, these shops can offer excellent buys. If you wear large sizes, you'll probably have trouble finding shoes that fit well.

Top-name Italian and other European shoes can be found in the department stores and shopping centers. But don't expect prices for designer shoes to be much less than they are back home.

Custom-made shoes for both men and women are readily and quickly available. Cobblers, even those with names such as **Lee Kee Boot & Shoe Makers** (65 Peking Rd., Tsimshatsui); are renowned for their skill in copying specific styles at reasonable prices. **Mayer Shoes** (Mandarin Hotel, Central) has an excellent range of styles and leathers. If you like cowboy boots in knee-high calfskin, try the **Kow Hoo Shoe Company** (Hilton Hotel, Central). The shops in Happy Valley will also make shoes and boots to order, and are particularly good at making shoes and bags, covered with silk or satin, to match an outfit. If you leave your size chart, you can make future purchases through mail order.

Sporting Goods Hong Kong is an excellent place to buy sports gear, thanks to high volume and reasonable prices. Tennis players and golfers can find a good range of equipment and clothing in **Hong Kong**

Sports Shop (19B, LG/F Connaught Centre, Central). Watersports enthusiasts will find sailing, waterskiing, surfing, and snorkeling gear (including wet suits) at **Bunns Diving Equipment** (188 Wanchai Rd., Wanchai). Fishermen can get outfitted at **Po Kee Fishing Tackle Company** (Ocean Terminal, Tsimshatsui). For a comprehensive range covering a variety of sports, visit the **World Top Sports Goods Ltd.** (351–352 Ocean Centre, Harbour City; 49 Hankow Rd.; and 9 Carnarvon Rd., all in Tsimshatsui).

Tailor-Made Clothing Despite the number of ready-to-wear clothing shops and off-the-peg fashion stores, you can still find Chinese tailors to make Western suits, dresses, and evening gowns. Here are some do's and don'ts.

For a suit, overcoat, or jacket, give the tailor plenty of time—at least three to five days, and allow for a minimum of two proper fittings plus a final one for finishing touches. Shirts *can* be done in a day, but again you will get better quality if you allow more time. Some shirtmakers like to give one fitting.

Choose a tailor whose shop is near your hotel, so you won't be too inconvenienced when you need to return for one or more fittings. Tailors located in hotels or other major shopping centers may be more expensive, but they will be more accustomed to Western styles and fittings.

Have a good idea of what you want before you go to the tailor. Often the best method is to take a suit you want copied. Go through the details carefully, and make sure they are listed on the order form, together with a swatch of the material ordered. When you pay a deposit (which should not be more than 50% of the final cost) make sure the receipt includes all relevant details: the date of delivery, the description of the material, and any special requirements. All tailors keep records of clients' measurements, so satisfied customers can make repeat orders by mail or telephone. Keep a copy of the original measurements in case you need to change them.

There are a number of reputable and long-established tailors in Hong Kong who provide for both men and women. **Sam's** (Burlington House, 94 Nathan Rd., Kowloon) has been patronized by members of the British Forces since 1957; one of the company's regular customers is the Duke of Kent. Another tailor is **Cheng and Cheng** (Regal Meridian Hotel, 71 Mody Rd., Tsimshatsui). **Ascot Chang** (Peninsula and Regent hotels, Kowloon; and Prince's Bldg., Central) has specialized in shirtmaking since 1949. Clients have included George Bush, Sammy Davis Jr., and Andy Williams.

Tea If you want to buy a ton of tea, you can probably do so in Hong Kong's most famous tea area—Western district on Hong Kong Island. Walk down Queen's Road West and Des Voeux Road West and you will find dozens of tea merchants and dealers, such as **Cheng Leung Wing** (526 Queen's Rd. W). If you want to enjoy a cup of *cha* (tea) in traditional style, stroll along Stanley Street in Central, where Hong Kong's greatest selection of teas is served in traditional teahouses. The beautiful **Luk Yu Teahouse** (24 Stanley St.) is the oldest and best known. Also, try the **Wan Lai** (484 Shanghai St., Yaumatei, Kowloon) for the experience of having *yam cha* (tea with small snacks called *dim sum*). As you sip your tea, you'll be able to watch "bird walkers" who come here with their caged birds after taking them for a morning stroll.

You can buy packages or small tins of Chinese tea in the tea shops of the Western district or at the various **China Product** stores and leading supermarkets, such as **Park'n Shop.**

For more sophisticated tea shopping go to the **Fook Ming Tong Tea Shop** (211, Prince's Bldg., Central). There you can buy superb teas in beautifully designed tins, or invest in some antique clay teaware.

Teas fall into three types: green (unfermented), black (fermented), and oolong (semifermented). Various flavors include jasmine, chrysanthemum, rose, and narcissus. Loong Ching Green Tea and Jasmine Green Tea are among the most popular, often available in attractive tins. These make inexpensive but unusual gifts.

TVs and Video Recorders   Color TV systems vary throughout the world, so it's important to be certain the TV set or video recorder you purchase in Hong Kong has a system compatible to the one in your country. Hong Kong, Australia, Great Britain, and most European countries use the *PAL* system. The United States uses the *NTSC* system, and France and Russia use the *Seacam* system. Before you buy, tell the shopkeeper where you will be using your TV or video recorder. In most cases you will be able to get the right model without any problems. The HKTA has a useful brochure called: *Shopping Guide to Video Equipment.*

Watches   You will have no trouble finding watches in Hong Kong. Street stalls, department stores, and shops overflow with every variety, style, and brand name, many of them with irresistible gadgets. (But remember Hong Kong's remarkable talent for imitation. A super-bargain gold "Rollex" may have hidden flaws—cheap local or Russian mechanisms, for instance, or "gold" that rusts). Stick to officially appointed dealers carrying the manufacturers' signs if you want to be sure you are getting the real thing. When buying an expensive watch, check the serial number against the manufacturer's guarantee certificate and ask the salesman to open the case to check the movement serial number. If an expensive band is attached, find out whether it is from the original manufacturer or locally made, as this will dramatically affect the price (originals are much more expensive). You should obtain a detailed receipt, the manufacturer's guarantee, and a worldwide warranty for all items.

For top-of-the-market buys, try **Artland Watch Co. Ltd.** (corner of Ice House St. and Des Voeux Rd., Central; and 62A Nathan Rd., Tsimshatsui). For less expensive brands, visit any of the 11 branches of **City Chain** (127–131 Des Voeux Rd. and Queen's Rd., Central; 10 stores on Nathan Rd., in Kowloon).

Women's Clothing   Hong Kong is more Western than many first-time visitors imagine. Nowhere is this more obvious than in fashions, especially in areas such as Central, where everyone wears Western-style clothing.

Some of the leading stores are **Green & Found** (Swire House, Landmark, and Peninsula Hotel), **Joyce Boutique** (Landmark and Peninsula Hotel), **Issey Miyake** (Swire House and Kowloon Hotel), **Boutique Bazaar** (Landmark and Peninsula hotel), **Celina Boutique** (Furama Inter-Continental and Kowloon hotels, Landmark, Repulse Bay Shopping Arcade), **Chanel Boutique** (Peninsula Hotel and Prince's Bldg.), **D'Urban** (Landmark; Matsuzakaya, Mitsukoshi, Daimaru, and Sogo department stores), **Giorgio Armani** (Mandarin Hotel), **Christian Dior** (Landmark and Peninsula and Kowloon hotels), **Gucci** (Sogo, Kowloon Hotel, and Landmark), **Hermès of Paris** (Landmark and Peninsula Hotel), **Loewe** (Landmark), and **Nina Ricci** (Prince's Bldg. and Regent Hotel).

For trendy or unusual fashions (though fairly expensive), **Jenny Lewis** (Shop 5, G/F Swire House) features exquisite, modern Asian-style fashions. Also try **Pavlova** (Shop 115, Swire House and Shop 20, G/F at Ocean Centre), **Diane Freis** (Shop 2590D and 258 3/F at Ocean Terminal; UG 25–26 Prince's Bldg.; Shop A & B Lobby at the Furama Inter-Continental Hotel; and Shop 56 at the Tsimshatsui Centre), and **Michel Rene** (Shop B11 at Landmark; Shop 5 at Prince's Bldg.; Shop 58, 2/F at Ocean Centre; Shop 2 at Paterson Plaza, Causeway Bay; and Shop 81, 2/F at Ocean Galleries Harbour City). **Kinsan Collections** (29 Wyndham St., Central) features the printed styles of Laura Ashley.

Medium-priced fashions in the latest styles for the young and young-at-heart can be found in such stores as **Toppy** (Shell House, 28 Queen's Rd., Central; Shop 64–66 at Landmark Shop G9 at New World Centre, Tsimshatsui; Shop 87, 2/F Ocean Terminal; and Shop 81, 2/F Ocean Galleries, Harbour City).

Other well-known designers located in Hong Kong include **Esprit** (88 Hing Fat St., at North Point; and in Prince's Bldg.), **Benetton** (25–27A Des Voeux Rd., Central; the Hong Kong Hotel, Tsimshatsui; and boutiques at Ocean Terminal), and **The Cotton Collection** (26 Wellington St., Central).

For uniquely designed T-shirts, sweat shirts, mohair sweaters, plus a host of designer goods, try the **Ben Sprout Shop** (inside Kowloon and Hong Kong terminals of Star Ferry). Dancers, exercisers, and those who like the latest in sexy bathing suits can browse through **Delilah** (Shop 54, New World Centre, Kowloon); **La Plume** (Shop 226, Edinburgh Tower, Central); and **Cliche** (Shop 203, Holiday Inn Golden Mile shopping arcade). For frothy negligees, try **Caetla** (Bank of East Asia Bldg., 10 Des Voeux Rd., Central).

For fancy hats, try **Renomee** (Shop 115, Melbourne Plaza, Queen's Rd., Central).

6 Sports and Fitness

Participant Sports

Golf Three clubs welcome visitors, but only those with reciprocal rights from a club at home.

The **Royal Hong Golf Club** allows visitors to play on its nine-hole course at Deep Water Bay, Hong Kong Island, or on its three 18-hole courses at Fanling, New Territories. *Fanling, tel. 0/901–211 for bookings, 0/900–647 for club rentals. Deep Water Bay, tel. 5/812–7070. Weekdays only.*

The **Clearwater Bay Golf and Country Club** in New Territories has tennis, squash, badminton, table tennis, and a health spa, in addition to golf. The Hong Kong Tourist Association (HKTA) and this club run a Sports and Recreation Tour for visitors (*see* Tours). *Clearwater Bay Rd., Sai Kung Peninsula. Tel. 3/719–1595. HKTA tour, tel. 5/244–191. Cost HK$190 adults, HK$150 children 12 and under.*

The **Discovery Bay Golf Club** on Lantau Island is open to visitors seven days a week. *Tel. 5/987–6080. Take hoverferry from Blake Pier in Central.*

Jogging Visitors can join members of the **Hong Kong Running Clinic** (a Far East chapter of the Honolulu Marathon Clinic) every Sunday morning, and two evenings each week. Beginners are especially welcome and looked after. These runs are in the Hawaiian tradition of conversation-speed jogging—if you can't talk to your neighbor, you must be running too fast. There is also a "Ladies Walking Group" for visitors, going along Bowen Road. *Meet in front of Adventist Hospital, 40 Stubbs Rd., Hong Kong Island, tel. 5/746–211, ext. 888 (ask for director of health). Sun. 7:30 AM; Tues. and Thurs. 6–6:30 PM; Ladies Walking Tues. 8:30–10 AM.*

Victoria Park at Causeway Bay has an official jogging track.

Pool Those who cannot do without their friendly neighborhood pool hall will be pleased to hear of two **American Pool Leisure Centres,** one in Kowloon, one on Hong Kong Island. *13 Man Tai St., Hung Hom area, in Kowloon; 21 Old Bailey St., in Central, tel. 5/264–825. Open 9–2.*

Roller Skating and Ice Skating There are two first-class roller-skating rinks, one at **Cityplaza II** on Hong Kong Island, the other at **Telford Gardens** in Kowloon. Cityplaza also has an ice-skating rink. *Taikooshing, Quarry Bay, tel. 5/670–400; Telford Gardens Housing Estates, Kowloon Bay, tel. 3/757–2211.*

Squash **Squash** is very much a club activity in Hong Kong. However, there are public courts at the **Hong Kong Squash Centre,** where you'll need a passport to make a booking, and the **Harbour Road Indoor Games Hall,** both on Hong Kong Island; and at Lai Chi Kok Park, in Kowloon. *Hong Kong Squash Centre, tel. 5/286–802. Lai Chi Kok Park, tel. 3/745–2796. Harbour Rd. Indoor Games Hall, tel. 5/893–7684.*

Tennis You will probably have to make arrangements with a private club if you want to play tennis. Although there are a limited number of public tennis courts, they are heavily booked in advance. To book a public tennis court you will need identification such as a passport. *Victoria Park, tel. 5/706–186; Bowen Rd.,* *tel. 5/282–983; Wongneichong Gap, tel. 5/749–122; and Kowloon Tsai Park, tel. 3/367–878.*

Water Sports **Junking**—dining on the water aboard large *junks* (flat-bottom Chinese fishing boats) that have been converted to pleasure craft—is unique to Hong Kong. This type of leisure has become so entrenched in the colony that there is now a fairly large junk-building industry that produces highly varnished, upholstered, and air-conditioned junks up to 80 feet long.

These floating rumpus rooms serve a purpose, especially for citizens living on Hong Kong Island who suffer "rock fever" and need to escape by spending a day on the water. Because so much drinking takes place, the junks are also known as "gin-junks," commanded by "weekend admirals." They also serve as platforms for swimmers, waterskiers, and snorkelers. If anyone so much as breathes an invitation for junking, grab it. To rent a junk, call **Boating Centre** or **Colony Cruises** (tel. 5/235–716) or **Simpson Marine Ltd.** (tel. 5/558–377). The junks, with crew, can hold up to 45 people, and cost HK$2,000 per day.

To **waterski** you will need a speedboat and equipment. Contact the **Waterski Club** (tel. 5/812–0391) or ask your hotel front desk for names and numbers.

Windsurfing is certainly not unique to Hong Kong, but the territory has welcomed it with open sails. A company called Kent operates four **Windsurfing Centres** throughout the territory, offering lessons and board rentals. The cost for lessons is about HK$250 for four hours (spread over two days). Cost for a windsurfing board is around HK$40 per hour. The centers are at **Stanley Beach** (tel. 5/660–320 or 5/660–425); **Tun Wan Beach** on Cheung Chau Island (tel. 5/981–8316 or 5/981–4872); **Tolo Harbour,** near Taipo in New Terrorities (tel. 0/658–2888); and **Sha Ha Beach,** in front of the Surf Hotel, Kowloon (tel. 3/792–5605).

Swimming is extremely popular with the locals, which means that most beaches are packed on summer weekends and public holidays. The more popular beaches, such as Repulse Bay, are busy day and night throughout the summer (*see* Beaches). Shortly after the Mid-Autumn Festival in September, local people stop using the beaches. This is a good time for visitors to enjoy them, especially since the weather is warm year-round.

Public swimming pools are filled to capacity in summer and closed in winter. Most visitors use the pools in their hotels, although not all hotels have them.

To go **sailing** you must belong to a yacht club that has reciprocal rights with one in Hong Kong.

A number of clubs have **scuba diving** trips almost year-round, but it is usually difficult for visitors to join them unless introduced by a friend. However, **Bunn's Diving Equipment Corporation** offers Sunday outings for qualified divers. *188 Wanchai Rd., Hong Kong Island, tel. 5/891–2113. Cost HK$250 for outings, HK$160 per dive for equipment rental.*

Spectator Sports

Horse Racing and Gambling Horse racing is the nearest thing in Hong Kong to a national sport. It is a multi-million-dollar-a-year business, employing thousands of people and drawing crowds that are almost suicidal in their eagerness to rid themselves of their hard-earned money.

The Sport of Kings is run under a monopoly by the Royal Hong Kong Jockey Club, one of the most politically powerful entities in the territory. Profits go to charity and community organizations. The season runs from September or October through May. Some 65 races are held at two race courses–**Happy Valley** on Hong Kong Island and **Shatin** in New Territories. Shatin's race course is only a few years old and is one of the most modern in the world. Both courses have huge video screens at the finish line so that gamblers can see what is happening each foot of the way.

Races are run at one track, on Wednesday nights, and at both tracks on either Saturday or Sunday. Even if you're not a gambler, it's worth going just to see the crowds.

Tourists can view races from the Members' Stand at both tracks by showing their passports and paying HK$50 for a badge.

In a place where gambling has developed into a mania, it may come as a surprise to learn that most forms of gambling are forbidden. Excluding the stock market, which is by far the territory's biggest single gambling event, the only legalized forms of gambling are horse racing and the lottery. Nearby Macau is another story—there you can get your fill of casino gambling (*see* Macau).

The ancient Chinese sport of cricket fighting (that's cricket as in insect, not as in the sport) is hidden from visitors, so you'll have to ask to get directions from a local friend. If you see someone wandering in a market, carrying a washtub, and softly calling, "tau, chi choot," follow him.

7 Dining

Introduction

by Harry Rolnick

Harry Rolnick has written more than a dozen books, including the only restaurant guide to the People's Republic of China, and The Best of Hong Kong and Macau. *The New York–born writer lives in Hong Kong and contributes to all magazines of the region as well as* New York, Diversion, Master Chef, *and other publications.*

It's true, East does meet West in Hong Kong. Luxury French restaurants do inhabit spaces cheek-by-jowl with outdoor noodle stalls. And while many chefs have been lured to London, New York, and San Francisco, the pleasure of doing "homecooking" in Hong Kong has kept many of the best here.

Unlike other Asian cuisines, Chinese restaurant food is considered better than "home-cooked," and the 6,000 restaurants do a roaring trade here. They stay open every day except two days during Chinese New Year, and are packed solid on Sunday lunchtimes with families. Trying to get seats then is almost impossible, but nobody considers it impolite to hang around behind a chair waiting for another person to finish eating.

Outside of the handful of Western restaurants that expect jacket and tie (listed on the following pages), eating out is a very informal affair. Although there are certain points of etiquette involved in eating Chinese food, Westerners are hardly expected to know what these are. Nobody will look askance at how you handle your chopsticks (most restaurants will supply Western cutlery if requested). Nobody will disapprove if you slurp your Szechuan pepper soup. (Actually, slurping is *de rigueur*.) And if you have children, they'll be supplied with high chairs and treated with respect.

Certain precautions should be taken. Although tap water is never injurious to residents, visitors sometimes have trouble adjusting to its quality, so hot tea is suggested during meals.

Don't worry too much about decor. While some restaurants are opulent, it doesn't follow that the food in these highly decorated palaces is especially good. Many of the best restaurants are basic: Formica tables, neon lights, the odd picture, a slightly scruffy wall. But the kitchens, though rudimentary, are clean, and the food is delicious.

The words "Chinese cuisine" don't mean much more than "European cuisine." The largest country in the world has dozens of different styles, though only five are prominent in Hong Kong. These are as follows:

Cantonese. As 94% of the population comes from Guangdong (or Canton) Province, this is the most popular style by far. This is fortunate, because the semitropical province has the largest selection of fruits, vegetables, and meats. And speaking of *great* Chinese styles, Cantonese is the finest. The styles of cooking are simple: The wok is used to stir-fry, boil, or steam. When oil is poured into the bottom and heated up, the food can be dipped in quickly or left for just a few seconds. The result is a natural taste. Says international gourmet William Mark: "Only Cantonese chefs understand simplicity, purity, and variety." The menus are enormous.

Shanghai. Shanghai is a city of immigrants, not unlike New York, and its cosmopolitan population has several different styles of food. Lying at the confluence of several rivers on the South China Sea, it has especially good seafood. Shanghai crabs (actually from Suzhou) are winter favorites. Many dishes are fried in sesame or soy sauce. Some find the dishes a bit oily, but nobody can forget the famous beggar's chicken or squirrel fish, so-called because the sauce poured over the fish sizzles or "chatters" like a squirrel. Again, this dish originated in Suzhou, but Shanghai restaurants feature it.

Peking. Of course Peking duck is a favorite, and nowhere is it better than in Hong Kong. This was an Imperial Mongolian favorite, and its two (or three) courses are inevitably ordered. This is a northern "noodle" culture rather than a rice one. The Peking noodles, along with Mongolian barbecue and onion cakes, are always ordered.

Szechuan. The spiciest Chinese food is now a favorite around the world. Rice, bamboo, wheat, river fish, shellfish, chicken, and pork dishes all have plenty of salt, anise, fennel seed, chili, and coriander. The ingredients are simmered, smoked, stirred, and steamed. Szechuan cuisine has integrated flavors —the opposite of Cantonese food, where each ingredient has its own taste.

Chiu Chow. Coming from near Canton, the Chiu Chow people have a gutsy, hearty cuisine which has never caught on in the West. It begins with "Iron Buddha" tea, goes on to thick shark's-fin soup, soya goose, whelk, bird's nest, and the irresistible "chuenjew leaves" usually served with chicken.

A few more hints:

Dim-sum restaurants serve tasty Chinese hors d'ouevres and must be tried at lunch (or a bit earlier, to avoid the crowds). The staff push trolleys around calling out the names of the dishes, and you point to what you want. Some dishes, such as congealed blood and giblets, are rather esoteric, but others, such as steamed pork buns or spring rolls, are readily acceptable to all.

Always check the prices of anything that says "market price." Anything from a typhoon to heavy traffic can determine the cost. Ask for the exact price for your party rather than a *tael* (Chinese weight system).

Our listings start with Cantonese and move on to Chiu Chow, Peking, Shanghai, and Szechuan.

Visitors are often surprised by the plethora of other Asian cuisines here, but Hong Kong has been an industrial magnet for many Asian nationalities. Indian, Pakistani, Japanese, Burmese, Thai, Sri Lankan, Malaysian, Indonesian, Filipino, and Vietnamese cuisines are all listed below and should be sampled.

The most highly recommended restaurants in each price category are indicated by a star ★.

At press time there were 7.8 HK dollars to the U.S. dollar.

Category	Cost*
Very Expensive	over HK$300
Expensive	HK$225–HK$300
Moderate	HK$100–HK$225
Inexpensive	under HK$100

per person plus 10% service charge

In more traditional Chinese restaurants, tips are not expected. However, it is customary to leave small change.

Dining

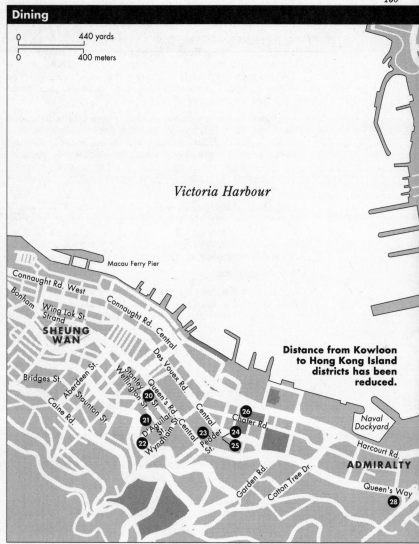

0 — 440 yards
0 — 400 meters

Victoria Harbour

Macau Ferry Pier

Connaught Rd. West

Bonham Strand

Wing Lok St.

SHEUNG WAN

Connaught Rd. Central

Bridges St.

Aberdeen St.

Caine Rd.

Staunton St.

Des Voeux Rd.

Stanley St.

Wellington St.

Queen's Rd. Central

D'Aguilar St.

Wyndham St.

Central

Pedder St.

Chater Rd.

**Distance from Kowloon
to Hong Kong Island
districts has been
reduced.**

Naval
Dockyard

Harcourt Rd.

ADMIRALTY

Garden Rd.

Cotton Tree Dr.

Queen's Way

20 · 21 · 22 · 23 · 24 · 25 · 26 · 28

American
Restaurant, **31**
Amigo, **40**
Ashoka, **22**
Au Trou Normand, **13**
Baron's Table, **8**
Benkay, **25**

Bloom, The, **23**
Chesa, **3**
Chili Club, **32**
Chinese Restaurant, **5**
Chiu Chow Garden, **35**
Eagle's Nest, **28**
Gaddi's, **4**
Golden Bull, **11**

Great Shanghai, **15**
Hugo's, **6**
Indian Curry Club, **17**
Koreana, **37**
Lai Ching Heen, **10**
Le Restaurant
de France, **18**

Luk Yu Teahouse, **20**
Omar Khayyam, **12**
Peking Garden, **1**
Pierrot, **26**
Plume, The, **9**
Rainbow Room, **39**
Rangoon, **36**
Red Pepper, The, **38**

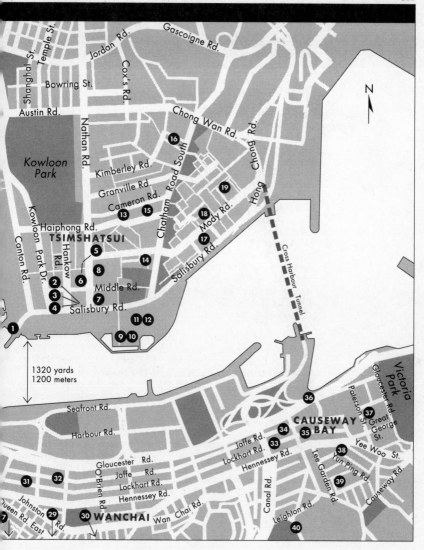

N

Kowloon
Park

TSIMSHATSUI

1320 yards
1200 meters

CAUSEWAY
BAY

Victoria
Park

WANCHAI

Royal Thai, **34**

Sichuan Garden, **24**

Spices, **27**

Spring Deer, **14**

Spring Moon, **2**

Stanley's French
Restaurant, **30**

Sze Chuan Lau, **33**

Szechuan Lau, **19**

Tien Heung Lau, **16**

Unkai Restaurant, **7**

Verandah, **29**

Yung Kee, **21**

Although major credit cards are widely accepted, many smaller establishments do not accept them. Ask before you sit down.

The following credit-card abbreviations are used: AE, American Express; CB, Carte Blanche; DC, Diners Club; MC, MasterCard; V, Visa.

Chinese

Cantonese
Expensive

Eagle's Nest. Some folks can't abide the setting here, which could be a supper club or a Continental restaurant—there's nothing very Chinese about it. The view of the harbor is superb, and so is some of the food. The suckling pig is good, the seafood is fresh, and the beggar's chicken (here called vagabond chicken) is memorable. Vegetarians have a great selection, and the family set luncheons are bargains. Service is Hilton service, which means the very best. Prices, alas, are also Hilton prices. *Hilton Hotel, 2 Queen's Rd., Central, Hong Kong Island, tel. 5/233–111. Dress: no jeans. Reservations necessary. AE, DC, MC, V.*

★ **Lai Ching Heen.** Another luxury Chinese restaurant, with some of the most unusual and best dim sum in the territory. The restaurant has beautiful cutlery, a lovely view of Victoria Harbour, delicious vegetable and chicken dishes, and baked stuffed lobster tails. Hardly traditional Chinese, but luxurious. *The Regent Hotel, Salisbury Rd., Kowloon, tel. 3/721–1211. Jackets required at dinner. Reservations suggested. AE, DC, MC, V.*

Spring Moon. This intimate, caring, and tiny restaurant has wonderful touches: Chinese vases, framed marble in glass cases, and real ivory chopsticks. The set meal is pricy, but it includes the best: shark's fin, king prawn, and crispy pigeon. Ordering à la carte is even more pricy, but the surprises are worth it—for instance, *kar luen lau* chicken (prepared like Peking duck), with skin coated with honey and left hanging overnight. The skin is carved at the table. The second course is the minced meat. Ask the waiter for specials not on the menu, such as lunch dim sum. If you're in the mood for something spicy, request the Peninsula X.O. Sauce, which is similar to a Thai hot garlic-pepper sauce with minced ham. The restaurant also has fine wines and a choice of five different Chinese teas. On Sundays and holidays, from 10 AM–midnight, special dim sum is offered. *The Peninsula Hotel, Salisbury Rd., Kowloon, tel. 3/666–251. Dress: informal. Reservations necessary. AE, DC, MC, V.*

Moderate

The Bloom. One of the more attractive Cantonese restaurants in Central. Bloom has a knowledgable and polite staff, recruited from the Regent Hotel. The decor is a snazzy pink and gray. Part of the cuisine is *nouvelle cantonoise:* spicy beef, for example, which isn't really spicy, but subtle—a bit sweet, a bit "chili-ish," with hints of garlic and shallot. The pork casserole consists of tender chunks of pork kept hot in sizzling oil. The restaurant has a good dessert menu, excellent dim sum, and serves afternoon tea. Don't bother with the pricy dishes. *Basement, Pedder Bldg., 12 Pedder St., Central, Hong Kong Island, tel. 5/218–421. Dress: informal. Lunch reservations recommended. AE, DC, MC, V.*

★ **Chinese Restaurant.** This newest addition to luxurious hotel dining is very special. The decor is 1920s Chinese teahouse style, with wood paneling, marble, and Chinese paintings. Chinese Restaurant has a superb seasonal menu, as well as an excellent regular menu. The spring menu, for example, includes shrimp mousse, and bird's nest, which is sautéed boneless chicken wings with ham and bamboo shoots. All the dishes, from deep-fried stuffed crab claw to boiled seafood rice with Chinese curry, are immaculately prepared. There are lunches and dinners for single diners and for larger groups as well. *Hyatt Hotel, 67 Nathan Rd., Tsimshatsui, Kowloon, tel. 3/662-321. Jackets required at dinner. Dinner reservations recommended. AE, DC, MC, V.*

★ **Jumbo Restaurant.** Residents scorn the "floating restaurants," but tourists unfailingly revel in the idea. To reach them, you board a boat behind Aberdeen Centre Housing Estate or off Wong Chuk Hang Road. Meals vary at Jumbo or the adjoining Sea Palace. The decks are huge, and the fish is fresh and well cooked—but be careful about ordering "market" or "seasonal" price; always ask for prices in advance. *Shum Wan, Aberdeen, Hong Kong Island, tel. 5/539-111. Dress: informal. Reservations not required. AE, DC, MC, V.*

Rainbow Room. Many believe that Rainbow Room has the best Peking duck in the territory. While this is arguable, it certainly has splendid meals as well as spectacular views from its top-floor location. The dim sum is wonderful, the seafood is fine. The Peking duck takes around 45 minutes to prepare, but the wait is worthwhile and the beginning courses are delightful. The Rainbow Room has good meals for one or two people, as well as for large groups. It's very friendly, with charming decor. *Lee Gardens Hotel, Hysan Ave., Causeway Bay, Hong Kong Island, tel. 5/893-3311. Dress: informal. Lunch reservations recommended. AE, DC, MC, V.*

Yung Kee. One of the oldest and best, this restaurant's specialties include succulent dumplings and huge prawns. Yung Kee is known mainly for its tender roast goose, the best in Hong Kong. Lunchtimes are crowded, but if you go after 2 PM an excellent meal is in store for you. *32 Wellington St., Central, Hong Kong Island, tel. 5/231-562. Dress: informal. Lunch reservations recommended. AE, DC, MC, V.*

Inexpensive **Luk Yu Teahouse.** Although this is reputedly the oldest teahouse in the city, many teahouses in run-down Western district are older, and Luk Yu has moved from its original 1920s location. Still, this is traditional Chinese, with large ceiling fans, big ebony tables, and Chinese calligraphy on the walls—very much a picture of the territory in post-Edwardian days. For atmosphere, go at breakfast time and order tea and dim sum. The restaurant also serves a fair dinner, but you'll find better food elsewhere. (Late at night, the service is a bit surly.) It's certainly worth a look inside. *24 Stanley St., Central, Hong Kong Island, tel. 5/235-463. Dress: informal. Lunch reservations recommended. No credit cards.*

Chiu Chow **Chiu Chow Garden.** From the opening thimbles of tea–stronger
Moderate than any coffee–to the sweet bird's nest, Chui Chow food is in a class by itself. Never having caught on in the West, this cuisine is one of extremes. Soya goose, shark's fin in vinegar, prawns with crisp scallions, and green, crispy *chinjew* (leaves) that melt in your mouth. The restaurant has excellent food and a good wine list. The richness of the food makes an expensive wine superfluous, so try Chinese rice wine or sorghum wine. *2nd floor, Hennessy Centre, 500 Hennessy Rd., Causeway Bay, Hong Kong Island, tel. 5/773-891. Dress: informal. Lunch reservations recommended. AE, DC, MC, V.*

Hangchow
Very Expensive

Tien Heung Lau. Two notes of warning before you eat here: a) this can be one of the most expensive of all restaurants, and b) your meal should be ordered, in Chinese, in advance, with all prices noted. Heeding these warnings, you can enjoy an extraordinary meal. The beggar's chicken—ordered 48 hours in advance—is fragrant and wonderful. Also excellent are the dried bamboo shoots covered with crispy snow pea pods, and the duck and wonton soup, which is half a duck boiled with hundreds of wontons in a huge clay cauldron. *18C Austin Ave., Tsimshatsui, Kowloon, tel. 3/662–414. Dress: informal. Dinner reservations recommended. No credit cards.*

Peking
Moderate

American Restaurant. This restaurant, which has been around for four decades, has an "Olde Hong Kong" feel to it. Although noisy and crowded, it's a good place to eat and a favorite with residents. It has wonderful onion cakes, prawns, and sizzling mutton (in winter). The paper-wrapped chicken is one of the best in town. The mushroom soup has huge black mushrooms, and the dumplings are very juicy. *20 Lockhart Rd., Wanchai, Hong Kong Island, tel. 5/277–277. Dress: informal. Reservations not required. No credit cards.*

★ **Peking Garden.** In addition to Peking food, this restaurant serves Szechuan and Hunan cuisine. The in-house noodle-maker delights visitors. The Peking duck is excellent and carved at the table, and there are many fine cold platters, as well as diced chicken in chili sauce, and all the famed dishes of Peking. Residents love the place. Visitors are especially well treated. *4 locations: Excelsior Shopping Arcade, Causeway Bay, Hong Kong Island, tel. 5/777–7231; Alexandra House, Central, Hong Kong Island, tel. 5/266–456; Empire Centre, Mody Rd., Tsimshatsui East, Kowloon, tel. 3/687–879; and 3rd floor, Star House, Star Ferry, Tsimshatsui, tel. 3/698–211. Dress: informal. Lunch reservations recommended. AE, DC, MC, V.*

★ **Spring Deer.** Some residents swear by the Peking duck at this restaurant. Hundreds of them—actually the same breed as Long Island (New York) duckling—are served each week. Be sure that the skin is cut thin. Served with *hoisen* (plum) sauce and thin pancakes, it is delicious. Order the begger's chicken a day in advance for another treat. The prawns and the cold dishes are all very good. This is an old-fashioned restaurant—noisy, crowded, and memorable. *42 Mody Rd., Tsimshatsui, Kowloon, tel. 3/664–012. Dress: casual. Reservations necessary. V.*

Inexpensive

Islamic Food. This restaurant specializes in North China Muslim food. The onion cakes are thin crepes stuffed with beautiful green onions, the beef dumplings are juicy and tender, the hot-sour soup is very tasty, the shrimp or chicken with cashews is deliciously tangy, and the bean curd with chopped beef is also delicious. It's crowded and very friendly. Located near Kai Tak Airport, it has tables outside where you can watch the planes coming in for a landing. *1 Lung Kwong Rd., Kowloon City, tel. 3/822–822. Dress: informal. Reservations not required. No credit cards. Closed Wed. on 2nd and 4th week of every month.*

Shanghai
Moderate

Great Shanghai. Shanghai food is actually a combination of different Central Chinese cuisines. This restaurant has wonderful eel, fried shrimp, hot chilied bean curd, and cabbage. The food is fairly oily. The restaurant is huge, without any noticeable decor and with so-so service, but it's the best place for trying out the dishes of Shanghai. *Prat Museum, 26 Prat Ave., Tsimshatsui, Kowloon, tel. 3/668–158. Dress: informal. Reservations not required. AE, DC, MC, V.*

Szechuan
Moderate
★ **Red Pepper.** Very popular with residents, this restaurant is tiny and crowded and everybody seems to know everybody else. The eggplant in garlic sauce is pungent, the spicy minced beef with "tree-climbing ants" vermicelli offers interesting contrasts in taste. That great Szechuan dish, duck smoked with camphor wood, is always juicy. *5 Lan Fong Rd. (behind Lee Gardens Hotel), Causeway Bay, Hong Kong Island, tel. 5/768–046. Dress: informal. Reservations required. AE, MC, V.*

Sichuan Garden. The chefs here were personally taught by the original chef who was from the Szechuan province. The restaurant is huge, with nearly 300 seats. It has many seasonal specials, such as quick-fried lobster balls with hot chili sauce. The smoked duck is wonderfully fragrant. A mundane-sounding dish such as panfried bamboo shoots is lovely, with chunky stems, onion, pork, and coriander. *3rd floor, Landmark, Central, Hong Kong Island, tel. 5/214–433. Dress: informal. Lunch reservations necessary. AE, DC, V.*

Sze Chuen Lau. To regular patrons, this is the place for hot-sour soup, prawns in chili, crispy beef, and seasonal pea sprouts. Parties of more than eight can reserve one of the private rooms. Lately, some "errors" have been found in the bill. But if you check the tab and politely point out any mistakes, they will be quickly rectified. *446 Lockhart Rd., Causeway Bay, Hong Kong Island, tel. 5/790–2571. Dress: informal. Dinner reservations recommended. AE, MC, V.*

Szechuen Lau. This restaurant is no relation to Sze Chuen Lau, but the food is equally good. *South Seas Centre, Tsimshatsui East, Kowloon, tel. 3/697–685. Dress: informal. Reservations recommended. AE, DC, MC, V.*

Other Asian
Restaurants
Very Expensive
Unkai Restaurant. Even for a Japanese restaurant, this one is expensive. A meal for one could run you over HK$250. Still, you get real artistry for your money, in the decor and in the food. The small, individual rooms are decorated in subdued red and brown colors and surrounded by cobblestone paths. The food presentation is equally artistic, with table settings representative of each season. It serves all the usual Japanese dishes in an atmosphere that will make any meal one to remember. *3rd floor, Sheraton Hotel, Kowloon, tel. 3/691–111. Jackets required. Reservations suggested. AE, DC, MC, V.*

Expensive
Benkay. A traditional Japanese restaurant, it has small rooms and a very cosmopolitan crowd—with expense-account tastes. The sushi, teppanyaki, broiled fish, and stuffed beef are all authentic. The *Udonsuki* (leeks, mushrooms, seafood, chicken, and two types of noodles in bouillon) is excellent. The teppanyaki bar has crisp vegetables and broiled meats. *1st basement, Landmark, Central, Hong Kong Island, tel. 5/213–344. Dress: informal. Reservations suggested for lunch. AE, DC, MC, V.*

Moderate
★ **Ashoka.** After almost two decades, this is still a favorite Indian restaurant, especially for lunch. It serves mainly Northern dishes and incredibly sensual sweets. *57 Wyndham St., Central, Hong Kong Island, tel. 5/249–623. Dress: informal. Lunch reservations essential. AE, DC, MC, V.*

★ **Golden Bull.** This is a Vietnamese restaurant with an especially fine atmosphere. It has a rock pool with fish, peasant cane chairs, Vietnamese murals, and very friendly service. Although Vietnamese food is fairly mild compared to other Southeast Asian foods, nobody can deny the variety of tastes. The cuisine includes beef cooked seven different ways and vermicelli cooked more ways than a variety of Italian pastas. Popular dishes include shrimp on sugarcane and barbecued suckling pig with bean curd (this must be ordered in advance). Bring a large party for the greatest variety from the large menu. *1st floor, New World Centre, Tsimshatsui, Kowloon, tel. 3/694–617. Dress: informal. Lunch reservations suggested. AE, DC, MC, V.*

Koreana. There are so many Korean restaurants in Hong Kong that no one is gospel. But for 15 years, Koreana has been a great favorite. The food is wonderful and includes Korean barbecue, spicy kimchee salad, barbecued beef, and ginseng tea. Try the *namool*: a base of spinach kimchi with bean sprouts, soy sauce, garlic, cayenne pepper, and fried sesame seeds. No wine, but saki or beer is available. *1 Paterson St., Causeway Bay, Hong Kong Island, tel. 5/775–145. Dress: informal. Lunch reservations suggested. AE, DC.*

Royal Thai Restaurant. This is an elegant-looking restaurant serving delectable curries, heavy on the cream. Some of the dishes are Chinese concoctions that don't exist in Thailand, such as shark's fin curry. But they're delicious, nevertheless. *Elizabeth House, 250 Gloucester Rd., Wanchai, Hong Kong Island, tel. 5/832–2111. Dress: informal. Lunch reservations suggested. AE, DC, MC, V.*

★ **Spices.** This restaurant serves a melange of foods from around Asia and is located on the site of the old Repulse Bay Hotel. The menu is an ambitious one, with curries from around the region and tandoori chicken, Malaysian sambai, and Filipino adobes. On a summer day it's especially worthwhile coming here for a buffet lunch, spending the day on the beach, and then having dinner on the verandah. *109 Repulse Bay Rd., Repulse Bay, Hong Kong Island, tel. 5/812–2711. Dress: informal. Dinner reservations suggested. AE, DC, MC, V.*

Inexpensive **Chili Club.** This is an excellent Thai restaurant. Quite good here are the *mee krob* noodles, fried rice, curries, and *khanom* desserts. The food is relatively mild, but you can have it spicier if you ask for *pet pet dee*. Also ask about the *Isarn* foods—Northeastern dishes, including green papaya salad and grilled chicken, that are tastier than ordinary central Thai food. There's no atmosphere whatsoever, but you'll enjoy a real Thai treat. Check your bill carefully. *68 Lockhart Rd., Wanchai, Hong Kong Island, tel. 5/272–872. Dress: informal. Lunch and weekend reservations essential. MC, V.*

Indian Curry Club. This serves the ultimate Indian buffet bargain, not because you can eat endlessly for very little but because the food is so good and it includes about 30 dishes from all sections of India, Pakistan, and Sri Lanka. It also has Afghan-style chicken drumsticks, lamb with almonds and eggs, and delicious sweets. The owner, Ranjan Dey, takes special care that the food is always delectable. *Basement, Tsimshatsui Centre, Tsimshatsui East, tel. 3/721–9873. Dress: informal. Lunch reservations suggested. MC, V.*

★ **Rangoon.** The food here is better than the food in Burma because it's less greasy and tastier. There's a large menu, with photographs of dishes such as Burmese curries, and 12 varieties of noodle soup, rich in garlic and coriander. Service is slow but very friendly. Be sure to ring the magic Burmese bell near the entrance. *265 Gloucester Rd., Causeway Bay, Hong Kong Island, tel. 5/893–2281. Dress: informal. Reservations not necessary. AE, MC, V.*

Padang Restaurant. Indonesian food is the specialty here. Dishes include shrimp with the bitter petai bean, which gives it a most unusual taste; *gado-gado* (vegetable salad) with a fresh peanut sauce, and a wide variety of chicken dishes. If you like your food especially spicy, ask for the *sambal*, an optional (free) dish of chopped peppers and garlic. Cafe-style dining with a very friendly staff from Surabaya. *85 Percival St., Causeway Bay, Hong Kong Island, tel. 5/761–828. Dress: informal. No reservations. No credit cards.*

Woodlands. You don't have to be a vegetarian to enjoy Indian vegetarian food. On each *thali* (round silver tray with 12 tiny dishes) are lentil beans, curries, eggplant, and sweets, as well as a variety of breads and chutneys. Choose from the Punjabi (north) or Madras (south) thalis, both under HK$50. This is a delightful place. Although alcohol is not served here, you may bring your own. *8 Minden Ave., Tsimshatsui, Kowloon, tel. 3/693–718. Dress: informal. Dinner reservations suggested. No credit cards.*

Western
Very Expensive

Amigo. A madly extravagant, romantic restaurant, Amigo has a wine cellar, 18th-century antiques and paintings, and a genuine Petrov piano. It's luxurious, vulgar, and exciting. Although some find the decor a bit heavy, most people enjoy the luxury of the food. This includes trolleys of salmon and Maine lobster, a menu of traditional French food (none of this nouvelle stuff for Amigo), wonderful salmon crepes, clam chowder, and chicken breast with cheese, plus a splendid cheese tray. The wine list is equally extravagant, and so are the prices—a 1911 Château Cheval Blanc goes for HK$6,500! The service is as considerable as the prices. If nothing else, Amigo is an experience. *79a Wongneichong Rd., Happy Valley, Hong Kong Island, tel. 5/772–202. Jackets required. Lunch and dinner reservations suggested. AE, DC, MC, V.*

Baron's Table. For those who want German food, game meat, cheesecake, and the like, this is the place. Baron's Table looks like the inside of a Rhine castle; lovers of Teutonic food enjoy it. In the fall it has fresh grouse, hare, venison, and pheasant. The smoked food (from the smokehouse in the hotel) is excellent. There's also fresh lobster, plus an excellent selection of German and Swiss wines. *Holiday Inn Golden Mile, 50 Nathan Rd., Tsimshatsui, Kowloon, tel. 3/693–111. Jackets required. Lunch and dinner reservations suggested. AE, DC, MC, V.*

★ **Chesa.** This is a Swiss restaurant, with stucco walls, dark wood ceilings, hand-painted butter molds, and Swiss linen. The food is heavenly, especially the à la carte dishes: bone-marrow bouillon, a splendid salmon cream soup, veal, and an escalope of fresh salmon with horseradish and a wine sauce. The desserts are delicious, and there's a long selection of Swiss wines. Service is extremely attentive. *1st floor, Peninsula Hotel, Salisbury Rd., Kowloon, tel. 3/666–251. Jackets required. Reservations required. AE, DC, MC, V.*

★ **Gaddi's.** The "flagship" restaurant of the Peninsula Hotel, it is praised by gourmets for its artistic presentation of food. Specialties include rack of lamb, crabmeat pancakes, and roast duckling. *Peninsula Hotel, Salisbury Rd., Kowloon, tel. 3/666–251. Jackets required. Reservations suggested. AE, DC, MC, V.*

Hugo's. The decor here is so striking and so strong that the food is often anticlimactic. The walls are deep browns and mahoganies and the room is filled with great leather chairs. At the entrance is a mammoth board loaded with breads and cheeses. The food is equally heavy, but excellent: saddle of venison or fillet steak, escalope of veal soaked in a heady portion of wine, pea soup with champagne, and fresh chocolate cake. The four-course Executive Lunch is one of the great bargains of Hong Kong. *Hyatt Regency Hotel, 67 Nathan Rd., Kowloon, tel. 3/662–321. Jackets required. Reservations required. AE, DC, MC, V.*

La Restaurant de France. The plainness of the decor here can't detract from the enjoyment of the food. It has a choice menu, ranging from truffle soup to lobster with rosemary and breast of duckling. The restaurant has a most unusual series of festive weeks. An especially memorable one was a 1988 Truffle Festival, with a complete menu planned around this heavenly fungus. Check for special events. *Hotel Regal, 71 Mody Rd., Tsimshatsui East, Kowloon, tel. 3/722–1818. Jackets required. Reservations suggested. AE, DC, MC, V. Open for lunch only.*

Pierrot. Some consider this restaurant the height of nouvelle cuisine. It is certainly an experience dining here, for the best French chefs have worked in its kitchen. The menus change constantly, but the food is always good and beautifully presented, and the wine list is excellent. *Mandarin Hotel, 5 Connaught Rd., Central, Hong Kong Island, tel. 5/220–111. Jackets required. Reservations required. AE, DC, MC, V. Closed lunchtime weekends, holidays.*

★ **The Plume.** Some consider this the very best restaurant in Asia. The luxury of sitting parallel with the harbor and watching the promenade, the 10,000-bottle wine cellar, the dishes that include cream of artichoke with caviar, prime beef, and lobster and prawn raviolini in sorrel sauce—all add up to a wonderful dining experience. *The Regent Hotel, Salisbury Rd., Tsimshatsui, Kowloon, tel. 3/721–1211. Jackets required. Reservations essential. AE, DC, MC, V.*

Expensive **Au Trou Normand.** This French restaurant has been managed ★ for over 20 years by Bernard Vigneau, who imports his own wines, cheeses, and other products. When he's in the kitchen, which is most of the time, you can expect splendid pâtés, terrines, soups, and original dishes of the most diverse kinds. Here you will find goose-liver mousse, Moroccan sausages, poached eggs with spinach and Gruyere cheese, and veal kidneys. The atmosphere is pure French village, and the restaurant is always crowded. *6 Carnavon Rd., Tsimshatsui, Kowloon, tel. 3/668–754. Dress: informal. Reservations required. AE, DC, MC, V.*

Beverly Hills Deli. This American-style delicatessen has two branches. Both serve huge sandwiches as well as gefilte fish, blintzes, salami, lox, and chili. The imaginative menu includes *pitcha* (jellied veal foot) and Cajun chicken. Their cooking includes dishes from North Africa, Eastern Europe, and the United States. Although not literally kosher, the food is basically kosher-style. The imported bagels are wonderful, as is the yogurt ice cream. The service is friendly and informal. *2 Lan Kwai Fong, Central, Hong Kong Island, tel. 5/265–809; L2-55, New World Centre, Tsimshatsui, Kowloon, tel. 3/698–695. Dress: informal. Lunch reservations suggested. AE, DC, MC, V.*

Casa Mexicana. This has the best Tex-Mex food in the territory, with good, hot chili, a Texas-style bar, and a friendly atmosphere. *Victoria Centre, Watson Rd., North Point, Hong Kong Island, tel. 5/665–525. Dress: informal. Reservations suggested. AE, DC, MC, V.*

Landau's. This restaurant, which is basically Scandinavian, recreates the aura of the 1920s. It's cozy and pretty, with blackboards filled with specials of the day. The menu is a sumptuous one and includes cold, thick vichyssoise, a tangy liver terrine, and black pepper steak. The desserts are rich—apple strudel and strawberry omelets are just two. The staff is very friendly. *257 Gloucester Rd., Causeway Bay, Hong Kong Island, tel.5/891–2901. Dress: informal. Reservations recommended. AE, DC, MC, V.*

★ **Lan Kwai Fong.** This is the new "bohemian" district, between the hills leading to mid-levels and the lowlands. It's near the Hollywood Road antiques shops. Some of the restaurants in this area include **California** (tel. 5/211–345), with its California-style food and trendy atmosphere; **Café de Paris** (tel. 5/890–4348), a tiny bistro with Parisian food; **Graffiti** (tel. 5/212–202), with pizzas, pastas, and an informal atmosphere; and **97** (tel. 5/260–303), with everything from caviar to pasta and Continental cuisine. *Central, north of Wellington St., Hong Kong Island. Prices, credit cards, times vary.*

Mistral. This is a Mediterranean-style restaurant with two superb choices of bouillabaisse, paella, pastas, and a few Greek dishes. Meals start off with pita bread and goat cheese and go on to Italian pizzas. The desserts are deliciously rich. There's live music at night. *Holiday Inn Harbour View, 70 Mody Rd., Tsimshatsui East, Kowloon, tel. 3/721–5161. Dress: informal. Reservations suggested. AE, DC, MC, V.*

San Francisco Steak House. This restaurant looks like an old railway carriage, with plush red upholstery and lots of wood. It has some of the best steaks and lobsters in town. The extras are equally good: onion rings, large baked potatoes, garlic bread, and fresh salads. *101 Barnton Court, Harbour City, Kowloon, tel. 3/722–7565. Dress: informal. Reservations suggested. AE, DC, V.*

Verandah. Visit this restaurant mainly for nostalgia. This is a replica of the fabled Verandah restaurant of the old Repulse Bay Hotel, where British soldiers were captured by invading Japanese troops during World War II. Some of the specialties include Scottish salmon, wild forest mushrooms with shallots, and flambéed pepper steak. The peppercorn dessert is most unusual. The wine selection is fair. *109 Repulse Bay Rd., Repulse Bay, Hong Kong Island, tel. 5/812–7533. Dress: no jeans. Reservations necessary for dinner. AE, DC, MC, V.*

Moderate **Adriatico.** This restaurant is operated by a Filipino group, but has primarily Mediterranean and Adriatic fare: paella from Spain, Greek-style calamares, and crispy-fried spinach. The atmosphere is unique and the food is unusual. *89 Kimberly Rd., Tsimshatsui, Kowloon, tel. 3/688–554. Dress: informal. Dinner reservations suggested. AE, DC, MC, V.*

★ **Bella Donna.** This Italian restaurant has a panoramic view of the harbor and a funky, friendly atmosphere. It also has an old pizza oven, delicious pastas, spaghetti, chicken with cheese, good minestrone, fine Italian wine selections, and a wine bar. *1st floor, 6–8 Harbour Rd., Wanchai, Hong Kong Island, tel.*

5/280–182. Dress: informal. Reservations required. AE, DC, MC, V.

★ **La Rose Noire.** Everybody loves this little French bistro. The atmosphere is Left Bank, with everything in black, including black silk roses. Although the restaurant is tiny, it breathes aura and ambience. The wines are good—those by the glass or the carafe are especially good bargains. Food includes baked goat cheese with basil, truffly foie gras, steak tartare, and excellent pastries. This one gets a lot of repeat customers because it's such a friendly place and the cuisine is always interesting. *1st floor, 8–13 Woo On La., Central, Hong Kong Island, tel. 5/ 265–965. Dress: informal. Reservations not required. AE, DC, V.*

Mozart Stub'n. Here, Austrian food is served in a "stub'n," which is a cozy kitchen farmhouse. Visitors from Austria love it for its authentic cuisine—terrines with cranberry sauce, cold cuts, goulash, boiled beef, and smoked pork loin, plus plenty of Austrian desserts. Strangely, only one Austrian wine is offered, but there are dozens of coffees on the menu. Try a few glasses of schnapps before dinner. *8 Glenealy, Central, Hong Kong Island, tel. 5/221–763. Dress: informal. Reservations suggested. MC, V.*

Omar Khayyam. This is the only Middle Eastern restaurant in the city. It has a salad bar with Turkish, Armenian, Greek, and Egyptian salads. It also has pita bread sandwiches with goat cheese, a good Sunday buffet, and set lunches. The atmosphere is pseudo-Arabian, with comfortable booths. Sometimes diners are entertained by belly dancers. *Level 2, New World Centre, Tsimshatsui, Kowloon, tel. 3/668–243. Dress: informal. Reservations suggested. AE, DC, MC, V.*

★ **Stanley's French Restaurant.** This is on the extreme southern tip of Hong Kong Island, but it's worth the trip. The restaurant is actually a beautiful three-story house, each floor resembling a picture gallery. Located near a beach, you can listen to the sound of the waves and winds as you dine. The fresh fish, rack of lamb, Cajun dishes, escargots, and salads are splendid. *86 Stanley Main St., Stanley, Hong Kong Island, tel. 5/813–8873. Dress: informal. Reservations suggested. AE, DC, MC, V.*

Inexpensive **Pizzeria.** This restaurant serves beautiful pizzas and pastas and has a great salad buffet. The lunchtime buffet, in particular, is probably one of the largest pasta buffets in the world. Try the "four cheese pizza" with olives, peppers, and oregano. The dessert list includes good ice creams, cheeses, and an excellent zabaglione. *Kowloon Hotel, 19–21 Nathan Rd., Tsimshatsui, tel. 3/698–698 ext. 3322. Dress: informal. Lunch reservations essential. AE, DC, MC, V.*

8 Lodging

Introduction

Until the early 1960s, Hong Kong didn't have a single international hotel. Today there are more than 60 hotels and some 24,000 hotel rooms (with another 4,500 to be added by the end of 1989) in a city that welcomes more than four million visitors annually. These figures only include hotels and lodging facilities that belong to the **Hong Kong Tourist Association (HKTA)**. There are others that market themselves to visitors from Taiwan, the People's Republic of China, and Southeast Asia, but such hotels have not been included in our listings. With two exceptions, the Surf Hotel in Sai Kung and the Silvermine Beach Hotel on Lantau Island, we only list hotels that belong to the HKTA or to the **Hong Kong Hotels Association (HKHA)**.

As price ranges indicate, Hong Kong isn't a budget traveler's paradise. The vast majority of hotel rooms are in the *Very Expensive* and *Expensive* categories. Visitors not on group tours must expect to pay at least HK$650 for a hotel room of normal international standards. For that price visitors probably won't get harbor views, but they will get reliable facilities—bathrooms with unfailing hot and cold running water, color TV, radio, same-day laundry and valet service, 24-hour room service, air-conditioning, telephones that always work, and an evening turn-down service by room attendants (generally called room "boys").

Due to the limited price ranges available for even halfway decent accommodations, economy-minded visitors are advised either to use tour-group bookings or to visit during the low season, generally June through August. Other quiet periods are the weeks on either side of Chinese New Year, a moveable feast that usually occurs in January or February; Christmas; and the Western New Year.

In the busy periods—spring and fall—advance bookings are strongly recommended. Even with the rash of new hotels, rooms can still prove scarce during the high seasons of March through June and September through early December.

The HKTA publishes a list of hotel members in a brochure, *Hotels*, that provides details of facilities and rates. Because the brochure is published twice a year, it is usually one price-hike behind the current situation. The HKTA does not arrange hotel reservations. The HKHA does, but only through its reservations office at Kai Tak International Airport, which is immediately beyond the Customs area.

Choosing where to stay in Hong Kong depends on the purpose of your visit. Time-wise, nothing is very far. Thanks to the Harbour Tunnel and the Mass Transit Railway (MTR) subway system, it no longer matters whether you stay "Hong Kongside" or "Kowloon-side." Either side of the harbor is only minutes away by MTR.

Central, on Hong Kong Island, is preferred by people needing to be near the city's financial hub. As busy as New York's Manhattan Island on weekdays, Central is quiet at night and on weekends. It has three hotels (with three more soon to open in nearby Queensway): the **Hong Kong Hilton, Furama Inter-Continental,** and **Mandarin Oriental.** All are very expensive.

Wanchai, east of Central, was once a sailor's dream of "Suzie

Wongs" and booze. Although it is still one of the city's more entertaining nightlife areas, land reclamation has given it an area of new harbor-fronting skyscrapers. Wanchai's few hotels will soon be supplemented by a **Grand Hyatt Hotel** and a **New World Hotel,** both part of the **Hong Kong Convention and Exhibition Centre.**

Causeway Bay, farther east on the island, has three major hotels: the **Lee Gardens, Excelsior,** and **Park Lane.** Ideal for those who like to try lots of different restaurants or are on shopping trips, Causeway Bay has become even more popular since the opening of the MTR Island Line, linking it to Central and Kowloon.

Tsimshatsui, the name of the harbor-fronting promontory at the end of mainland Kowloon, can be divided into three areas as far as its hotel and shopping facilities are concerned:

"Old" Tsimshatsui lies on and off the fabled shopping "Golden Mile" of Nathan Road. Warrens of back streets are filled with restaurants, boutiques, stores, and old-style hotels. Large international hotels—notably, the **Peninsula, Sheraton, Hyatt-Regency, Holiday Inn Golden Mile,** and **Ramada Renaissance**— are at the harbor end of Nathan Road, a short walk from the Star Ferry or the Tsimshatsui MTR Station.

Tsimshatsui East is the newly developed "mini-Miami" of Hong Kong. A grid of office blocks and luxury hotels, it's not a cheap place to stay. It is only a short walk from old Tsimshatsui. Of the area's four new hotels—**Regal Meridien, Royal Garden, Shangri-La,** and **Holiday Inn Harbour View**—the Shangri-La and Holiday Inn face the harbor with uninterrupted views. The nearby **New World** and **Regent Hotels** are closer to old Tsimshatsui's action.

Harbour City, on the western side of the Tsimshatsui promontory, is the preserve of the Peninsula Group, whose owners are associated with the development of Harbour City (Asia's largest air-conditioned shopping and commercial complex), along with the Hong Kong, Prince, and Marco Polo hotels.

Kowloon, generally taken as beginning north of Jordan Road (and the Jordan MTR Station), contains a lot of moderate, smaller, older hotels. Most are still on Nathan Road, within the magic "Golden Mile" and are probably the best bets for economy-minded visitors. Excellent bus service and the MTR ensure that Kowloon and North Kowloon are not far, timewise, from the center of old Tsimshatsui.

Our indicated hotel rates show published price ranges for a double room for two people at press time. Few of the major hotels have specially designed single rooms, but the price difference between single and double rates is usually minimal. All rates are subject to a 10% service charge and a 5% government tax, which is used to fund the activities of the HKTA. There are few rooms at the lower end of the range. Widespread hotel renovations, refurbishments, upgrading, and price hikes have given the city a top-heavy concentration of good-quality but fairly expensive accommodations.

The most highly recommended properties in each price category are indicated by a star ★.

At press time there were 7.8 HK dollars to the U.S. dollar.

Lodging

0 ————— 440 yards
0 ————— 400 meters

Victoria Harbour

Macau Ferry Pier

22
Connaught Rd. West
23

Connaught Rd. Central

Bonham
Wing Lok St.
Strand

SHEUNG WAN

Bridges St.

Aberdeen St.

Caine Rd.

Staunton St.

Wellington St.

Stanley St.

Queen's St.

D'Aguilar St.

Wyndham St.

Des Voeux Rd.

Queen's Rd. Central

Central

Pedder St.

Chater Rd.
24 **26**

Garden Rd.
25

Cotton Tree Dr.

Distance from Kowloon to Hong Kong Island districts has been reduced.

Naval Dockyard

Harcourt Rd.

ADMIRALTY

Queen's Way

Ambassador, **7**
Caravelle, **31**
Emerald, **22**
Empress, **14**
Excelsior, The, **33**

Furama Inter-Continental, **26**
Grand, **11**
Guangdong, **15**
Harbour, **30**
Harbour View International, **29**

Holiday Inn Golden Mile, **5**
Holiday Inn Harbour View, **19**
Hongkong, The, **3**
Hong Kong Hilton, **25**

Hotel New Harbour, **27**
Hotel Nikko, **20**
Hyatt Regency, **4**
Imperial, **6**
Lee Gardens, **32**
Mandarin Oriental, **24**
Marco Polo, **1**

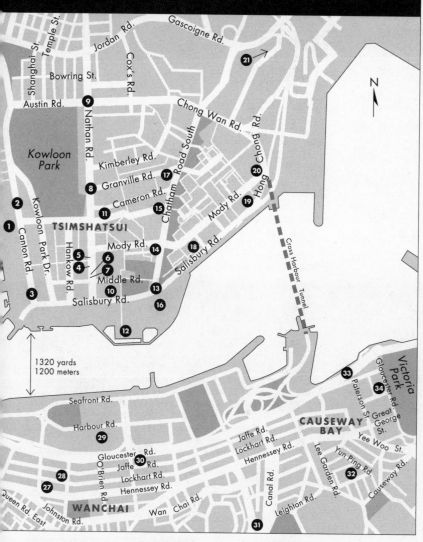

Miramar, **8**
New World, **16**
Park, **17**
Park Lane, **34**
Peninsula, **10**
Prince, **2**
Ramada Inn, **28**

Regal Airport, **21**
Regent, **12**
Ritz, **9**
Shangri-La, **18**
Sheraton, **13**
Victoria Hotel, **23**

Category	Cost*
Very Expensive	over HK $2,000
Expensive	HK $1,000– HK $2,000
Moderate	HK $800– HK $1,000
Inexpensive	under HK $800

double room; add 15% for taxes

The following credit-card abbreviations are used: AE, American Express, CB, Carte Blanche; DC, Diners Club; MC, MasterCard; V, Visa.

Our hotel categories are arbitrary. Hong Kong has no official hotel rating system. Our *Very Expensive* hotels are the few that are genuine world-beaters, recognized as such by prestigious international surveys. Our *Expensive* and *Moderate* hotels are usually chain-associated international hotels with extremely high quality guest rooms and facilities. *Inexpensive* hotels are more humble, but many have undertaken renovations that make them comfortable and easy to recommend.

Inexpensive accommodations are difficult to find. For single rooms, the best bets are the **YMCAs** and the **YWCA**. Rates for their double rooms are in the Moderate range. The most popular of the Ys is the YMCA on Salisbury Road, Kowloon (tel. 3/692–211), no doubt because of its central location and swimming pool. The other YMCA in Kowloon is on Waterloo Road (tel. 3/771–911). The YWCA, also in Kowloon, is on Man Fuk Road, Waterloo Hill (tel. 3/713–9211). The YMCA in Wanchai, Hong Kong Island, is listed as **Harbour View International House** in our *Inexpensive* category (tel. 5/201–111). The least expensive rooms of all can be found in the **Chung King Mansions** in Kowloon, on Nathan Road, between the Sheraton and Holiday Inn Golden Mile hotels. If the noise and the unusual aromas from the block's many Indo-Pakistani cafes don't bother you, you will find the prices and the central location a bargain.

On the **Outlying Islands,** accommodations are very limited. On some of the islands, such as Cheung Chau Island, visitors will find a booming little business in rooms to rent. Placards of photographs line the waterfront opposite the ferry pier. For something very different, consider staying in a monastery, such as the huge **Po Lin Monastery** or the beautiful **Trappist Monastery**, both on Lantau Island. Such retreats require advance reservations. The rooms are spartan, but they're the closest thing to solitude one can get in Hong Kong. Check with the HKTA for information and reservations.

Massive development in **New Territories** north of Kowloon is resulting in fewer country-style guest houses and more international-standard hotels in the urban areas. There is one hotel included in our listing, and Shatin and Tsuen Wan each have a new hotel opening in 1989. Tsuen Wan's Panda Kowloon will be the biggest in Hong Kong, with 950 rooms.

As one might expect in the world's third most important financial center, Hong Kong is a business executive's paradise. Every hotel in the *Very Expensive* or *Expensive* categories has some form of Business Center providing secretarial services, translators, easy access to telex and fax machines, and libraries of local publications. It also has front-desk personnel who attend promptly to an executive's needs. Most of the *Moderate* hotels can arrange for secretarial services quickly.

With almost every hotel involved in renovation and modernization plans, this guide's listing will soon be outdated. But one thing won't be changing: Good service is the name of the hotel game in Hong Kong, and the city's top 15 or so hotels probably provide the best all-around hotel services of any city in the world. The fact that they also contain some of Asia's finest restaurants is another major plus.

Hong Kong Island

Very Expensive ★ **Hong Kong Hilton.** Recent revamping of the guest rooms has given this long-established hotel fresh favor with Central business visitors. There are now five Executive Floors for business travelers. The second-floor lobby has a popular Dragon Boat Bar, a very elegant grill, and the Jade Lotus Restaurant. The rooftop Chinese restaurant, the Eagle's Nest, has great food, views, and a romantic evening ambience. Genji, a Japanese restaurant in the basement, specializes in teppanyaki and sushi. The hotel offers private cruises around the harbor and beyond on a two-masted brigantine. *Queen's Rd., Central, tel. 5/233–111. 780 rooms. Facilities: heated outdoor pool, health spa, business center. AE, CB, DC, MC, V.*

★ **Mandarin Oriental.** In the heart of Central, this 20-year-old hotel combines British rectitude with Oriental splendor. It's the flagship of the Hong Kong-based Mandarin Oriental Hotels Group, and has been consistently voted one of the world's best hotels. The hotel covers one square block, with two sides facing the harbor. Its balcony windows have double-glazing to keep out the roar of the waterfront road traffic. All rooms, including 60 suites, have been completely renovated. The British influence is obvious in the clubbish Chinnery Bar (for men only), named after a 19th-century South China Coast artist whose portrait smiles down on a lunchtime roast beef wagon and silver tankards. Off the lobby, the popular cocktail lounge, the Captain's Bar, also has a luncheon roast beef wagon. A band entertains here after 9 PM. Seafood and roasts are the specialties at the Mandarin Grill. On the 25th-floor rooftop, there's the *nouvelle cuisine* of Pierrot, one of Hong Kong's better and most expensive restaurants. Similar stylishness graces the adjacent Man Wah Chinese restaurant, which shares the Harlequin Bar with Pierrot. The ground-floor coffee shop, with a Greco-English indoor garden, and the all-day Clipper Lounge, on the mezzanine, serve light meals and snacks and are the best of their kind in town. *5 Connaught Rd., tel. 5/220–111. 240 rooms. Facilities: rooftop health club with pool, business center, shopping arcade, beauty salon. AE, CB, DC, MC, V.*

Expensive ★ **The Excelsior.** The city's second largest hotel, this harborfronting skyscraper overlooks the Royal Hong Kong Yacht Club marina and the flight path into Kowloon's Kai Tak Airport. Ideally located for shopping trips into Causeway Bay, the hotel is only a few minutes by MTR from Wanchai's nightlife or Central's banks. There's good dining in Cammino, an Italian restaurant, and in Excelsior Grill, adjacent to the jolly Noon Gun Bar. Managed by the Mandarin Oriental Hotels Group, the Excelsior houses one of Hong Kong's most popular watering holes, The Dickens Bar, and one of its best-established discos, The Talk of the Town. *Glouster Rd., Causeway Bay, tel. 5/767–365. 930 rooms. Facilities: business center; covered, air-conditioned tennis courts; jogging path in park setting; shopping arcade; beauty salon. AE, CB, DC, MC, V.*

Furama Inter-Continental. Overlooking City Hall from the front, and Chater Gardens from the back, the Furama is in a quiet section of Central. The rooms tend to be small but are much favored by business travelers. A major renovation has added 55 suites, including attractive Junior Suites. There are also fine rooms with convertible pull-down beds on the sixth floor. The 13th floor has a revolving rooftop restaurant, La Ronda, offering 75-minute panoramic trips and buffet feasts; the Rotisserie is a lunchtime favorite, and there's also a good Japanese restaurant. *Connaught Rd., tel. 5/255–111. 521 rooms. Facilities: business center, health club, shopping arcade, beauty salon. AE, CB, DC, MC, V.*

Lee Gardens. Popular with European and Australian groups, this hotel is well located for shopping and is surrounded by good restaurants. The rooftop Chinese restaurant, Rainbow Room, is justifiably famed for dim sum and Peking duck. The hotel also has a fine Japanese restaurant and a Korean restaurant. *Hysan Ave., Causeway Bay, tel. 5/895–3311. 810 rooms. Facilities: business center, beauty salon. AE, CB, DC, MC, V.*

Park Lane. This hotel, in the heart of the Causeway Bay shopping area and adjacent to Victoria Park, has been completely renovated. Its elegant restaurant, Park 27, serves Continental cuisine and has one of Hong Kong's best panoramic views. Its Gallery Bar and Lounge has live entertainment nightly. The hotel has a Premier Club floor for business travelers. *311 Gloucester Rd., tel. 5/890–3355. 850 rooms. Facilities: business center; health spa with sauna, steam bath, and Jacuzzi; beauty salon. AE, CB, DC, MC, V.*

Victoria Hotel. The hotel occupies the top 15 floors of a 40-story building. The Dynasty Club, for business travelers, occupies two of those floors. Restaurants include Bocarinos Grill, with mesquite charcoal specialties; Dynasty, with superb and original Cantonese food; and the Cafe Terrace coffee shop. *Shun Tak Centre, 200 Connaught Rd., Central, tel. 5/407–228. 540 rooms. Facilities: business center, health club with pool and sun deck, tennis courts, shopping arcade. AE, CB, DC, MC, V.*

Moderate **Caravelle.** Overlooking the Happy Valley Race Course, near Queen Elizabeth Stadium, this hotel is a short walk from Causeway Bay shops and Wanchai night spots. It has a brightly decorated and cheerful coffee shop, a grill room, and a bar. *84 Morrison Hill Rd., Happy Valley, tel. 5/754–455. 102 rooms, all with TV. AE, DC, MC, V.*

Emerald. This is the first hotel in the colony's Western district. It has a lounge and three restaurants serving Cantonese and European food. *152 Connaught Rd. West, tel. 5/468–111. 288 rooms, all with TV. AE, CB, DC, MC, V.*

★ **Harbour.** Renovated and taken over by Chinese interests, this hotel is favored by budget-minded travelers and delegations from the People's Republic of China. It has a restaurant that serves good dim sum and Cantonese food. *116–122 Gloucester Rd., Wanchai, tel. 5/748–211. 200 rooms; all with TV and minibar. Facilities: sauna; China Trade Counter; and cable, telex, and fax facilities. AE, CB, DC, MC, V.*

Harbour View International Hotel. Part of the YMCA group, this hotel is next to the Arts Centre and Academy for Performing Arts and a short stroll from the heart of Wanchai. The hotel has a coffee shop and two restaurants serving Western and Cantonese food. *4 Harbour Rd., Wanchai, tel. 5/201–111. 300 rooms, all with TV and refrigerator. AE, DC, MC, V.*

Hotel New Harbour. Many will remember this as the Singapore Hotel. Taken over by Chinese interests, it is now a favorite of visitors from the People's Republic of China. It has a coffee shop, a restaurant serving Western and Chinese cuisine, and a lobby lounge. *41–49 Hennessy Rd., Wanchai, tel. 5/861–1166. 173 rooms. Facilities: secretarial services, telex, cable, and fax available. AE, DC, MC, V.*

Ramada Inn Hong Kong. This hotel is aimed at the budget-conscious business traveler. It has a coffee shop, Abe's, which serves Western and Oriental food, and a lounge, the Captain's Bar. *61–73 Lockhart Rd., Wanchai, tel. 5/861–1000. 284 rooms, all with TV and minibar. Facilities: business center. AE, CB, DC, MC, V.*

Kowloon

Very Expensive **Kowloon Shangri-La.** Managed by Westin Hotels, the Shangri-La will soon be joined by a sister hotel on Hong Kong Island. The hotel overlooks the harbor road and pedestrian promenade. The lobby, also a tea lounge, contains two massive Chinese-style paintings by a Western artist. Escalators link the cavernous lobby and its reception desk to the various restaurants. These include an excellent branch of the Japanese Nadaman chain; a lush, imperial Shang Palace Chinese restaurant; the comfortable, French, Margaux dining salon, which also serves a good Sunday brunch; and a spacious Coffee Garden with a Steak Place. The large, smart guest rooms all have minibars and TVs and were recently refurbished. *64 Mody Rd., Tsimshatsui East, tel. 3/721–2111. 710 rooms. Facilities: indoor pool and health club, beauty salon, gift shop gallery. AE, CB, DC, MC, V.*

★ **The Peninsula.** The grand old lady of Hong Kong hotels, "The Pen" was built in 1928, when travelers took many weeks, and trunks, to reach Hong Kong by train from London's Victoria Station. Almost a British colonial institution, with a baroque lobby reminiscent of Europe's great railway lounges, the hotel was built by a Shanghai-based company. It has long been managed by traditionalist Swiss hoteliers. Two adjoining towers are being built to add more guest rooms. The Pen's glory as a monument to good taste is first encountered in the ornate-columned and gilt-corniced lobby. This is the place to see and be seen eating scones and cucumber sandwiches. The "in" side is on the right as you pass the white-clad page boys holding open the etched glass doors that face a fountained driveway filled with the hotel's fleet of Rolls-Royces. Gaddi's, arguably Hong Kong's most distinguished gourmet restaurant, has its own elevator, famed squire lunches, and very formal evening dining. The chaletlike Swiss Chesa restaurant serves fine Swiss cuisine, including glorious fondues. The discreet, clublike atmosphere of the Verandah Bar and Lounge, adjacent to the Verandah Grill, is open until 2 AM. There is now a Japanese restaurant, Inagiku, and a Cantonese one, Spring Moon. The Peninsula's old-world style (large, high-ceiling bedrooms, attentive room valets) isn't outdated and has consistently put the hotel among the top 10 in opinion surveys of the world's best hotels. *Salisbury Rd., tel. 3/666–251. 210 rooms, with 230 more being added. Facilities: shopping arcade, beauty salon. AE, CB, DC, MC, V.*

★ **The Regent.** Flagship for the Regent International Hotels group, this elegantly modern hotel is a symbol of the new Hong Kong. The lobby, which has mirrorlike polished granite flooring and windows 40 feet high, has a cocktail lounge where you can enjoy a spectacular harbor view. Plume, an expensive dinner-only restaurant, also overlooks the harbor. Plume has glass elevators, antiques, an open-to-view 10,000-bottle wine cellar, an Indian tandoori oven for baking bread, and fine French cuisine. The Lai Ching Heen Cantonese restaurant, with its table settings of jade and ivory, is considered one of the finest in town, and the American-style Steakhouse has a splendid fresh salad and berry bar. *Salisbury Rd., Tsimshatsui, tel. 3/721–1211. 600 rooms. Facilities: luxurious health center, with private rooms and Hong Kong's largest outdoor pool; business center; shopping arcade; beauty salon. AE, CB, DC, MC, V.*

Expensive **Holiday Inn Golden Mile.** Right in the thick of old Tsimshatsui's action, this hotel is a well-established favorite with Europeans and Australians. The popular and crowded lobby bar, coffee shop, and completely renovated Baron's Table, a German gourmet restaurant, attract a loyal local clientele. The elegant Loong Yuen Chinese restaurant boasts one of Hong Kong's best Cantonese chefs. You'll also find a superb Delicatessen Corner, where all smoked items are from the hotel's own smokehouse. *46 Nathan Rd., tel. 3/693–111. 600 rooms. Facilities: business center, rooftop pool, health spa, shopping arcade, beauty salon. AE, CB, DC, MC, V.*

★ **Holiday Inn Harbour View.** At the "far" end of the new Tsimshatsui East belt of hotels, which is not really far from anywhere, this hotel has been voted among the top 10 business hotels in the world. It has good harbor views from 60% of the rooms, all of which are handsomely decorated. A fine collection of eating places includes a coffee shop, Cafe Rendezvous, with splendid harbor view; The Mistral, an interesting Mediterranean restaurant; Matsubishi, a top Japanese restaurant; The Belvedere, a gourmet Continental restaurant; Tsui Hang Village, a very popular Chinese restaurant; and two elegant cocktail lounges. It also has an Executive Club floor for business travelers. *70 Mody Rd., tel. 3/721–5161. 597 rooms. Facilities: business center, rooftop pool with snack bar and fitness center, shopping arcade, beauty salon. AE, CB, DC, MC, V.*

The Hongkong. Managed by Marco Polo International, this hotel has enhanced its up-market image with extensive renovations. It's always been a favorite with visitors, primarily because of its location as an integral part of the Ocean Centre-Harbour City shopping complex. The Star Ferry and bus terminals are next door, and old Tsimshatsui is a short walk away. The enormous range of restaurants in the hotel and shopping complex include the fine Asian Spice Market and the cozy Tai Pan Grill. A new coffee shop on the first floor is open until 2 AM. Other recent additions include two Executive Floors. *3 Canton Rd., Tsimshatsui, tel. 3/676–011. 800 rooms. Facilities: business center, outdoor pool and health center, beauty salon. AE, CB, DC, MC, V.*

Hyatt Regency Hong Kong. Soon to be joined by the Grand

Hyatt on Hong Kong Island-side, this hotel has been given a sparkling new image following a huge facelift. Haute cuisine is still the specialty of Hugo's gourmet restaurant, one of Hong Kong's finest. Added to this is Nathan's, a brightly lit restaurant serving luncheon buffets and snacks; the adjacent Chinese Restaurant, serving Cantonese specialties; and the Cafe, serving both Western and Chinese cuisine. There are two lounges, Nathan's and the Chin Chin Bar, the latter one of Kowloon's most popular bars. The Regency Club, for business travelers, occupies two floors. The hotel is near shops, restaurants, transportation, and nightlife. *67 Nathan Rd., Tsimshatsui, tel. 3/ 311–1234. 723 rooms. Facilities: business center, use of nearby fitness center, shopping arcade. AE, CB, DC, MC, V.*

The Marco Polo Hong Kong. The flagship of Marco Polo International, this hotel has small functional guest rooms and a price range that suits economy-minded business travelers. Its restaurants include La Brasserie, a popular French restaurant; the Coffee Mill, serving international cuisine; and The Patisserie, featuring European cuisine. A popular lounge is The Tartan Bar. *Canton Rd., Harbour City, tel. 3/721–5111. 440 rooms. Facilities: business Center, use of pool at Hongkong Hotel, shopping arcade. AE, CB, DC, MC, V.*

Miramar. A massive redevelopment program has upgraded the Miramar. It has six restaurants, including two Chinese restaurants, and a lounge, Princess Bar. *130 Nathan Rd., Tsimshatsui, tel. 3/681–542. 542 rooms. Facilities: pool and health center, shopping arcade, beauty salon. AE, CB, DC, MC, V.*

New World. This hotel, smack in the middle of a huge shopping complex, has beautifully landscaped gardens totaling 40,000 square feet, with pool and terraces. In addition to a Cantonese restaurant there's the Panorama, serving Continental food, good luncheon buffets, and living up to its name by offering a sweeping view of the harbor; Faces, one of Hong Kong's top discos; and Lobby and Penthouse lounges. The Dynasty Club offers two floors for business travelers. *22 Salisbury Rd., Tsimshatsui, tel. 3/694–111. 720 rooms. Facilities: business center, pool and health spa, jogging path, shopping arcade, beauty salon. AE, CB, DC, MC, V.*

Hotel Nikko Hong Kong. Part of the Japanese Nikko chain, the hotel has four restaurants. Toh Lee serves Cantonese cuisine; Sagano, Japanese; Les Celebrites, French; and Cafe Serena, international—and three lounges. It has special floors for business executives. *72 Mody Rd., Tsimshatsui East, tel. 3/739– 111. 461 rooms. Facilities: business center, outdoor pool, fitness center, gift shops, beauty salon. AE, CB, DC, MC, V.*

Prince. Surrounded by a large shopping complex, this hotel is also run by Marco Polo International. It has two restaurants— The Rib Room, serving Western cuisine, and The Coffee Shop, serving both Western and Oriental food, plus two cocktail lounges, one in the lobby. The hotel is linked to more than 600 shops by an air-conditioned walkway. *Harbour City, Canton Rd., Tsimshatsui, tel. 3/723–7788. 401 rooms. Facilities: business center, use of pool at Hongkong Hotel, shopping arcade. AE, CB, DC, MC, V.*

Regal Airport. Part of the Regal International chain, this hotel is connected to Kai Tak Airport's passenger terminal by an air-conditioned walkway and a luggage conveyer belt. It is ideal for visitors in transit or anyone with business in northern Kowloon. The rooms are soundproof and comfortable. There are two lounges and five restaurants, including the fine French restaurant on the rooftop, Five Continents, overlooking the airport and harbor; and The China Coast Pub serving English and German food. The China Trader's Centre is a well-equipped business center used by those on short stays. It has 10 offices for rent and a China consultancy service for those doing business with China. *30–38 Sa Po Rd., Kowloon, 3/718–0333. 400 rooms. Facilities: business center, shopping arcade, beauty salon, dental clinic. AE, CB, DC, MC, V.*

★ **Regal Meridien.** Chic and stylish, this hotel has well-designed rooms, some with harbor views. There is gourmet dining at the Restaurant de France and French country cuisine at the Brasserie. Regal Seafood serves Cantonese food, and Nishimura features Japanese specialties. On the basement level is one of Hong Kong's top discos, Hollywood East. There's also a Meridien Club lounge for business travelers. *71 Mody Rd., Tsimshatsui, tel. 3/722–1818. 590 rooms. Facilities: business center, health club, beauty salon. AE, CB, DC, MC, V.*

Royal Garden. This is Hong Kong's only atrium hotel. If you like exquisite atriums, you'll love the hotel's glass elevators, fairy lights, trailing greenery, and trickling pools. The third-floor atrium leads to the fine Lalique French restaurant, a coffee shop, and terraces. The lower atrium contains the "lakeside" Flower Lounge Cantonese restaurant. Falcon is an English-style pub during the day and a disco at night. *Mody Rd., Tsimshatsui East, tel. 3/721–5215. 433 rooms. Facilities: business center, health center, shopping arcade, beauty salon. AE, CB, DC, MC, V.*

Sheraton Hong Kong Hotel & Towers. Ideally located in the middle of the "Golden Mile," the Sheraton has renovated its rooms and facilities. The Someplace Else American-style diner has good Tex-Mex food, and the Grandstand Grill offers traditional roasts. Take a ride on Hong Kong's first set of glass-walled external elevators, and visit the rooftop Pink Giraffe supper club, with its nouvelle cuisine, and the Sky Lounge. Both have excellent city views. Other restaurants include Unkai, serving Japanese food, and Sidewalk Cafe, featuring both American and Chinese food. *20 Nathan Rd., Tsimshatsui, tel. 3/691–111. 922 rooms. Facilities: business center, pool and health spa, shopping arcade, beauty salon. AE, CB, DC, MC, V.*

Moderate **Ambassador.** This hotel, which fronts Nathan Road's "Golden Mile," is a reliable business and group-tour hotel. Its rates reflect the central value of its location. The hotel has an expansive lobby lounge, a coffee shop, and two restaurants. The Caliph Room serves Western cuisine and the Dynasty Room serves Chinese cuisine. *4 Middle Rd., Tsimshatsui, tel. 3/666–321. 300 rooms, all with TV and minibar. Facilities: shopping arcade, beauty salon. AE, CB, DC, MC, V.*

Empress. This balconied hotel belongs to a small local hotel group. Guest rooms on the top floors have good views of the undeveloped spaces of Tsimshatsui East. The hotel is close to both old Tsimshatsui's shops and restaurants and to new Tsimshatsui's office blocks and shopping complexes. It has one restaurant, the Mayfair Coffee Shop, serving American, French, and Chinese food. *17 Chatham Rd., Tsimshatsui, tel. 3/660–211. 190 rooms, all with TV and minibar. Facilities: secretarial services, telex, cable, and fax. AE, CB, DC, MC, V.*

Fortuna. A fair way up Nathan Road, the Fortuna is favored by groups who like being in the heart of a Hong Kong shopping scene that's geared more toward locals than tourists. It has a coffee shop, Highland Cafe, and a reasonably priced Chinese restaurant, Tan Kok, plus a bar and lounge. *351 Nathan Rd., tel. 3/851–011. 186 rooms, all with TV and minibar. Facilities: business center. AE, DC, MC, V.*

Grand. One of the older Tsimshatsui hotels, the Grand has a pleasant restaurant, the Viking, serving an international buffet for both lunch and dinner, plus a coffee shop, lobby bar, and cocktail lounge. *14 Carnarvon Rd., Tsimshatsui, tel. 3/669–331. 220 rooms, all with TV and minibar. Facilities: secretarial services. AE, DC, MC, V.*

Grand Tower. This is a good place for travelers who want the "real" Hong Kong. It's surrounded by side streets teeming with people. The hotel, adjacent to the Mongkok MTR Station, has a coffee shop and three Asian restaurants, one of them serving Chinese Chiu Chow cuisine. *624–641 Nathan Rd., tel. 789–0011. 545 rooms, all with TV and minibar. Facilities: business center, beauty salon. AE, DC, MC, V.*

★ **Imperial.** Centrally located between the Sheraton and the Golden Mile Holiday Inn, the Imperial is a small, comfortable hotel catering to commercial visitors. Its restaurant, the Gardena, is above average and serves international cuisine. The hotel has automatic tea boilers and vending machines on each floor, something that's still a rarity in Hong Kong. *32 Nathan Rd., Tsimshatsui, tel. 3/662–201. 220 rooms, all with TV. AE, DC, MC, V.*

International. Quiet and simple, the International is one of several small hotels in the heart of old Tsimshatsui. Its guests are from Western and Northeast Asian countries. Treetops, a restaurant and lounge, serves French food and Chinese food from the province of Swatow. *33 Cameron Rd., tel. 3/663–381. 89 rooms, all with TV. MC, V.*

Nathan. At the far end of Nathan Road's "Golden Mile," the hotel has four restaurants and a snack shop. Three of the restaurants serve Cantonese food, the fourth features Continental cuisine. It isn't far from the heart of Tsimshatsui by MTR. *378 Nathan Rd., tel. 3/885–141. 186 rooms, all with TV and refrigerator. Facilities: business center. AE, DC, MC, V.*

Park. Tsimshatsui's largest independent hotel, the Park has been extensively renovated. It has three restaurants and two bars. *61 Chatham Rd., South Tsimshatsui, tel. 3/661–371. 420 rooms, all with TV and refrigerator. Facilities: business center, shopping arcade, beauty salon. AE, DC, MC, V.*

Inexpensive **Bankok Royal.** Tucked into a back street behind the London theater, the Bangkok has one of Hong Kong's few Thai restaurants. It also has a restaurant serving both Western and Asian dishes. Its lobby, coffee shop, and rooms are somewhat scruffy, but the atmosphere is friendly. The Jordan MTR Station is nearby. *2–12 Pilkem St., tel. 3/679–181. 70 rooms, all with TV. AE, DC, MC, V.*

Booth Lodge (The Salvation Army). This guest house, built in 1985, is pleasant, clean, and close to the Jade Market. It has one coffee shop which serves only Western food. *11 Wing Sing La., Yau Ma Tei, tel. 3/771–9266. 33 rooms. No credit cards.*

Caritas Bianchi Lodge. This hotel is also close to the Jade Market and the nightly Temple Street Market. It's clean and friendly and serves both Chinese and Western food. *4 Cliff Rd., Yau Ma Tei, tel. 3/881–111. 90 rooms. No credit cards.*

First. This hotel is near Mongkok, and far away, by Hong Kong standards, from the heart of Kowloon. However, the adjacent Argyle MTR Station makes it an easy commute to the center of the city. *206 Portland St., tel. 3/780–5211. 50 rooms, some with TV. No credit cards.*

Guangdong. This hotel appeals to many Southeast Asians and Western-born Chinese visitors. It has two restaurants, one serving Chinese cuisine, another serving Japanese and Western food. *18 Prat Ave., tel. 3/739–3311. 245 rooms, all with TV and minibar. Facilities: business center with special Chinese section. AE, CB, DC, MC, V.*

King's. This small hotel is best known for its tiny, six-table Thai restaurant. It also has a restaurant serving Chinese and Western food. It's located near the Waterloo MTR Station. *473 Nathan Rd., tel. 3/780–1281. 80 rooms, all with TV. No credit cards.*

Ritz. Located north of the Tsimshatsui area, close to the Jordan MTR Station, this hotel is a bargain for anyone looking for somewhere to rest his or her head between shopping and dining experiences. It has a coffee shop that serves both Western and Chinese cuisine. *122 Austin Rd., tel. 3/692–282. 60 rooms, all with TV and minibar. AE, DC, MC, V.*

★ **Shamrock.** This comfortable hotel is the pick of the Inexpensive bunch of hotels along northern Nathan Road. Its 10th-floor restaurant serves Chinese, Malaysian, and Western food. The lobby is brightly decorated, Oriental-style. *223 Nathan Rd., tel. 3/662–271. 150 rooms, all with TV. Facilities: Cable, telex, fax services. AE, DC, MC, V.*

New Territories

Expensive **Regal Riverside Hotel.** This is the first luxury hotel in New Territories. Situated on a river in the town of Shatin, it has several good restaurants: Asian Delights, featuring food of Thailand, Indonesia, Malaysia, Singapore, and Japan; Bottania Cafe, serving Continental food; and Regal Seafood, specializing in Chinese seafood dishes. It also has a disco. *Ta Chung Kiu Rd., Shatin, tel. 0/649–7878. 836 rooms. Facilities: business center, free shuttle service to Tsimshatsui, health center. AE, CB, DC, MC, V.*

Outlying Areas and Islands

Expensive **Silvermine Beach Hotel.** This Moorish/Iberian-style hotel is Lantau Island's first resort. It is on the beach at Silvermine Bay, not far from the ferry pier. The hotel has a swimming pool and a children's playground, emphasizing the fact that it caters to local families as well as to overseas visitors. The modest restaurant serves Chinese food. *Silvermine Bay, Mui Wo, tel. 5/ 984–8295. 76 rooms. AE, CB, MC, V.*

Warwick. On Cheung Chau Island, the Warwick soars above Tung Wan Beach and faces across miles of water to Hong Kong Island. The hotel features a swimming pool with sunken bar, a weekend disco, and two restaurants serving Chinese and Western food. A windsurfing center is nearby. The hotel, eight stories high with balconies, is Hong Kong's first luxury seaside hotel. Cheung Chau, which has no cars, is an hour away by ferry from Hong Kong Island. It's popular with local families. *East Bay (Tung Wan), tel. 5/981–0081. 70 rooms, all with TV. AE, DC, MC, V.*

Moderate **Surf.** The Surf, on Sha Ha Beach in Sai Kung, is a popular weekend retreat for locals getting out to the unspoiled eastern side of the Kowloon peninsula. Near the old fishing community of Sai Kung, the hotel has rentals for windsurfing, rowboats, canoes, and motorboats. It also has good swimming pools and all-weather tennis and badminton courts. It serves reasonably priced Western and Chinese food and is a 20-minute drive from Tsimshatsui (in nonrush-hour traffic). *Tai Mong, Tsai Rd., Sai Kung, tel. 3/792–4411. 32 rooms. MC, V.*

9 The Arts and Nightlife

The Arts

The best daily calender of cultural events is the *South China Morning Post* newspaper, which has a daily arts and culture page. You can read previews in the *Sunday Post.* The *Hong Kong Standard* also lists events. Weekly listings are in the *TV and Entertainment Times*, which comes out on Thursdays. The government radio station, RTHK 3, announces events during the 7 AM–10 AM "Hong Kong Today" program.

City Hall (by Star Ferry, Hong Kong Island) has posters and huge bulletin boards listing events and ticket availability, and booths where tickets can be purchased, although finding the right booth can be a bit confusing. The monthly *Urban Council* newspaper, which also lists events, is free and available at City Hall. The following is a list of locales that present events and display posters of Hong Kong cultural events.

Performance Halls

Hong Kong Island   **City Hall** (Edinburgh Pl., by Star Ferry, Central, tel. 5/229–928). This complex has a large auditorium, a recital hall, and a theater. Classical music and legitimate theater are presented here.

Hong Kong Arts Centre (2 Harbour Rd., Wanchai, tel. 5/280–626). Here you will find 15 floors of auditoriums, rehearsal halls, and recital rooms. Local as well as visiting groups of entertainers perform here.

Hong Kong Fringe Club (2 Lower Albert Rd., Central, tel. 5/217–251). Locally run, this has some of Hong Kong's most interesting visiting and local entertainment and art exhibitions. Shows and exhibits range from the blatantly amateur to the magically professional. It also has good jazz, avant-garde drama, and events for and by both young and old.

Queen Elizabeth Stadium (Oi Kwan Rd., Wanchai, tel. 5/756–793). Although this is basically a sports stadium with a seating capacity of 3,500, it frequently presents ballet, orchestra concerts, and even disco.

Hong Kong Academy for Performing Arts. (Harbour Rd., Wanchai, tel. 5/823–1500). This arts school has two major theaters seating 1,600 people, plus a 200-seat studio theater and outdoor theater.

Lee Theatre. (99 Percival St., Causeway Bay, tel. 5/795–4433). This is mainly a movie theater, but it also has performances by visiting Chinese opera and pop stars.

Kowloon   **Hong Kong Coliseum.** (Hung Hom Railway Station, Hung Hom, tel. 3/765–9234). This stadium has seating capacity for more than 12,000 and presents everything from basketball to ballet. It was the site of a David Bowie concert.

Academic Community Hall (224 Waterloo Rd., Kowloon Tong, tel. 3/386–121. Take the MTR to Kowloon Tong Station, then a taxi). This is a very modern auditorium belonging to Baptist College. Mainly it has rock and pop groups, but it offers other concerts, too.

New Territories **Tsuen Wan Town Hall** (Tel. 0/440–144. Take the MTR to Tsuen Wan Station). Although off the beaten track, this auditorium has a constant stream of performers. Groups include everything from the Warsaw Philharmonic to troupes of Chinese acrobats. It has seating capacity for 1,424 and probably the best accoustics in the colony.

Shatin Town Hall (tel. 0/694–2510). This is an impressive building attached to an enormous shopping arcade. It usually shares cultural events with Tsuen Wan through the Regional Council.

Festivals and Special Events

No other Asian territory has as many festivals as Hong Kong. Many festivals are ad hoc—somebody comes up with the idea for a Chinese dance festival or an Asian acrobatic festival, and suddenly it's there, taking even the residents by surprise. Following are the regular cultural festivals—but don't be surprised if a festival turns up that's not on the list.

Hong Kong Arts Festival (Jan.–Feb.). This includes four weeks of music and drama from around the world. Information abroad can be obtained through Cathay Pacific Airline offices. In Hong Kong, City Hall has all the schedules.

Hong Kong Fringe Festival (Jan.–Feb.). Running simultaneously with the Arts Festival, it starts off with Sunday street theater in Central. There are shows at the Fringe Club, near Star Ferry pier, and just about anywhere.

Hong Kong International Film Festival (Apr.). This includes two weeks of films from virtually every country in the world. Quality varies, but since this festival is neither for selling films nor for competition, the spectrum is far wider than anywhere else. It's difficult to get tickets for evening performances, but daily shows, beginning at 10:30 AM, are available (tel. 5/739–595 for information). Brochures are available at City Hall.

Free Chinese Cultural Shows sponsored by the Hong Kong Tourist Association (HKTA) are performed in the *Ocean Terminal, New World Centre,* and *Tsim Sha Tsui Centre,* all in Kowloon, and in the *Landmark* and *Cityplaza* on Hong Kong Island. A monthly schedule and program is published by the HKTA.

Chinese Opera Fortnight (Sept.). This is two weeks of Cantonese, Peking, Soochow, Chekiang, and Chiu Chow opera presented in City Hall Theatre, Concert Hall, and Ko Shan Theatre.

Festival of Asian Arts (Oct.–Nov.). Perhaps Asia's major cultural festival, this draws over 150 artistic events from as far afield as Hawaii, Bhutan, and Australia. It is staged not only in City Hall and Queen Elizabeth Stadium but also at playgrounds throughout the territory. It occurs biennially in even-numbered years.

Performing Arts Ensembles

Several permanent arts ensembles are indigenous to Hong Kong, some with government support, some subsidized by private organizations. The following are the major groups:

Hong Kong Philharmonic Orchestra. More than 100 artists from Hong Kong, the United States, and Europe perform everything from classical to avant-garde to contemporary music by Chinese composers. Soloists have included Ashkenazy, Firkusny, and Maureen Forrester. Performances are mostly on Friday and Saturday at 8 PM in City Hall or recital halls in New Territories (tel. 5/832–7121 for ticket information).

Hong Kong Chinese Orchestra. Created in 1977 by the Urban Council, this group performs only Chinese works. The orchestra is divided into strings, plucked instruments, wind, and percussion. Each work is arranged and orchestrated especially for the occasion. Weekly concerts are given throughout Hong Kong.

Chinese Opera

Cantonese Opera. There are 10 Cantonese opera troupes in Hong Kong, as well as many amateur singing groups. Many perform "street opera," as in the Shanghai Street Night Market on Sundays, while others perform at temple fairs, in City Hall, or in playgrounds under the auspices of the Urban Council. Visitors unfamiliar with the form are sometimes alienated by the strange sounds of this highly complex and extremely sophisticated art form. Every gesture has its own meaning; in fact, there are 50 different gestures for the hand alone. Props attached to the costumes are similarly intricate and are used in exceptional ways. For example, the principal female will often wear five-foot-long pheasant tails attached to the headdress. Anger is shown by dropping the head and shaking it in a circular fashion so the feathers move in a perfect circle. Surprise is shown by "nodding the feathers." One can also "dance with the feathers" to show a mixture of anger and determination. The orchestral instruments punctuate the singing. It is best to have a friend translate the gestures, since the stories are so complex that they make Wagner or Verdi librettos seem almost simplistic.

Peking Opera. Some people like this less than Cantonese opera, because the voices are higher-pitched. This is an older opera form and more respected for its classical traditions. Several troupes visit Hong Kong from the People's Republic of China each year, and their meticulous training is of a high degree. They perform in City Hall or at special temple ceremonies.

Dance

Dancescope (tel. 5/833–9922). Founded in 1977 by American dancer Daryl Ries, this group presents dance troupes from abroad, works with dancers from the People's Republic of China, and with most dancers in the region.

Hong Kong Dance Company (tel. 5/737–398). The Urban Council created the Hong Kong Dance Company in 1981 to promote the art of Chinese dance and to present newly choreographed work on Chinese historical themes. They give about three performances a month throughout the territory and have appeared at the Commonwealth Arts Festival in Australia. The 30-odd members are expert in folk and classical dance.

Hong Kong Ballet (tel. 3/349–974). This is Hong Kong's first professional ballet company and vocational ballet school. It is Western-oriented, both classical and contemporary, with the dancers performing at schools, auditoriums, and various festivals.

City Contemporary Dance Company (tel. 3/268–597). This group is dedicated to contemporary dance inspired by Hong Kong, and has very innovative programs.

Drama

The Fringe Club. An enormous amount of drama, ranging from one-man shows to full dramatic performances, is presented by this club. Regular groups include Chung Ying Theatre Company, a professional company with British and Chinese actors performing plays in English and Cantonese, mostly in schools and churches. The British Council (tel. 5/831–5138) can give more information.

Zuni Icosehedron (tel. 5/893–8419). The most important avant-garde group puts on new drama in Cantonese and English at various locations.

Nightlife

Hong Kong's nightlife offers something for everybody. For some, a night out means a visit to a street market, a long dinner at a harborside restaurant, or a bout of window-shopping. For others, it means elegant piano bars and rollicking British pubs, funky jazz dens, high-tech, super-strobed discos, topless bars, and hostess clubs. For still others, it includes marble massage parlors, American-style bar-lounges, old-fashioned ballrooms, sing-along cafes, *karaoke* (sing-a-song) bars for Japanese amateur crooners, and cabaret restaurants.

All premises licensed to serve alcohol are subject to stringent fire, safety, and sanitary controls by police and local authorities. True clubs, as distinct from public premises, are less strictly controlled, and wise visitors should think twice before succumbing to the city's raunchier club hideaways. If you stumble into one, check out cover and hostess charges *before* you get too comfortable, pay for each round of drinks as it's served (by cash rather than credit card), and never sign any blank checks. As in every tourist destination, the rip-off is a well-practiced art. To be safest, visit spots that are sign-carrying members of the Hong Kong Tourist Association (HKTA). You can pick up its free membership listing (including approved restaurants and night spots) at any HKTA Information Office.

Take note, too, of Hong Kong's laws. You need to be over 18 to be served alcohol. Drugs, obscene publications, homosexual acts, and unlicensed gambling are ostensibly illegal. There is some consumer protection, but the generally helpful police, now mostly English-speaking, expect every visitor to know the meaning of "caveat emptor" (buyer beware!).

Following is a checklist of some suggested drinking and dancing spots (with telephone numbers where reservations are possible or wise). Many of Hong Kong's smarter night spots are located in hotels *(see* the Hotels section for addresses and telephone numbers).

Fast-paced, competitive Hong Kong is a world of change where buildings seem to vanish overnight and new fads emerge weekly. Don't be surprised if our listing includes some spots that have changed their decor or name, or have closed down since these words were written.

Cabaret and Nightclubs

Some hotels have dinner shows on a now-and-then basis. The **Hilton** is the major dinner-theater destination, often featuring short seasons of British theater companies staging three-act comedies for nostalgic British expatriates.

Stand-up comedians, usually British, also visit Hong Kong, appearing at the **Sheraton, Holiday Inn Harbour View,** or **China Fleet Club** (6 Arsenal St., Wanchai, tel. 5/296–001). Check newspaper listings or the weekly *TV & Entertainment Times* for details.

The biggest and best old-fashioned nightclub-restaurants are Chinese. The cuisine is Cantonese, and so are most of the singers. Big-name local balladeers and "Cantopop" stars make guest appearances. Though modest by Las Vegas standards, the shows can be entertaining, as at the massive **Ocean City Restaurant & Night Club** in New World Centre (tel. 3/699–688). It claims to be the world's biggest Chinese restaurant.

Ocean Centre's **Ocean Palace Restaurant & Night Club** (tel. 3/677–111) is another favorite for Hong Kong family and wedding parties.

On Nathan Rd., at 36 and 66, check out the **Capital** (tel. 3/681–844) and **Golden Crown** (tel. 3/666–291) nightclub-restaurants. Here you will see Hongkongers dining and dancing the night away.

One of the few hotel restaurants to feature a band and singers is Hilton's rooftop **Eagle's Nest** Chinese restaurant (5/233–111). Another good, old-style "supper-club," with nouvelle cuisine and Caucasian singers, is the Sheraton's rooftop **Pink Giraffe** (tel. 3/691–111). Both can be pricy, even if you order the set dinners.

In Causeway Bay, the Lee Gardens Hotel's **Pavilion** (tel. 5/895–3311) is a less expensive dinner-dance Western-style restaurant, much favored by Australian and British tourists.

Duddell's, a duplex operation in Central (tel. 5/845–2244), serves European cuisine and has a live band, a resident magician, and other lively entertainers. It's a favorite with Western yuppies and local chuppies (Chinese yuppies).

Cocktail and Piano Bars

Every luxury hotel has at least one piano bar. Some serve food, and many have live music (usually jolly Filipino trios with a female singer) and a handkerchief-size dance floor. Hong Kong's Happy Hours usually run from late afternoon to early evening, with drinks at half price.

Harbor-gazing is the main attraction at the Shangri-La's **Tiara Lounge,** Sheraton's **Sky Lounge** (go up in the bubble lift), and Excelsior's **Talk of the Town.**

Feeling pampered is the pleasure at the Peninsula's clublike **Verandah** or the Mandarin Oriental's mezzanine **Clipper Lounge.** The socially aware go to the Peninsula's **Lobby** or Regent's two lobby lounges to see and be seen. Sit on the right of the Peninsula's entrance to be where the cream of society traditionally lounges; be ready to chat about the fashion industry if you sit in the Regent's lobby.

Pubs

Pubs have become popular with young beer-loving Hong Kongers as well as British residents and troops. Drinks are cheaper than in bars, pub "snacks" are filling fare, and there is usually a game of darts or chess, and some free musical entertainment.

Off-duty Central business folks flock to Connaught Centre pirate-galleon **Galley** (tel. 5/263–061).

Central's oak-beamed, British-managed **Bull & Bear** is in Hutchison House, on Lambeth Walk (tel. 5/257–436).

Another popular spot is **The Jockey Pub,** tucked away in Swire House (2nd-floor shopping arcade Chater Rd., tel. 5/261–478).

In Wanchai, pub-hopping is practiced by the fit and less fastidious. **The Horse & Groom** (126 Lockhart Rd., tel. 5/272–083) and its neighboring **Old China Hand Tavern** (104 Lockhart Rd., tel. 5/279–174) are reliable starting points. End up at the Excelsior Hotel's **Dickens Bar** (go there first on a Sunday afternoon for its jazz sessions).

Cool off at an outdoor table at Causeway Bay's **King's Arms,** on Sunning Plaza (tel. 5/895–6536), one of Hong Kong's few city-center "beer gardens."

Over in Tsimshatsui, a mixed, happy crowd can be found in the window-fronted **Kangaroo Pub** (11 Chatham Rd., tel. 3/723–9439). The set-up includes the **Windjammer Restaurant.**

The **Blacksmith's Arms** (16 Minden Ave., tel. 3/696–696), is a cozier gathering place. Go to 4 Hart Avenue to taste the varying styles of **Rick's Cafe** (tel. 3/672–939), a pioneer in live jazz sessions.

Neighboring **Grammy's Lounge** (2A Hart Ave., tel. 3/683–833) features Filipino-led sing-alongs. The **Stoned Crow** (12 Minden Ave., tel. 3/668–494) is Aussie-style, with beer and filling grub. One of Hong Kong's best drinking scenes for non-Asian visitors is in Central, in the Lan Kwai Fong area *(see* For Singles).

Wine Bars

Western stockbrokers and financial types unwind in **Central's Brown's Wine Bar** (Tower 2, Exchange Sq., tel. 5/237–003). It has good food and a splendid bar. Accents tend to be British.

At **La Rose Noire,** a chic little bistro (8 Wo On La., Central, tel. 5/265–965), the owners are a formidable piano-singing team.

Even more intimate is **Le Tire Bouchon** (9 Old Bailey St., tel. 5/235–459), whose owner dispenses tasty bistro meals and fine wines by the glass.

Jazz Clubs

Although there are few professional jazz players in town, regular sessions are mounted by part-timers at some bars. **Rick's Cafe** (4 Hart Ave., Tsimshatsui, tel. 3/672–939) promotes jazz fusion in a Bogie-honoring *Casablanca* setting.

Ned Kelly's Last Stand (11 Ashley Rd., Tsimshatsui, tel. 3/660–562) is an Aussie-managed home for pub grub and Dixieland. Get there early, before 10 PM, to get a comfortable seat.

Sunday afternoon sessions at the Excelsior Hotel's **Dickens Bar** are always worth checking out. So are the Wednesday-night gigs at the **Godown** bar-restaurant, in the basement of Chater Road's Sutherland House in Central (tel. 5/221–608).

Seasons, a two-deck bistro (17 On Lan St., Central, tel. 5/268–429) has jazz evenings sometimes, and light classical music at other times.

There's a rousing Filipino version of Country Western music most evenings in **Bar City** in New World Centre, in Tsimshatsui (tel. 3/698–571), which is popular with young Hong Kongers.

Hardy's Folk Club (35 D'Aguilar St., Central, tel. 5/224–48) is another Hong Kong rarity—the singers tend to be self-conscious Western transients singing for their supper in a pub setting.

Discos

Hong Kong young people fill the discos, a major outlet for letting off steam. Entry prices are high by American standards, and you'll see thousands of fashionably dressed fun-seekers if you do a grand disco tour. Entrance to the smarter spots, around HK$100 or more (much more on major public holiday eves), usually entitles you to two drinks. The trendsetter is still **Canton** (World Finance Centre, Harbour City, Canton Rd., Tsimshatsui, tel. 3/721–0209), a two-story high-energy maze of gangways, video monitors, and gathering areas packed with a young crowd. Its members-only room is a live music lounge.

Slightly older nightlifers frequent the adjacent **Hot Gossip** (tel. 3/721–6884), which has a separate café-style cocktail lounge.

Other discos on this side of Tsimshatsui, such as **Apollo 18** (Silvercord, Canton Rd., tel. 3/722–6188), attract milling crowds of local youngsters. There is a more cosmopolitan scene at **Hollywood East,** in the basement of Tsimshatsui East's Regal Meridien Hotel (tel. 3/722–5597). Smallish, it boasts ever-changing light effects.

Its reliable neighbor is the Royal Garden Hotel's **Royal Falcon.** The daytime pub operation goes disco at night. So does the Excelsior's **Talk of the Town** in Causeway Bay.

Japanese tourists gravitate to the Park Lane Raddison Hotel's **Starlight** disco, also in Causeway Bay. Some check out the self-styled Japanese high-tech **Shesado** disco in the New World Centre's **Bar City** drinking complex (tel. 3/698–571). One ticket admits you to the City's three operations. It's another place for Chinese youngsters enjoying a night out on the town.

Chuppies and conversationalists head upstairs, to the New World Hotel's **Faces,** which has quiet corners. Similar types, many of the boat-owning class, take a taxi or chauffeur out to **Casablanca Supper Club** in Aberdeen's Marina Club (tel. 5/540–044) on the south side of Hong Kong Island.

The **Godown** disco bar-restaurant, in Central's Sutherland House (Chater Rd., tel. 5/221–608), is another popular night spot. **Joe Bananas** (23 Luard Rd., Wanchai, tel. 5/291–811) is a high-ceiling, American-style disco-café, busiest when the fleet's in town. The original trendsetter, and Hong Kong's first really mixed disco in which all classes and races mingled, is **Disco Disco** (40 D'Aguilar St., Central, tel. 5/235–863). It is still popular with singles and, like almost all discos, has midweek ladies' nights.

Topless Bars

With a few notable exceptions, most topless bars are scruffy dives. A beer may seem reasonably priced, at around HK$20, but the "champagne" the women drink is not. Charges for conversational companionship can also be unexpected extras.

Bottoms Up (14 Hankow Rd., Tsimshatsui, tel. 3/721–4509) was immortalized by its use in a James Bond film. Cozy circular bar counters are tended by topless women. This place is so respectable that visiting couples are welcomed.

Over in Wanchai, once known as "The World of Suzie Wongs," the friendliest faces are those of off-duty Filipina *amahs* (household servants), either working or lounging on the dance floors of spots like the **Makati Inn** (15 Luard Rd., tel. 5/270–117) and the **Island Cavern Pub & Disco** (18 Fenwick St., tel. 5/292–977).

Other bars, with or without door touts, in Wanchai or old Tsimshatsui (on the side roads off Nathan Road), warrant sober assessment by potential visitors. Avoid the so-called "fishball stalls" farther out, in Kowloon, unless you are a Cantonese-speaking anthropologist who likes working in the dark. Ditto for massage parlors.

A popular cluster of Wanchai haunts are to be found on and off Wanchai's Fenwick Street—stick your nose in **An-An, Crossroads, Club Mikado, Pussycat,** and, of course, the **Suzie Wong Club.**

Hostess Clubs

These are clubs in name only. Hong Kong's better ones are multimillion-dollar operations, with hundreds of presentable hostess-companions of many races. Computerized time clocks on each table tabulate companionship charges in timed units— the costs are clearly detailed on table cards, as are standard drink tabs. The clubs' dance floors are often larger than a disco's, and they have one or more live bands and a scheduled line-up of singers. They also have dozens of fancily furnished private rooms with sofas or partitioned drinking lounges, often palatially comfortable. Local and visiting businessmen adore them—and the numbered, multilingual hostesses. Business is so good that the clubs are willing to allow visitors *not* to ask for companionship. The better clubs are on a par with deluxe hotels' music lounges, and they cost little more. Their Happy Hours start in the afternoon, when many have a sort of tea-dance ambience, and continue through to mid-evening. Peak hours are 10 PM–4 AM.

Club Volvo is the grandest, in Tsimshatsui East's Mandarin Plaza (tel. 3/692–883). Executives, mostly Hong Kongers, entertain here, tended by a staff of over 1,000. If one's VIP room is too far from the entrance, one can hire an electrified vintage Rolls and purr around an indoor roadway. Close by is another drinkers' dreamland, **China City Night Club,** in Peninsula Centre (tel. 3/723–0388). Along the harbor, in New World Centre, are **Club Cabaret** (tel. 3/698–431) and **Club Deluxe** (tel. 3/721–0277), both luxurious dance lounges.

As its name implies, **Club Kokusai** (81 Nathan Rd., Tsimshatsui, tel. 3/676–969) appeals to visitors from the land of the risen Yen. So does Causeway Bay's **Club Dai-Ichi** (257 Gloucester Rd., tel. 5/831–0935).

Two comfortably grand Wanchai nightclubs are the **Mandarin Palace** (24 Marsh Rd., tel. 5/756–551) and the **New Tonnochy** (1 Tonnochy Rd., tel. 5/754–376).

For Singles

Many Westerners and chuppies choose to meet in crowded comfort in the Lan Kwai Fong area, a hillside section around Central's D'Aguilar Street. It contains many appetizing bistros, wine bars, and ethnic cafés.

Singles mix happily at **Disco Disco** *(see* Disco) and around the bar of **California** (tel. 5/211–345) a laid-back American-style restaurant for all ages. It has a late-night disco most nights.

The bar area of the cosy **Nineteen '97** restaurant (tel. 5/260–303) is also favored by conversationalists, though they tend to arrive, and stay, in cliques. So does most of the cheery Western crowd in a Scottish-Victorian pub farther up the hill: **Mad Dogs** (33 Wyndham St., tel. 5/252–383).

Schnurrbart (Winner Bldg., D'Aguilar St., tel. 5/234–700) is a friendly German pub. Next door is *Hardy's Folk Bar.* One place nearby where the arts-minded can mingle is the **Fringe Club** (2 Lower Albert Rd., tel. 5/217–251), in the historic red-brick building that also houses the Foreign Correspondents Club. The Club is Hong Kong's "alternative" arts scene.

Lonely businessmen can be talked to at hotel bars. The Hilton's **Dragon Boat,** Hyatt's **Chin Chin** or **Nathan's,** and Sheraton's **Someplace Else** have their fans.

Owing to the supposedly reserved natures of both the British and the Chinese, Hong Kong is one of the more difficult places for striking up conversations with strangers. Most Hong Kong singles go hunting in discos or pubs with same-sex friends, or wander in groups through the shopping complexes. Central's **Landmark,** on Des Voeux Road, is a favored place for "eye-talking," up to 6 PM. As in most destinations, singles usually meet each other during the day (on coach tours or on business assignments).

10 Macau

Introduction

by Shann Davies

A British freelance writer, Shann Davies, has lived and traveled in many countries, but she always comes back to Macau, which she first visited in 1962. She is the author of Viva Macau!, Chronicles in Stone, *and* Macau *(Times Edition).*

If history balanced its books, no one would today be skimming over the 40-mile (64-km) waterway from Hong Kong to Macau. After all, the Portuguese-administered enclave of six square miles (15.6 sq km) tucked into China's back pocket ceased to have any commercial or political significance a century and a half ago.

How and why has it survived? One clue can be found on the vessel en route to Macau. Most of the passengers will be Hong Kong Chinese heading for the casinos, which have provided the territory with much of its revenue since legal gambling was introduced in the 1840s as an attempt to compensate for the loss of entrepôt trade to newly founded Hong Kong.

Also on board might be Jesuit priests and Roman Catholic nuns, both Chinese and European, who run vital, centuries-old charities and tend to one of Asia's oldest and most devout Christian communities. Just as likely, there are Buddhist priests, who help maintain Macau's firm faith in its Chinese traditions. Then there are the tourists—more than three-quarters of a million a year—textile and toy buyers, British engineers, Swiss chefs, French showgirls and bar hostesses from Southeast Asia. In their different ways they all prove that there's plenty of life left in the grande dame of the China Coast.

The voyage is a pleasant progress between hilly green islands, some belonging to Hong Kong, some Chinese, and most uninhabited. As it appears on the skyline, Macau jolts the imagination. Hills crowned with a lighthouse and church spire, a blur of pastel buildings, and tree-lined avenues all confirm that this is a bit of transplanted Iberia. It was settled in 1557 by the Portuguese as Europe's first outpost in China.

Macau is 90 miles (144 km) south of Canton, the traditional port for China's trade with foreign "barbarians." In the 16th century, however, her traders were forbidden by the emperor to deal with Japan, whose Shogun had imposed a ban on China trade. The Portuguese saw their chance and soon were making fabulous fortunes from their command of trade between the two Asian countries and Europe. Among the cargoes that passed through Macau were silk, tea, and porcelain from China, silver and lacquerware from Japan, spices and sandalwood from the East Indies, muslin from India, gems from Persia, wild animals and ivory from Africa, foodstuffs from Brazil, and European clocks, telescopes, and cannons.

Macau's golden age came to an abrupt end with the closure of Japan and the loss of Portugal's mercantile power to the Dutch and English. The northern Europeans and the Americans sent their India-men and clipper ships to Macau to barter ginseng, furs, woolens, and opium for tea and silk. Their merchants treated the city as their own but, with their rents and customs duties, helped Macau survive. Then, in the mid-19th century, Hong Kong was founded and the merchants moved out, leaving Macau a backwater.

In the early part of this century, Macau was cast by movie producers and novelists as a den of sin, sex, and spies. True, it had casinos, brothels, opium divans, and secret agents; but, in fact, it was a small, pale shadow of Shanghai or even Hong Kong. Today, any traveler in search of wild and wicked Macau will be disappointed, and so will romantics looking for a colonial twilight. As you approach through the ocher waters of the silt-heavy Pearl River estuary, the reality of modern Macau is unavoidable. High-rise apartments and office blocks mask the hillsides, multistory factories cover land reclaimed from the sea, and construction hammers insist that this is no longer a sleepy old town.

The modern prosperity comes from taxes on gambling and the export of textiles, toys, electronics, furniture, luggage, fireworks, and artificial flowers. Like Hong Kong, Macau is a duty-free port where anyone can set up a business with minimal taxation or government restrictions. As a result, there is little evidence of city planning and many of the new skyscrapers are grotesque. However, some building projects have benefited Macau. These include the University of East Asia and the Trotting Club on Taipa Island, a handsome handful of good hotels, and a number of superbly restored or re-created historical buildings.

Relations with China have never been better, with ever increasing two-way trade and joint ventures in Zhongshan, the neighboring Chinese county. Macau's close proximity to China also makes it a popular gateway for excursions across the border. Following the Sino-British agreement to hand Hong Kong back to China in 1997, the Portuguese negotiated the resumption of Chinese sovereignty over Macau, which will take place on December 20, 1999.

Macau has a population of about 450,000, and most live in the 2.5 square miles (6.5 sq km) of the mainland peninsula, with small communities on the mostly rural islands of Taipa and Coloane. About 95% of the inhabitants are Chinese, many of them of long-standing residence. About 7,000 people speak Portuguese as their first language, but only a few come from Portugal, the others being Macanese from old established Eurasian families. The more transient residents are expatriate Europeans, Americans, and Australasians, plus a few hundred Vietnamese refugees and several thousand nightclub hostesses from Thailand and the Philippines. Although Portuguese is the official language, and Cantonese the most widely spoken, English is generally understood in places frequented by tourists.

Arriving and Departing

The Hong Kong–Macau route is possibly the busiest international water highway in the world, with more than 5½ million round-trip passages a year, or a daily average of over 15,000. The crossing procedure is very efficient, but this is not to say it's problem-free. Tickets are hard to get on weekends and public holidays, when the Hong Kong gamblers travel en masse. And services are disrupted when typhoons are in the area.

Travel Documents Visas are *not* required by Portuguese citizens or nationals of the United States, Canada, the United Kingdom, Australia, New Zealand, France, West Germany, Austria, Belgium, the Netherlands, Switzerland, Sweden, Denmark, Norway, Italy, Greece, Spain, Japan, Thailand, the Philippines, Malaysia, Brazil (up to a six-month stay), or Hong Kong residents. There is unlimited stay for Chinese, 20 days for non-Chinese. Other nationals need visas, available on arrival: HK$50 for individuals, HK$75 for a family, and HK$25 for group members. Visas are good for one or two visits within 20 days.

Tickets Travel agents and most Hong Kong hotels can arrange for tickets. There are also 11 Ticketmate computer-booking outlets in Hong Kong that sell tickets up to 28 days in advance for the Jetfoils headed for Macau. They are located in Exchange Square (Central, Hong Kong Island) and the major Mass Transit Railway (MTR) stations. It's best to get the return ticket at the same time because it can be inconvenient to do so in Macau. If you change your mind about the time of your return, you can change tickets in Macau or go to the harbor and return on a stand-by basis. Tickets can also be booked in Hong Kong by phone and with credit cards (Jetfoil 5/859–3288, AE, DC, V; hydrofoils and Jetcats, 5/232–136, AE, V). There is a HK$15 departure tax from Hong Kong, none from Macau.

By Plane At the time of writing, helicopter service between Hong Kong and Macau was scheduled to begin in 1989. Plans are for 10 round-trips a day, leaving from a heli-pad on top of the Hong Kong Shun Tak Centre terminal and landing at Macau's Outer Harbour. Flight time is expected to be 20 minutes.

By Sea The vast majority of sailings for Macau use the Macau Terminal in the Shun Tak Centre (200 Connaught Rd.), a 10-minute walk west of Hong Kong's Central District.

Booking offices for all shipping companies, most Macau hotels and travel agents, excursions to China, and the MTIB are located in the Shun Tak Centre.

In many cases information is hard to obtain over the phone; it's best to call the MTIB (tel. 5/408–180).

A fleet of Boeing Jetfoils provides the most popular service between Hong Kong and Macau. Carrying about 260 passengers, these craft ride comfortably on jet-propelled hulls at 40 knots and make the 40-mile trip in about an hour. Beer, soft drinks, and snacks are available on board, as are telephones and Macau's instant lottery tickets. Jetfoils depart at least every half hour from 7 AM to dusk, with frequent sailings between 6:30 PM and 1:30 AM. The top deck of each vessel is first class, and there are non-smoking sections on both decks.

Fares for first class are HK$66 on weekdays, HK$72 on weekends and public holidays, and HK$88 on the night service. Lower-deck fares are HK$57 weekdays, HK$63 weekends, and HK$77 at night. The Jetfoils are operated by Far East Jetfoil Company, a division of Shun Tak Shipping, which runs two conventional ferries on the route. These provide a pleasant, leisurely way of getting to Macau and take about three hours. They make two round-trips a day, with extra sailings on holidays. The fares range from HK$30 for aircraft-type seats to HK$150 for a VIP cabin.

The other long-established company on the route is Hong Kong Macau Hydrofoil Company (HMH). It operates a fleet of hydrofoils which take about 75 minutes and make 22 round-trips a day between 8 AM and dusk. These craft can be uncomfortable in choppy seas, but they have the advantage of small, open decks for picture-taking and wind-swept rides. Fares are HK$46 on weekdays, HK$58 on weekends and holidays. The HMH also operates three jet-propelled catamarans called Jetcats. They carry 215 passengers and make the trip in about

70 minutes, with 10 round-trips a day. Fares are HK$46 on weekdays, HK$58 on weekends.

The newest vessels on the Macau run are High Speed Ferries, which take about an hour and a half on five round-trips daily between 8 AM and 10:30 PM. These sleek, comfortable craft have a sun deck and first-class lounge. On all three decks the seats are comfortable, there's Chinese-language TV and slot machines for entertainment, plus a variety of snacks and drinks. Fares are HK$46 first class, HK$38 economy class weekdays, HK$57 weekends, and HK$45 holidays. Bookings can be made at Ticketmate and the wharf.

Another relatively new service is by Sealink's hover-ferries. They carry 250 passengers and take about an hour. Fares are HK$45 weekdays, HK$56 weekends and holidays. They make eight round-trips a day and, unlike those mentioned above, sail from Taikoktsui ferry pier on the Kowloon peninsula. This pier Jetcats, but is too out-of-the-way and ramshackle for tourists' use.

Important Addresses and Numbers

Tourist Information In Macau, the **Department of Tourism** offers information, advice, maps, and brochures about the territory. It has an office at the arrival terminal, open 9 AM–6 PM every day. There is also an office at Travessa do Paiva, next to Government Palace, open during office hours (tel. 772–18).

Probably more useful is the MTIB in Hong Kong. It has a wide range of maps, brochures, and up-to-the-minute information on hotels and transport. The office is located on the same floor as the wharf entrance. *305 Shun Tak Centre, tel. 5/408–180 outside office hours, 5/408–198. Open weekdays 9–5, Sat. 9–1.*

In addition, there is a Macau information desk at Hong Kong's Kai Tak Airport, just outside the Arrivals Hall. *Open daily 8 AM–10 PM.*

Business visitors to Macau can get information about all aspects of local commercial conditions from the Macau Business Centre, Edificio Ribeiro, in the square between the Praia Grande and Rua do Campo (tel. 864–62). For trade information call the Export Promotion Department (tel. 782–24).

Getting Around

In the old parts of town and shopping areas, walking is the best means of transportation. Here the streets are narrow, often under repair, and invariably crowded with vehicles weaving between sidewalk vendors and parked cars, so that pedestrians often make the fastest progress. Otherwise transport is varied, convenient, and often fun.

By Pedicab This tricycle-drawn, two-seater carriage has been in business as long as there have been bicycles and paved roads in Macau, and a few look like originals. They cluster at the wharf and their drivers hustle for customers, usually offering guide services. In the past it was a pleasure to hire a pedicab for the ride from the wharf to downtown, but no longer. Construction along the Outer Harbour and the outrageous prices asked by today's drivers make it a hassle. To appreciate the pedicab, especially on a sunny day, take one along the Praia Grande and admire the avenue of ancient trees and the seascape of islands and fishing junks. The city center is not a congenial place for pedicabs, and the hilly districts are impossible. Of course you have to haggle, but you shouldn't pay more than HK$10 for a short trip.

By Taxi There are usually plenty of taxis at the wharf, outside hotels, and cruising the streets. All are metered and most are air-conditioned and reasonably comfortable, but the cabbies speak little English and probably won't know the English or Portuguese names for places. It is highly recommended that you carry a bilingual map or name card in Chinese. Flag-fall is 4.50 patacas for the first 1,500 meters (about 1 mile), and 60 avos for each additional 250 meters (about ¼ mile). Drivers don't expect more than small change as a tip. For trips to Taipa there is a five-pataca surcharge, and to Coloane 10 patacas.

By Bus The public buses that rattle around Macau are cheap—no more than one pataca in the city—but usually crowded and uncomfortable. Some bus services, however, can be recommended. One is the no. 3 and no. 3A, which link the wharf with the Lisboa and Sintra hotels, the main street, and A-Ma Temple. The others are those that commute between the city and the islands. Among those that serve Taipa, for one pataca, are some open-topped double-deckers which provide a roller-coaster-like ride across the bridge. Less dramatic are the single-deck buses that go to Coloane village and Hac Sa beach, for 1.50 and two patacas, respectively. They stop outside the Lisboa. The newest buses in town are replicas of 1920s London buses known as "Tour Machines." Their depot is in front of the Lisboa hotel, and they can be hired for parties of up to nine people, for 200 patacas an hour. They are also often used to transfer groups to and from hotels. Finally, they ply set routes for 20 patacas a ticket good for all sections of the route. For information call 865–22.

By Bicycle Bicycles are available for rent at about 10 patacas an hour from shops on Avenida Dom Joao 1V in the city and near the Taipa bus station. The Mandarin Oriental Hotel also has bikes for rent. They are newer and more modern but cost more.

By Hired Car Self-drive Jeeplike mini vehicles called mokes are fun and ideal for touring. International and most national driving licenses are valid. Rates are HK$250 for 24 hours weekdays, HK$280 weekends; special packages in conjunction with hotels are available. For Macau Mokes contact 5/434–190 or Ticketmate in Hong Kong, or the office at the wharf in Macau (tel. 788–51). For Avis mokes call 5/422–189 in Hong Kong, or their office in the Mandarin Oriental hotel (tel. 5/555–686, ext. 3004).

Guided Tours

Regular and customized tours, for individuals and groups, by bus or car, are easily arranged in Macau, and provide the maximum amount of sightseeing in a short space of time.

There are two basic tours. One covers mainland Macau with stops at the Chinese border, Kun Iam Temple, St. Paul's, and Penha Hill. It lasts about 3½ hours. By bus it costs HK$67 for one to three passengers, HK$62 each for four or more, and includes lunch. By car, the cost is HK$150 for one, HK$100 each for two or more. The other standard tour consists of a two-hour trip to the islands across the bridge, to see old Chinese villages, temples, beaches, the trotting track, and the University of East Asia. The bus tour costs HK$15 each for four or more.

The most comfortable way to tour is by chauffeur-driven car. For a maximum of four passengers it costs HK$100 an hour. Taxis can also be rented for touring. Depending on your bargaining powers, the cost will be HK$80 or more an hour *(see* Getting Around).

Most people book tours with Macau agents while in Hong Kong or through travel agents before leaving home. If you do it this way, you will have transport from Hong Kong to Macau arranged for you and your guide waiting in the arrival hall. There are many licensed tour operators in Macau. Among those specializing in English-speaking visitors, and who have offices in Hong Kong, are

Able Tours (Hoi Kwong Building, Travessa do Pe. Narciso, Macau, tel. 897–98; in Hong Kong, 8 Connaught Rd. West, 5/459–993); **Estoril Tours** (Lisboa Hotel, Macau, tel. 736–14; in Hong Kong, Macau Wharf, tel. 5/591–028); **International Tourism** (9 Travessa do Pe. Narciso, Macau, tel. 865–22; in Hong Kong, 143 Connaught Rd., tel. 5/412–011); **Macau Tours** (9 Ave. da Amizade, Macau, tel. 855–55; in Hong Kong, 287 Des Voeux Rd., tel. 5/422–338); and **Sintra Tours** (Sintra Hotel, Macau, tel. 863–94; in Hong Kong, Macau Wharf, tel. 5/408–028).

Exploring Macau

Like any territory with a long, eventful past, Macau is packed with points of interest that overlap and overlay each other. For those who would rather explore than sightsee, we have divided Macau into the following areas, which can be seen separately or back to back.

The Outer Harbor

Numbers in the margin correspond with points of interest on the Macau map.

The history of Portuguese Macau almost came to an end at this spot in 1622, when the Dutch fleet landed a large invasion force to capture the rich port. From here the troops attacked Guia and Monte forts, only to be defeated by a ragtag army of Jesuit priests, Portuguese soldiers, and African slaves.

❶ Today the **Outer Harbour** is designed to welcome all arrivals. On the mile-long (1.6 km) avenue from the wharf are the Mandarin, Oriental, Presidente, and Lisboa hotels, the **Jai Alai**
❷ **Stadium** and its casino, the new **Macau Forum** for conferences
❸ and sports events, and the grandstand for the annual motor and motorcycle Grand Prix events.

❹ Overlooking the harbor are the slopes of **Guia Hill,** embossed with new homes, a convent, and a hospital, and topped with a fort and the oldest lighthouse on the China coast, still a beacon for ships. The seascape presents a changing panorama, with fishing junks bobbing through the quiet, ocher water, ferries chugging to Canton, and the arcs of white wake as foilborne vessels and hovercraft land and take off like giant waterfowl.

Another kind of aircraft used to appear in the outer harbor: the flying clippers of Pan American Airways, which gave Macau a brief, and accidental, place in aviation history. On April 28, 1937, the Hong Kong Clipper left Manila on a flight that would inaugurate air service between the West Coast of the United States and China. The plane was supposed to land in Hong Kong, but at the last minute the British authorities held back landing permission, in order to gain rights for their own Imperial Airways. The seaplane landed in Macau and was greeted by most of the population before flying on to Hong Kong. The service continued intermittently until the outbreak of war; the Pan Am terminal stood on the site now occupied by the Mandarin Oriental Hotel.

Downtown

In theory, Macau is small enough to allow a visitor to cover all of the main attractions in a day, and with unswerving determination you could do it. However, it's almost impossible to resist the casual pace of Macau, where meals are enjoyed at leisure and traffic slows to pedicab or pedestrian speed in many parts of town. For a relatively straightforward introduction to the many-layered and often contradictory character of the city, you
❺ can stroll the mile (1.6 km) or so of the main street, **Avenida Almeida Ribeiro,** generally known by its Chinese name, **Sanmalo.** It begins a short walk from the Lisboa and ends at the floating casino in the inner harbor.

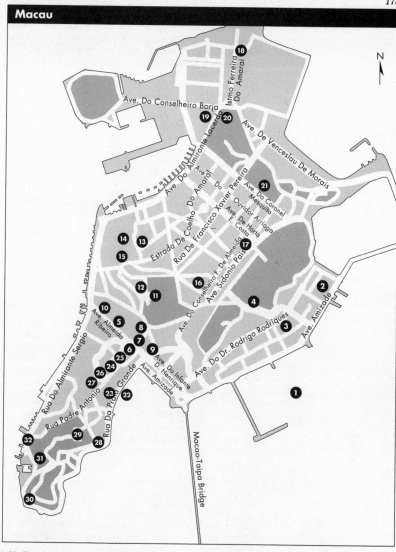

A-Ma Temple, **31**
Avenida Almeida
Ribeiro, **5**
Bela Vista Hotel, **28**
Bishop's Palace, **29**
Camoes Grotto and
Garden, **14**
Camoes Museum, **13**
Canidrome, **19**

Dom Pedro, **24**
Guia Hill, **4**
Jai Alai Stadium, **2**
Kun Iam Temple, **21**
Leal Senado, **6**
Lin Fung Miu, **20**
Lou Lim Ieoc
Garden, **16**
Macau Forum, **3**
Maritime Museum, **32**
Memorial Home of
Dr. Sun Yat-Sen, **17**

Monte Hill, **11**
Old Protestant
Cemetery, **15**
Outer Harbour, **1**
Palacio, **23**
Portas do Cerco, **18**
Post Office, **9**
Pousada de São
Tiago, **30**

Praia Grande, **22**
Rua Cinco
do Outubro, **10**
St. Augustine, **25**
St. Lawrence, **27**
St. Paul's, **12**
Santa Casa
da Misericordia, **7**
São Domingos
Church, **8**
Seminary of
St. Joseph's, **26**

Within this short distance you find colonial Portugal, traditional China, and modern Asia locked in architectural and social
embrace. Logically, it is an unworkable misalliance; in Macau
it's an enduring marriage of convenience. One reason is that
buildings, institutions, and even lifestyles have survived because enough people wanted them to, not because their
preservation was officially decreed. Sanmalo might look and
sound casually chaotic, but it works.

Like a European city, the focal point of this downtown is a large
square with a fountain and plaza surrounded by several impressive buildings. The **Leal Senado** (Loyal Senate) has a classically
simple facade, garden courtyard, and Edwardian council chambers. The Senate acts as a municipal government, taking care
of parks, garbage collection, the police force, and traffic regulations.

The library in the Leal Senado, a superb copy of a classic Portuguese library, contains possibly the best collection of books in
English about China's history, society, economy, and culture.
Much was inherited from the British- and American-managed
Chinese Customs House. In addition, the library has some rare
books from the early days of the Portuguese empire and bound
copies of old Macau newspapers. Scholars and others are welcome to browse or study. *Open Mon.–Sat. 1–7.*

The Senate president is by tradition the president of the **Santa
Casa da Misericordia** (Holy House of Mercy), the oldest Christian charity on the China Coast. Its headquarters occupy a
handsome baroque building in the square, and its offices ad-
minister homes for the elderly, kitchens for the poor, clinics,
and a leprosarium. Behind the Santa Casa is the beautiful **São
Domingos** church, with a magnificent altar.

The central **Post Office** and telephone exchange, as well as some
handsome old commercial buildings with arcades at street level, are also in the square. The São Domingos produce market,
its narrow streets packed with stalls selling fruit, vegetables,
and wholesale-price clothing from local factories, leads off the
square.

Sanmalo has some regular clothing stores, but the majority of
shoppers come here for gold jewelry, watches and clocks, Chinese and Western medicines, brandy, biscuits, and salted fish.
Interspersed are banks, lawyers' offices, and the Central Hotel. Now a rather dingy, inexpensive place to stay, the Central
used to contain the city's only casinos, where the *fan tan* (button game) attracted the high rollers and the top-floor brothel
did a thriving business.

The heart of the old red-light district was Rua da Felicidade
("Street of Happiness"), which runs off Sanmalo. Few brothels
have survived competition from sauna and massage parlors,
but you can still see the large picture-windows (some now
boarded up) where the women once displayed themselves. The
area does preserve the atmosphere of a prewar China-coast
community, especially in the evening. After sunset, food stalls
with stools and tiny tables are set out. Lights blaze from open-
front restaurants, laundries, tailor shops, and family living
rooms. The pungent smell of cooking pervades the streets, and
it seems as if most of Macau's 450,000 people have fled their tiny
apartments to eat out, relax, and socialize.

Another side street off Sanmalo worth a detour is **Rua Cinco do**

Outubro, which contains one of the best-looking traditional Chinese medicine shops anywhere. The Farmacia Tai Ning Tong has an elaborately carved wood facade and a cavernous interior, its walls lined with huge apothecary jars of medicinal roots, deer horn, and other assorted marvels. In a corner are mortars and pestles for making potions to order.

On the opposite side of the street is the Lok Kok teahouse. It looks undistinguished from the outside, but climb up to the third floor and discover an incredible room with pyramid-vaulted wood ceilings, skylights, brightly carved pillars, stained-glass windows, and walls hung with scrolls and mirrors. It is open from 4 AM to mid-afternoon and caters to a wide cross-section of the population, from wharf workers to bankers, market porters to students.

The Old Citadel

11 The most remarkable early buildings in Macau were on **Monte Hill.** Built by the Jesuits, they included a fort, a college, and the collegiate church of the Mother of God, commonly known as **12** **St. Paul's.** By the early 17th century, the college had become a university for scholar-missionaries en route to the courts of China and Japan. The church was declared the most magnificent in Asia, and a small town of merchants, clerics, and craftsmen grew up around the Monte.

Today this area is the heart of old Macau for visitors and is easily reached from Senate Square via Rua da S. Domingos. The college was destroyed in a disastrous fire in 1835, and the ruins of the fort are now a quiet belvedere. Of the church, only the great stone facade remains, but it is less a ruin than a dramatic symbol of Macau and certainly the leading attraction.

Traditional craftsmen, still in business carving camphorwood chests and family shrines, hand-beating metal utensils, making barrels and mattresses, and weaving bird cages, still occupy the jumble of narrow streets below the church. Tercena and Estalagens are the most interesting streets.

13 Following either Rua de S. Paulo or Tercena, you reach Praça Luis de Camões and the **Camões Museum.** Named for Portugal's greatest poet, the museum's finest exhibit is the building itself. Built in the 1770s, it is a superb example of Iberian colonial architecture, with spacious, high-ceilinged rooms and tall windows shaded by louvered shutters. In the late 18th and early 19th centuries it was rented by the British East India Company as a residence for the men who controlled much of the China trade of their time. Two of the museum's rooms recall this era, with four-poster beds, period furniture, and Chinese bric-a-brac. Other rooms display ancient Chinese pottery, Buddhist statues, and some fine Exportware made in Canton for the Macau government. The museum also has an art gallery with a permanent collection of paintings, drawings, and lithographs by Borget, Chinnery, and their contemporaries. *Admission: 1 pataca. Open 10–5; closed Wed.* (At the time of writing, plans were being made to totally renovate the museum, so it's best to check whether it is open.)

14 Next to the museum is the **Camões Grotto and Garden,** today Macau's most popular public park, frequented from dawn to dusk by people practicing t'ai chi ch'uan (shadowboxing), men carrying their caged songbirds for a country walk, young lovers, students, and groups huddled over games of Chinese chess.

The garden was originally the private grounds of the old house, and in 1785 was used by French cartographer La Perouse for a small observatory aimed at China. The garden was taken over by the city in 1886, when a heroic bronze bust of Camoes was installed in a rocky alcove. Nearby a wall of stone slabs is inscribed with poems praising Camoes and Macau by various contemporary writers. *Open dawn–dusk.*

⑮ The **Old Protestant Cemetery,** a "corner of some foreign field" for over 150 Americans and British, is opposite the entrance to the garden. It is a well-kept and tranquil retreat, where tombstones recall the troubles and triumphs of Westerners in 19th-century China. Some of the names are familiar: George Chinnery; Captain Henry Churchill, great granduncle of Sir Winston; Joseph Adams, grandson of John Adams, the second U.S. president; Robert Morrison, who translated the Bible into Chinese; Thomas Beale, the opium king; and traders James B. Endicott and Samuel Proctor. In addition, there are graves of sailors who were victims of battle, accident, or disease.

Restoration Row

One of the most incredible, and illogical, aspects of Macau is the physical survival of so much of its past. Given the city's shortage of land, revenue, and investment possibilities, it would have made economic sense to follow Hong Kong's lead and replace old buildings and gardens with high-rise office and apartment blocks. It's true that this has frequently happened, the most glaring example being the Praia Grande, but history is more than holding its own. One reason is the Macanese power of positive procrastination, which infuriates businessmen today as it doubtless did the would-be developers of the past. It's not that the government and public enterprises are not enthusiastic about development projects, it's that they rarely get past the discussion stages.

Happily for Macau's heritage, when it comes to maintaining public buildings procrastination is overcome by family pride, and every year or two buildings are given a new coat of white or pastel wash and generally spruced up. In some cases, such as the governor's residence and the government palace, the interiors have been redecorated and air-conditioned. Following suit, all of the churches and Chinese temples have also been restored to their old splendor.

Conservation and common sense don't always go together, but there is an outstanding example of such a match in Macau's Restoration Row. Actually it is a row of houses built in the 1920s in symmetrical arcadian style, on the **Avenida do Conselheiro Ferreira de Almeida,** a block or so from the Royal and Estoril hotels. The owners of the houses were persuaded to forego huge profits and sell to the government. The houses were then converted into homes for the Archives, the National Library, the Education Department, and university offices. The exteriors were extensively repaired and the interiors transformed. In the case of the library, the building had to be completely gutted to accommodate the stacks and rooms for the vast collection of old books. The Archives building has space for researchers and a small auditorium.

(16) Continuing along the avenue, you come to Estrada de Adolfo Loureiro and the **Lou Lim Ieoc Garden,** a classic Chinese garden modeled on those of old Soochow. It was built in the 19th century by a wealthy Chinese merchant named Lou. With the decline of the Lou family fortunes early this century, the house was sold and became a school. The garden fell into ruin until it was taken over by the city in 1974 and totally restored. Enclosed by a wall, it is a miniaturized landscape with miniforests of bamboo and flowering bushes, a mountain of sculpted concrete, and a small lake filled with lotus and golden carp. A traditional nine-turn bridge zigzags (to deter evil spirits, which can move only in straight lines) across the lake to a colonial-style pavilion with a wide veranda. This is used occasionally for exhibitions and other events. *Admission: 50 avos. Open dawn–dusk.*

(17) Another place of interest in this area is the **Memorial Home of Dr. Sun Yat-Sen.** Dr. Sun, father of the 1911 Chinese revolution, worked as a physician in Macau from 1892 to 1894, and some of his family stayed here after his death. The memorial home, in strange mock-Moorish style, was built in the mid-1930s. It contains some interesting photographs, books, and souvenirs of Sun and his long years of exile in different parts of the world. *1 Rua Ferreira do Amaral. Admission free. Open 10–1 weekdays, 3–5 weekends. Closed Tues.*

On the Doorstep of China

(18) The date of Mesquita's victory and a solemn quotation from Camões are inscribed on the stone gate—**Portas do Cerco**—that leads to China. Today the gate is closed at night, but throughout the day it is used by a steady stream of two-way traffic. From China come farmers carrying morning-fresh produce in bamboo baskets or on trucks, along with Chinese officials involved in joint business ventures and Macau and Hong Kong residents returning from visits with their families. From Macau the traffic consists of bus loads of tourists and groups of businesspeople.

(19) (20) Close by the border are two very different attractions. On one side is the **Canidrome,** where greyhound races are enthusiastically followed. On the other side of the road is the **Lin Fung Miu,** or Temple of the Lotus. In the old days this used to provide overnight accommodations for mandarins traveling between Macau and Canton. Today it is visited for its exquisite facade of clay bas-reliefs and classic architecture.

(21) **Kun Iam Temple,** nearby on the Avenida do Coronel Mesquita, should not be missed. A Buddhist temple, it has a wealth of statuary and decoration and a courtyard with a stone table where the first Sino-American treaty was signed in 1844 by the Viceroy of Canton and President John Tyler's envoy, Caleb Cushing.

Peninsula Macau

The narrow, hilly peninsula stretching from the main street to Barra Point and the Pousada de Sao Tiago is quintessential

(22) Macau, very Portuguese and very Chinese, ancient and uncomfortably modern. It is bounded on one side by the **Praia Grande** and its extension, Avenida da Republica, a graceful, banyan-shaded boulevard where people fish from the sea wall or play Chinese chess. Unfortunately, parts of the promenade have been taken over by parked cars, but there are also plenty of benches and the traffic is well diluted by pedicabs.

The cargo and fishing wharfs of the inner harbor, with their traditional Chinese shop houses—the ground floors occupied by ship's chandlers, net makers, ironmongers, and shops selling spices and salted fish—are on the opposite side of the peninsula.

In between there are several areas of historic or scenic interest. One is Largo de Sto. Agostinho, or St. Augustine Square, which is reached by climbing the steep street next to the Sen-
(23) ate, or from the Praia Grande and the pink-and-white **Palacio,** which houses government offices.

Taking the Travessa do Paiva to the right of the Palacio, you pass the trimly restored headquarters of the Department of Tourism. Beyond is the dimple-stone ramp to the square, which looks as if it came all of a piece from 19th-century Portugal. To
(24) the left is the **Dom Pedro V** theater, modeled after a European
(25) court theater. Opposite is the imposing church of **St. Augustine,** and next door is Casa Ricci, offices for one of the most active
(26) Catholic charities in Macau. Across the square is the **Seminary of St. Joseph's,** home of preeminent local historian and living legend Father Manuel Teixeira and a collection of religious art by 17th-century European and Japanese painters. Completing the scene is the memorial home of Sir Robert Hotung, the Hong Kong millionaire, who gave his house to the city in thanks for giving him refuge during the Pacific War. It is now headquarters for the new Cultural Institute.

Retracing your steps down the ramp and continuing along the Rua de São Lourenco, you reach the elegant twin-tower church
(27) of **St. Lawrence** and the Salesian Institute, a technical school that stands on part of the site of the headquarters of the British East India Company. From here you can take the Rua do Pe.
(28) Antonio to the **Bela Vista Hotel** or return to the Praia Grande and follow it to the Calcada do Bom Parto. Either way, you'll want to stop and visit the Bela Vista, a century-old landmark hotel.

Farther up the hill is one of the best lookouts in Macau, the
(29) courtyard of the **Bishop's Palace** and Penha Chapel. The Palace is always closed and the Chapel is opened only on the feast day of Our Lady of Penha, patroness of seafarers, and on the Feast of Fatima.

(30) At the far end of the peninsula is Barra Point with the **Pousada de São Tiago,** a Portuguese inn built into the ruined foundations
(31) of a 17th-century fort (*see* Lodgings), the **A-Ma Temple,** Macau's oldest and most venerated place of worship, and the
(32) new **Maritime Museum.** This gem of a museum has been a consistent favorite since its doors opened at the end of 1987. It is ideally located, where the first Chinese and later first Portuguese made landfall, and it is housed in an imaginatively restored colonial house facing the harbor. The old number one wharf was restored to provide a pier for a fishing junk, tug,

dragon boat, sampan, Vietnamese refugees' boat, and a copy of one of the "flower boat" floating pleasure palaces that once sailed along the China coast. Inside the museum are displays of the local fishing industry, models of historic vessels, charts of great voyages by Portuguese and Chinese explorers, navigational aids such as an original paraffin lamp once used in the Guia lighthouse, and much, much more. *Admission free. Open 10–6. Closed Tues.*

Taipa Island

Numbers in the margin correspond with points of interest on the Taipa and Coloane Islands map.

Linked to the city by the graceful 1.6-mile (2.5-km) bridge, Taipa can be reached by bus (including a double-decker with open-top roof deck) or taxi. Some residents jog over it daily. Up until the end of the 19th century, Taipa was two islands and provided a sheltered anchorage where clipper ships and East India-men could load and unload cargoes, which were then carried by junks and barges to and from Canton. Gradually the islands were joined by river silt and land reclamation, but Taipa, with its mansion—which now houses a museum—offers a reminder of the old days.

Taipa and Coloane, its neighbor, are Macau's New Territories, having been ceded by China only in 1887. Until the building of the bridge, both islands led a somnolent existence, interrupted only by occasional pirate raids. Taipa's economy depended on the raising of ducks and the manufacture of firecrackers. There are still some duck farms to be seen, as well as some firecracker factories, which look like ancestral Chinese villages but now produce fireworks for the American and European markets.

1 The **village of Taipa** is a tight maze of houses and shops in the traditional mold. It is changing, due to the island's new prosperity, and now boasts banks, a two-story municipal market, air-conditioned shops, and several excellent restaurants. Be-
2 low the church of Our Lady of Carmel is the **Taipa House Museum.** This finely restored 1920s mansion contains authentic period furniture, decorations, and furnishings that recapture the atmosphere and lifestyle of a middle-class Macanese family in the early part of the century. *Taipa Praia. Admission free. Open 9–5. Closed Mon.*

3 Another restored building worth a visit is the **Pou Tai Un Temple,** a short walk from the Hyatt Regency. It is famed for its vegetarian restaurant (the vegetables are grown in an adjoining garden), and has been embellished with a new yellow tile pavilion and statue of the Buddhist goddess of mercy.

For Buddhists, Taoists, and Confucians, Taipa is a favored, last, earthly address. They are buried or their bones stored in
4 the massive **United Chinese Cemetery,** which covers the cliff on the northeastern coast of the island. It is lavishly decorated with colored tiles and assorted religious images.

The northeast section of Taipa provides a stunning contrast, thanks to a recent building boom. Just across the bridge is the
5 luxurious Hyatt Hotel and the hilltop **University of East Asia.** Directly facing the bridge is a monument sculpted with images from Macau's history. On the western side of the island is the

Chapel of St. Francis
Xavier, **9**

Coloane Park, **10**

Hac Sa, **8**

Macau Horse
Racing Club, **6**

Pou Tai Un Temple, **3**

Pousada de Coloane, **7**

Taipa House Museum, **2**

United Chinese
Cemetery, **4**

University of East
Asia, **5**

Village of Taipa, **1**

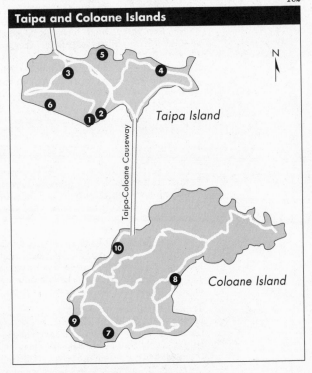

Taipa and Coloane Islands

⑥ raceway of the **Macau Horse Racing Club,** 50 acres of reclaimed land with an ultramodern, five-story grandstand, and track that is scheduled to open in mid-1989.

Coloane Island

Situated at the end of a 1.5-mile (2.4-km) causeway from Taipa, the larger, hillier island of Coloane has so far been spared from development. About a 25-minute drive from the city, it is generally considered to be remote. This makes it a popular spot for ⑦ relaxed holidays, especially at the attractive 22-room **Pousada de Coloane.** There is a long beach below the pousada and anoth- ⑧ er at **Hac Sa** (Black Sands). Both are clean, although the water is Pearl River ocher. There are plenty of cafes for food and drink.

The village of Coloane, with its old tile-roof houses, the Tam ⑨ Kong Temple, and the **Chapel of St. Francis Xavier,** are interesting to overseas visitors. The picturesque chapel, with its cream-and-white facade and bell tower, was built in 1928. Outside its door is a monument surrounded by cannon balls commemorating the local defeat of a pirate band in 1910, Macau's last encounter with old-style pirates. There are some important relics inside the chapel. The most sacred is an arm bone of St. Francis Xavier, who died in 1552 on an island 50 miles (80 km) from here while waiting to begin his mission in China. The bone, now in an ornate silver reliquary, was destined for his church in Japan, but by then the Japanese had closed their doors on the Christian church.

Other relics are the bones of the martyrs of Nagasaki and those of Vietnamese Christians executed in the early 17th century. By a strange irony, although it is not so strange for Macau, Coloane has a sizable Vietnamese community of boat people who fled their country and now await resettlement in a large, open camp administered by the Catholic church.

⑩ Coloane Park, on the west coast of the island, is the newest of Macau's natural preserves. Its centerpiece is a walk-in aviary containing more than 200 species of birds, including the rare Palawan peacock and the crested white pheasant. Nearby is a pond with black swans, a playground, a European restaurant, a picnic area, and a nature trail around the hillside. Developed by the Forestry Department, the park has an impressive collection of exotic trees and shrubs. *Admission: 5 patacas for park, 5 patacas for aviary. Open 9–7.*

Historic Sites

With more than four centuries of history-making, it's not surprising that Macau has a wealth of historic buildings. What is remarkable is how well they have survived the assault of time, climate, and schemes for modernization. One reason is that they have all been in constant and practical use. They are also valued as part of a proud heritage and so are regularly restored and redecorated, even as they are obscured by graceless skyscrapers and gimcrack architecture.

St. Paul's (São Paulo) has long been a popular symbol of Macau. The richly carved baroque facade is all that remains of what was called "the greatest church in Asia." Built between 1602 and 1627 by exiled Japanese Christians and local craftsmen under the direction of Jesuits, St. Paul's was the collegiate church for the Jesuit college, which was the first Western-style university in Asia. Such scholars as Matteo Ricci and Adam Van Schall studied here before going to the court in Peking. The church fell into disuse when the Jesuits were expelled in 1762. Later, the army was billeted in the college, and in 1835 a fire destroyed everything except the facade.

Monte Fort, on the hill overlooking St. Paul's, was also built by the Jesuits and completed in 1623. In 1622, the year before it was completed, the fort was the scene of Macau's most famous battle. The Dutch, jealous of Portugal's power in Asia, invaded the territory, which was protected by a small force of soldiers, African slaves, and priests. As the Dutch closed in on Monte, a lucky cannon shot, fired by one of the priests, hit the enemy's powder supply and in the ensuing confusion the Dutch were driven back to sea. In 1626, the first full-time governor of Macau evicted the Jesuits from the fort. For the next century-and-a-half it was the residence and office of Macau's governors. The fort's buildings were destroyed in the 1835 fire, but the great walls remain, along with their cannon. Today the meteorological office maintains a station here, and the fort is a popular belvedere for residents and tourists. Its gates are open from 7 AM to dusk.

The Loyal Senate (Leal Senado) stands in the heart of the city, on the main street facing a European-style square. It is a superb example of colonial architecture, with a simple, elegant facade dating from 1876. The main building was constructed in the late 18th century to house the senate of leading citizens who were at the time far more powerful than the governors, who served their short terms and then returned to Portugal. Today the senate, with some elected and some appointed members, acts as the municipal government, with its president holding the same power as a mayor. Inside the building, a beautiful stone staircase leads to a wrought-iron gate and a charming garden. The upper floor contains the senate chambers and the original national library, modeled on that of Mafra in Portugal. The foyer and garden are open during working hours, and there are art and history exhibitions in the foyer and adjoining galleries.

Holy House of Mercy (Santa Casa da Misericordia) stands in the square opposite the senate. Behind the imposing white facade are the headquarters of the first Western charity in Asia. Founded in 1569, it established orphanages, clinics, homes for the aged, free food supplies for the poor, and a leprosarium. On the second floor (open during office hours) is a reception room with paintings of benefactress Marta Merop and Macau's first bishop, Dom Belchior, as well as the latter's cross and skull.

St. Dominic's (São Domingos), Largo de São Domingos, adjoining senate square, is possibly the most beautiful church in Macau, with a magnificent cream-and-white baroque altar of graceful columns, fine statues, and a forest of candles and flower vases. Built in the 17th century by the Dominicans, it has a stormy history. In 1644 a Portuguese officer involved in civil strife was murdered by a mob at the altar during mass. In 1707 the church was besieged by the governor's troops when the Dominicans sided with the Pope against the Jesuits over a controversy as to whether or not ancestor worship should be permitted among Chinese Christian converts. After three days, the soldiers broke down the doors and briefly imprisoned the priests. Today those doors are open only during services; at other times, visitors should ring the bell on the green gate next to the entrance.

Guia Fort and Lighthouse, built in the 1630s, is on the highest point in Macau. Several roads lead up to the fort. The gate is open from 7 AM to dusk, and the views from the fort's platform are truly panoramic. Within the fort is the lighthouse, erected in 1865 and the oldest on the China coast, and a small, simple, white-stone chapel, built in 1707 and dedicated to Our Lady of Guia. The fort is used by the Marine Police. When there are typhoons in the area, typhoon signals in the form of specially shaped black bamboo baskets are hoisted on a yardarm on the platform. Permission is needed to enter the lighthouse and chapel (not easy, but you can ask the Department of Tourism to try).

The Border Gate (Portas do Cerco) marks the traditional boundary of Macau. Beyond is the Chinese border town of Gongbei. The present gate was built in 1870 and bears the arms of Portugal's navy and artillery, along with a quotation from Camões, which reads, in translation: "Honor your country for it looks after you." On either side of the gate is written the date 1849. This commemorates the year when the governor, Ferreira do Amaral (whose statue stands outside the Lisboa Hotel), was assassinated by the Chinese. The local warlord planned to invade Macau but a Macanese colonel, Nicolau Mesquita, with 37 men, slipped across the border and captured the Chinese fort. Today there is a steady flow of vegetable farmers, businessmen, and tourists at the gate. *Open daily 7–9.*

Temple of the Lotus (Lin Fung Miu), Ave. do Almirante Lacerda, is close to the border gate. This superb temple, dedicated to both Buddhist and Taoist deities, was built in 1592 and used for overnight accommodations by mandarins traveling between Macau and Canton. It is famous for its facade of intricate clay bas-reliefs depicting mythological and historical scenes and an interior frieze of colorful writhing dragons. *Open dawn–dusk.*

Kun Iam Temple (Kun Iam Tong), Avenida do Coronel Mesquita, is in the north of the city. This Buddhist temple, dedicated to Kun Iam (also known as Kwan Yin), the goddess of mercy, was founded in the 13th century. The present buildings are richly endowed with carvings, porcelain figurines, statues, old scrolls, antique furniture, and ritual objects. The temple is best known among Western visitors for the stone table in the courtyard, where, on July 3, 1844, the first Sino-American treaty was signed by the Viceroy of Canton and the United States envoy, Caleb Cushing. The temple has a large number of funeral chapels, where you can see the offerings of paper cars, airplanes, luggage, and money, which are burned to accompany the souls of the dead. *Open dawn–dusk.*

Dom Pedro V Theater, Largo de Sto. Agostinho, is on the hill above the Praia Grande and behind the Loyal Senate. The oldest Western theater on the China coast, it was built in 1859 in the style of a European court theater. Until World War II, it was in regular use with local performers and international artists. In recent years it has been extensively restored and equipped with sophisticated stage lighting. It is now used for concerts and other entertainment, such as plays in Macanese. Although not officially open to visitors during the day, one of the doors is usually open and no one objects to people looking around at the marvelously Victorian foyer and auditorium. The facade is also very fine.

St. Augustine's (Sto. Agostinho) is in the Largo de Sto. Agostinho, opposite the theater. This superb baroque building dates from 1814, when it replaced the burned-out 17th-century original. In the marble-clad high altar is the large statue of Our Lord of Passos, which is carried through the streets on the first day of Lent. Among the tombs in the church is that of Maria de Moura, a romantic heroine who in 1710 married the man she loved, even though he had lost an arm when attacked by another of her suitors. She died in childbirth and is buried with her baby and her husband's arm. The church is open daily.

St. Joseph's (São Jose), also in Largo de Sto. Agostinho, was once an important seminary with a superb church. Today it is in great need of repair and houses only Father Manuel Teixeira, Macau's resident historian, and some brilliantly restored 16th-century paintings. It is closed to the public.

Government Palace, Praia Grande, a distinctive pink-and-white mansion that contains the offices of the governor and his ministers, was built in 1849 by Macau's greatest architect Tomas de Aquino. Unfortunately, the public is not permitted inside to see the regal banquet hall and dining room. The exterior is very impressive.

Government House (Palacio de Santa Sancha) was also built by Aquino, and it shows the same mastery of elegant, simple lines. Surrounded by attractive gardens, it is the residence of the governor, and it is closed to the public. But the house can be easily seen from the road or the Bela Vista Hotel.

Penha Hill, above the Bela Vista on the highest point of the narrow peninsula, is the dominant landmark for arrivals by sea. At one time it was crowned with a church, where seafarers would worship before setting out. The present building is the bishop's residence and includes a small chapel built in 1935 (but which is usually closed to the public).

Temple of A-Ma (A-Ma Miu) is at the far end of the peninsula. Dating from the early 16th century, this is the most picturesque temple in Macau, with ornate prayer halls and pavilions built among the giant boulders of the waterfront hillside. The rocks are inscribed with red calligraphy telling the story of A-Ma (also known as Tin Hau), the favorite goddess of fishermen, who allegedly saved a humble junk from a storm. One of the many Chinese names for the area was Bay of A-Ma, or A-Ma Gau, and when the Portuguese arrived they adopted it as Macau. The temple is open dawn to dusk.

Shopping

At first glance, Macau is a poor country cousin to Hong Kong when it comes to shopping. Most stores are small and open to the street, the clerks might be eating snacks at the counter, and the merchandise is likely to be haphazardly arranged. There is also very little for sale here that isn't available in far greater abundance and variety in Hong Kong.

So why shop in Macau? First, the shopping areas are much more compact. Second, sales staff are in general much more pleasant and relaxed (although their command of English might not be as good as in Hong Kong). And, most important, many goods are cheaper. Like Hong Kong, Macau is a duty-free port for almost all items. But, unlike the British territory, commercial rents are reasonable and wages low, keeping overheads to a minimum.

Macau's shops are open every day of the year, except for a short holiday after Chinese New Year for family-run businesses. Opening hours vary according to the type of shop, but usually extend into mid-evening. Major credit cards are generally accepted, but not for the best discounts. Friendly bargaining is expected, and is done by asking for the "best price," which produces discounts of 10% or more. Larger discounts on expensive items should be treated with suspicion. Macau has its share of phony antiques, fake name-brand watches, and other rip-offs. Be sure to shop around, check the guarantee on name brands (sometimes fakes come with misspellings), and be sure to get receipts for expensive items.

The major shopping districts of Macau are the main street, Avenida Almeida Ribeiro, commonly known by its Chinese name Sanmalo; Mercadores and its side streets, Cinco de Outubro, and Rua do Campo. One of the pleasures of shopping here is the shop names that reflect Macau's dual heritage, for example, *Pastelarias Mei Mun* (pastry shops), *Relojoaria Tat On* (watches and clocks), *Sapatarias Joao Leong* (shoes).

Antiques

The days of discovering treasures from the Ming among the Ching Chinoiserie in Macau's antiques shops are long gone, but there are still plenty of old and interesting pieces available. Collectors of old porcelain can find some well-preserved bowls and other simple Ming ware once used as ballast in trading ships. Prices for such genuine items run into the hundreds or thousands of dollars. Far cheaper are the ornate vases, stools, and dishware from the late Ching period—China's Victorian era, which are in vogue. This style of pottery is still very popular among the Chinese and a lot of so-called Ching is faithfully reproduced today in China, Hong Kong, and Macau. Many of these copies are excellent and hard to distinguish from their antique cousins.

Over the years, dealers and collectors have made profitable trips to Macau, so it's interesting to ask where new supplies of antiques are coming from. The standard answer used to be "from an old Macau family" that was emigrating or had fallen on hard times. Today there is another explanation: They are brought out of China by legal and illegal immigrants in lieu of capital or foreign currency. Most of these smuggled items are small but some are rare and precious. Among them are such things as 2,000-year-old bronze money in the shape of knives, later types of coins with holes in the middle, jade *pi* (discs), ivory figurines, and old jewelry. In addition, you can still sometimes find Exportware porcelain, made for the European market in 19th-century China, and old bonds from the early 20th century.

Antiques shops that have earned excellent reputations over the years include the two stores of **Veng Meng** (114 Ave. Almeida Ribeiro and 8 Travessa do Pagode), **Wing Tai** (1A Almeida Ribeiro), and **The Antique House** (opposite Kun Iam Temple at 11 Ave. Coronel Mesquita). *All are open 9–6.*

Clothing

There are many shops in Macau that sell casual and sports clothes for men and women at bargain prices. Most are made in Macau or Hong Kong and carry big-name labels. In some cases these are fakes, but more often they are genuine overruns or rejects from local factories that manufacture, under license, garments for Yves Saint Laurent, Cacharel, Van Heusen, Adidas, Gloria Vanderbilt, and many others. Name-brand jeans cost about HK$150 and shirts HK$120. There are also padded jackets, sweaters, jogging suits, windbreakers, and a very wide range of clothes for children and infants at very low prices. The best shopping areas are on Rua do Campo or around Mercadores. For the very best bargains you should visit the street markets of São Domingos (off Leal Senado Square) and Cinco de Outubro. Credit cards are accepted at larger shops.

Crafts

Many traditional Chinese crafts are followed in Macau, and the best place to watch the craftsmen at work is along Tercena and Estalagens. These old streets are lined with three-story shop-houses with open-front workshops on the ground floor (living quarters and offices are above). Some shops produce beautifully carved chests and other furniture made of mahogany, camphorwood, and redwood, some inlaid with marble or mother-of-pearl. Other craftsmen make bamboo bird cages, family altars, "lucky" door plaques, and colorful sandals. Macau also makes modern furniture, lacquer screens, modern and traditional Chinese pottery, and ceremonial items such as lion dance costumes, giant incense coils, and temple offerings.

Gold and Jewelry

Macau's jewelry shops are not as lavish as those in downtown Hong Kong, but they offer much better prices. Each store displays the current price of gold per *tael* (1.2 troy ounces), which changes from day to day or even hour to hour according to the Hong Kong Gold Exchange. Some counters contain 14- and 18-carat jewelry, such as chains, earrings, pendants, brooches, rings, and bangles. There are also ornaments set with pearls or precious stones (usually made in Hong Kong), as well as pieces of costume jewelry and fanciful traditional Chinese items. Most important, however, are the counters with 24-carat jewelry and gold in the form of coins and tiny bars, which come with assays from a Swiss bank. Pure gold is very popular with the Chinese as an investment and as a hedge against the vagaries of the stock exchange and currency fluctuations.

Prices for gold items are based on the day's price plus a small percentage profit, so a limited amount of bargaining is possible.

Among the best known are: **Tai Fung** (36 Ave. Almeida Ribeiro), **Chow Sang Sang** (58 Ave. Almeida Ribeiro), **Pou Fong** (91 Ave. Almeida Ribeiro), **Sheong Hei** (Ave. Almeida Ribeiro). *All are open 9–7. The staffs are helpful and English-speaking. AE, DC, MC, V.*

Sports

For most regular visitors to Macau, the sporting life means playing the casinos, but there are plenty of other sports, albeit often with gambling on the side. The Macanese are keen on team sports and give creditable performances at interport soccer and field hockey matches. In addition to traditional annual events such as the Grand Prix, there are also international table tennis championships. Many events are held in the new Macau Forum. Participant sports activities have also increased, with some excellent routes for joggers and sports facilities in hotels.

Dragon Boat Racing

This newest of international sports derives from an ancient Chinese festival in which fishing communities would compete in long, shallow boats with dragon heads and tails, in honor of a poet who drowned himself to protest official corruption. At the time, about 2,000 years ago, his friends took to boats and pounded their oars in the water while beating drums to scare away the fish who would have eaten the poet's body. The festival and races have been revived in recent years in many parts of Asia, with teams from Hong Kong, Nagasaki, Singapore, Thailand, Malaysia, and Macau, plus crews from Australia, the United States, Europe, and China's Guangdong Province. The races are held in the Outer Harbour, where the waterfront provides a natural grandstand for spectators. The Dragon Boat Festival takes place on the fifth day of the fifth moon (usually some time in June) and is attended by a flotilla of fishing junks decorated with silk banners, and fishing families beating drums and setting off firecrackers.

Golf

No, of course it's not possible to play golf in Macau, but the Zhongshan and Zhuhai international-standard clubs are just a short distance across the border (see Side Trips to China).

Greyhound Racing

The dogs are very popular with residents and Hong Kong gamblers. The races are held in the scenic, open-air Canidrome, close to the Chinese border. Most dogs are imported from Australia. The 10,000-seat stadium has rows and rows of betting windows and stalls for food and drink. *Ave. General Castelo Branco. Races, 8 PM, Sat. and Sun., holidays, year-round. Admission: 2 patacas for public stands, 5 patacas for members' stand, 80 patacas for 6-seat box.*

Horse Racing

The raceway, built for Asia's first trotting track, is located on three million square feet of reclaimed land close to the Hyatt Regency Hotel.

The Macau Trotting Club spared no expense in building the facility. The five-story grandstand can accommodate 15,000 people, 6,000 of them in air-conditioned comfort. There are restaurants, bars, and some of the most sophisticated betting equipment available. Unfortunately, trotting races did not bring in sufficient revenue and the track is being converted into a larger venue for flat racing. It is scheduled for completion in mid-1989.

Jai Alai

Played in a custom-built stadium opposite the ferry pier, jai alai has never really caught on in Macau. Local cynics claim that human players can't be trusted the way horses and dogs can. This means that the stadium is poorly attended and the games less than passionately contested. Most of the players are from the Basque region of Spain, others are locally trained. A large electronic board lights up with the odds and results, and bettors have plenty of windows to choose from. *Nightly 7 PM–midnight, Sat. and Sun. 2 PM.*

Motor Racing

The Macau Grand Prix takes place on the third or fourth weekend in November. From the beginning of the week, the city is shattered with supercharged engines testing the 3.8-mile (6-km) Guia Circuit, which follows the city roads along the Outer Harbour to Guia Hill and around the reservoir. The route is as challenging as that of Monaco, with rapid gear changes demanded at the right-angle Statue Corner, the Dona Maria bend, and the Melco hairpin.

The Grand Prix was first staged in 1953 and the standard of performance has now reached world class. Today cars achieve speeds of 140 miles per hour (224 kph) on the straightaways, with the lap record approaching 2 minutes 20 seconds. The premier event is the Formula Three championship, with cars brought in from around the world. There are also races for motorcycles and production cars. Many internationally famous drivers have raced here, including Alan Jones, Ricardo Patrese, and Keke Rosberg.

Hotel bookings during the Grand Prix are made long in advance, and the weekend should be avoided by anyone not interested in motor racing.

Running

The 26-mile (41.6-km) Macau Marathon takes place in November or early December. All are welcome to try the fairly grueling course beginning and ending with the Macau-Taipa bridge and including the roads around both islands.

Stadium Sports

Since the opening of the Macau Forum's multipurpose hall, it has been possible to stage a variety of sporting events here. The world table tennis championships have been held here, as have regional basketball and badminton matches. Visitors interested should check with their hotel front desk staff to find out if something special is on.

Tennis and Squash

Both the Hyatt Regency and Mandarin Oriental hotels have tennis and squash courts for use by guests. At the Hyatt there is also a tennis coach.

Dining

Although East and West have clashed in many respects, when it came to cooking there was instant rapprochement and it happened in Macau. By the time the Portuguese arrived, they had learned a lot about the eating habits of countries throughout their new empire. They adopted many of the ingredients grown and used in the Americas and Africa, and brought them to China. The Portuguese were the first to introduce China to peanuts, green beans, pineapples, lettuce, sweet potatoes, and shrimp paste, as well as a variety of spices from Africa and India. In China, the Portuguese discovered tea, rhubarb, tangerines, ginger, soy sauce, and the Cantonese art of fast frying to seal in the flavor.

Over the centuries a unique Macanese cuisine developed, with dishes adapted from Portugal, Brazil, Mozambique, Goa, Malacca, and, of course, China. Today some ingredients are imported, but most are available, fresh each day, from the bountiful waters south of Macau and the rich farmland just across the China border. A good example of Macanese food is the strangely named Portuguese chicken, which would be an exotic alien in Europe. It consists of chunks of chicken baked with potatoes, coconut, tomato, olive oil, curry, olives, and saffron. Extremely popular family dishes include *minchi* (minced pork and diced potatoes panfried with soy), pork baked with tamarind, and duckling cooked in its own blood, all of which are served with rice.

The favorites of Portuguese cuisine are regular menu items. The beloved *bacalhau* (codfish), is served baked, boiled, grilled, deep fried with potato, or stewed with onion, garlic, and eggs. Portuguese sardines, country soups such as *caldo verde* and *sopa alentejana*, and dishes of rabbit are on the menus of many restaurants. Sharing the bill of fare are colonial favorites: from Brazil come *feijoadas*, stews of beans, pork, spicy sausage, and vegetables; Mozambique was the origin of African chicken, baked or grilled in fiery *piri-piri* peppers. In addition, some kitchens prepare baked quail, curried crab, and the delectable Macau sole that rivals its Dover cousin. And then there are the giant prawns that are served in a spicy sauce— one of Macau's special dining pleasures.

Not surprisingly, Chinese restaurants predominate in Macau. In addition, there are several restaurants offering excellent Japanese, Thai, Korean, Indonesian, and even Burmese meals, not to mention grills and various fast-food outlets. Visitors should take the unique opportunity of dining Macau-style. Food prices here are generally so reasonable that it's well nigh impossible to categorize restaurants by price except at the very top and bottom of the market.

One of the best bargains in Macau is wine, particularly the delicious Portuguese *vinho verde*, a slightly sparkling wine, and some reds and whites, such as the Dao family of wines. Restaurant wine prices range from 25 patacas (compared to 15 in the wine shops) at the inexpensive **Riquexo** to 90 patacas a bottle at the **Mandarin Oriental Grill**. The standard price is 55 patacas a bottle. Except in hotels, beer and spirits—including some powerful Portuguese brandies—are very reasonably priced.

All restaurants are open every day of the year except, for some, a few days' holiday after Chinese New Year. In most cases there is no afternoon closure for cleaning, and both lunches and dinners tend to be leisurely affairs, with no one urged to hurry up and leave. Most people order wine, relax, look at the menu, note what other diners are eating, talk to the waiter, and then make their decision. Dress is informal, and nowhere are jackets and ties required. The Department of Tourism's brochure, "Eating Out in Macau," is very useful.

The most highly recommended restaurants are indicated with a star. ★

At press time there were 7.8 patacas to the U.S. dollar.

Category	Cost*
Expensive	over 150 patacas
Moderate	50–150 patacas
Inexpensive	under 50 patacas

*per person including service and half a bottle of wine

The following credit card abbreviations are used: AE, American Express; CB, Carte Blanche; DC, Diners Club; MC, MasterCard; V, Visa.

Macanese-Portuguese

Expensive **Fortaleza.** The setting of this exquisite restaurant would be reason enough to dine here. Located in the traditional Portuguese inn built into the 17th-century Barra fortress, it offers vistas, between the branches of gnarled trees, onto an idyllic seascape of green islands and sailing junks. The decor and atmosphere recall the days of the Portuguese empire, with crystal lamps, hand-carved mahogany furniture, blue and white tiles, and plush drapes. The food is almost as marvelous, with a good selection of classic Macanese dishes, such as baked codfish, quail, and spicy prawns, and Continental dishes, too. There is a special businessman's lunch each weekday. Service is attentive, and prices expensive only by Macau standards. *Pousada de Sao Tiago, Ave. Republica, tel. 78111. Dress: informal. Reservations recommended for evenings. AE, DC, MC, V.*

Moderate **A Galera.** This is the new A Galera, very different but just as
★ good as the one that used to be in the hotel basement. It is an elegant, handsomely decorated restaurant, with blue-and-white-tile wall panels, black-and-white-tile floors, pearl-gray table linen, Wedgewood dishware, a bar with high-back armchairs, and views of the S. Francisco fortress. The atmosphere and menu indicate high prices, but in fact this is not so. Main courses, such as *bacalhau a bras* and squid stuffed with spiced meat, cost around 40 patacas; rich, homemade soups are 12 patacas and dessert souffles 15 patacas. As for wine, there is *vinho verde* and reds and whites for 48 patacas a bottle. *Lisboa Hotel, 3rd floor of new wing, tel. 577–666 ext. 1103. Dress: informal. Reservations not necessary. AE, DC, MC, V.*

Afonso's. This is one of the most attractively designed restaurants in Macau. It is horseshoe shaped, with Portuguese tiles on the wall, floral cushions on the rattan chairs, spotless table linen, and dishware made to order in Europe. Picture windows frame the gardens outside, and there is space for musicians when the hotel has promotions such as "April in Portugal." The menu is imaginative and the prices incredibly reasonable, with entrees costing about 30 patacas. The menu is a good balance of Macanese favorites, such as spicy prawns, and regional Portuguese dishes, including *açorda* bread, seafood soup, and *frango na pucara*, chicken in a clay pot. There is an excellent wine list and the service is cheerful and efficient. *Hyatt Regency Hotel, Taipa Island, tel. 2/7000. Dress: informal. Reservations recommended. AE, DC, MC, V.*

Fat Siu Lau. Opened in 1903, this is the oldest European restaurant in Macau and one which has maintained the highest standards of food and service. Years ago it looked like the average Chinese cafe, but now each of its three floors is elegantly furnished and decorated. The top two are perfect for romantic candle-lit dinners, while the ground floor seems to have been transported from Portugal. The walls of bare brick are partly covered with white stucco, blue tiles, and green vines. There is also a false half-roof with Cantonese tiles. The menu is tried and true. Regulars automatically order the roast pigeon (42 patacas) Fat Siu Lau made famous. Other favorites are African chicken (34 patacas), sardines (25 patacas), and ox breast with herbs (18 patacas). Wines are 33–38 patacas a bottle. *64 Rua da Felicidade, tel. 573–585. Dress: informal. Reservations not necessary. No credit cards.*

Flamingo. Designed like a European pavilion, with verandas on three sides, this restaurant is ideally located in the gardens of the Taipa Island Resort. There are no flamingos, but there are some very well-fed ducks in the surrounding pond. At night there is music by a Filipino group in the main room, with its Portuguese decor. At all times there is a wonderfully carefree atmosphere, and even if sometimes a dish doesn't work out properly, no one complains. First of all, Flamingo has the greatest bread (a whole fresh cottage loaf) in Asia, and wine for 25 patacas a bottle. The food is reasonable, with Portuguese steak for 32 patacas, bacalhau fried rice for eight patacas, and African chicken for 37 patacas. *Taipa Island Resort, Hyatt Regency Hotel, tel. 2/7000 ext. 1874. Dress: informal. Reservations recommended on sunny days and weekend evenings. AE, DC, MC, V.*

Galo. This new restaurant proves what can be done, with flair and dedication, to transform a traditional Taipa village house into a delight for all the senses. The owners—he was with the Portuguese military, she (his wife) is Macanese—gutted the two-story building. Then they decorated it in bright Iberian colors and added Macanese touches, such as Chinese rattan hats for lamp shades and big porcelain plant pots, plus a fireplace and country-style bar. The food is also country-style. One specialty is from Madeira and consists of chunks of orange-flavored lamb on a suspended skewer; others include *pipis*, rice with chicken in a hot sauce (15 patacas), codfish salad with tomatoes and green olives (25 patacas), and curry crabs. Topping off the pleasure of dining here are scenes of village life viewed through the lattice windows. *47 Rua do Cunha, Taipa Island, tel. 2/7318. Dress: informal. Reservations not necessary. No credit cards.*

Henri's Galley. Situated on the banyan-lined waterfront (with some tables on the sidewalk), this is a favorite with local residents and visitors from Hong Kong. The decor reflects owner Henri Wong's former career as a ship's steward. There is a complete "alphabet" of signal flags strung from the ceiling, pictures of old ships on the walls, and red and green lights to keep passengers on an even keel. The food is consistently good, with probably the biggest and best spicy prawns in town, delicious African and Portuguese chicken (48 patacas), Portuguese soups (13 patacas), and fried rice, complete with hot Portuguese sausage. Wines are 44 patacas a bottle. *4 Avenida da Republica, tel. 762–07. Dress: informal. Reservations recommended especially on weekends. MC, V.*

Pinocchio's. Until the opening of the Hyatt Hotel, the only reason most visitors went to Taipa was to eat at this restaurant. Owned by a former marine policeman (Senhor Pina, which explains the name), it has grown rather gracelessly from the original small, air-conditioned rooms and open courtyard. Now the courtyard is covered with a corrugated tin roof and lighted with harsh fluorescent strips. The simple cafe chairs and tables are rickety and service can be very casual, especially on busy weekends or when the boss is not there. Neither is much English spoken. However, there's no better place for curry crabs, baked quail, and steamed shrimps. Another special is superlative leg of lamb and roast suckling pig, which have to be ordered in advance. *4 Rua do Sol, Taipa Island, tel. 2/7128. Dress: informal. Reservations essential on weekends. Closed first Mon. and Tues. of the month.*

Portugues. The big attraction of this restaurant is its reliability. It is an unpretentious, family-style place, with prints of Macau scenes on the walls and plastic grapes hanging from the ceiling. It is conveniently located, with a fine menu featuring all the regular favorites. The bacalhau a bras (28 patacas) and feijoada (25 patacas) are particularly good. The Portugues also has the best *pregos* in town; these are crusty rolls filled with spiced steak, and cost nine patacas. Wine costs 36 patacas a bottle. The staff is friendly and efficient. *16 Rua do Campo, tel. 75445. Dress: informal. Reservations not needed. MC, V.*

Pousada de Coloane. This is 20 minutes by car from the city, by Macau standards a long, long way to go for a meal, but many residents and Hong Kong regulars consider it well worth the trip. The setting is fine, with a large open terrace outside the restaurant. When the weather is good, an alfresco lunch overlooking the beach and water is marvelous. For indoor dining, the restaurant is reminiscent of many in Lisbon, with dark wood panels, colorful tile floors, and folk art decorations. Service can be rather haphazard, but the food is usually excellent. Among the specialties are feijoadas, grilled sardines, and stuffed squid. Best of all is the Sunday buffet, with a great selection of Macanese dishes for only 65 patacas per person. Regular meals cost less than 100 patacas, including wine. *Praia de Cheoc Van, Coloane Island, tel. 2/8144. Dress: informal. Reservations not necessary. MC, V.*

Solmar. For many, many years the Solmar has been an unofficial club for local Portuguese and Macanese men, who gather here to drink strong coffee and gossip. It has a pleasantly lived-in atmosphere and a good range of dishes. Service can be slow, but the meals are worth waiting for, especially the baked Portuguese chicken and spicy African chicken (each 48 patacas). Wine is 55 patacas a bottle. *11 Praia Grande, opposite the Met-*

ropole Hotel, tel. 574–391. Dress: informal. Reservations not necessary. No credit cards.

Inexpensive **Riquexo.** This self-service cafe was created by and for lovers of authentic Macanese food at family prices. Each day half a dozen dishes (see introduction for examples) are prepared in private kitchens and delivered to the Riquexo (Portuguese for rickshaw and pronounced the same) in large tureens, which are kept heated in the restaurant. Beer and wine (regulars have their own bottles in the big refrigerator) are offered at little more than shop prices, as well as soups, salads, and desserts. The place is bright and basic, with the atmosphere of a family get-together. The staff doesn't speak much English but is very helpful. Prices average 35 patacas a meal, including wine. The best entrees are the first to go. *69 Sidonio Pais, tel. 762–94. Dress: informal. No reservations. No credit cards. Lunch only.*

Asian

Expensive **Ginza.** As befits a member of the Dai-Ichi group, the Royal's Japanese restaurant has an elegant, classic simplicity, with tatami rooms, sushi and tempura counters, and grill-topped tables for teppanyaki. There are a variety of set meals as well as à la carte, and prices are relatively reasonable, about 150 patacas per person for a full meal with beer or sake. *Royal Hotel, tel. 552–22. Dress: informal. Reservations recommended. AE, DC, MC, V.*

Moderate **Chiu Chau.** This is probably the best, and certainly most sumptuous, restaurant in Macau serving the Chiu Chow cuisine of Swatow. Many Hong Kong and Thai Chinese (and therefore many gambling visitors to Macau) are originally from Swatow Province. The food is richer than Cantonese and more spicy, with thick, strong shark's fin soup, chicken in hot *chinjew* sauce, and crabs in chicken sauce. *Lisboa Hotel, tel. 776–66 ext. 83001. Dress: informal. Reservations not necessary except on weekends. AE, DC, MC, V.*

East Garden. Locals say this restaurant offers the best dim sum in town as well as other excellent Cantonese fare. It is attractively decorated in garden style and the staff is eager to please. *11 Rua Dr. P. J. Lobo, behind the Sintra Hotel, tel. 562–328. Dress: informal. Reservations not necessary. AE, DC, MC, V.*

Four Five Six. Lovers of Shanghainese food flock to this restaurant, where the specialties are lacquered duck, braised eel, and chicken boiled in rice wine, plus steamed crabs during the winter. The atmosphere is generally cheerful, noisy, and welcoming. *Lisboa Hotel, mezzanine of new wing, tel. 884–74. Dress: informal. Reservations recommended on weekends. AE, DC, MC, V.*

Long Kei. This is one of the oldest and most popular Cantonese restaurants in Macau. It has a huge menu, plus daily specials of the best dishes (printed only in Chinese, so ask the waiter to translate). Like all good Chinese restaurants in this part of the world, it is noisy and apparently chaotic, with no attempt at glamour or sophistication. The total focus is the food and few will be disappointed here. *7 Largo do Senado, tel. 573–970. Dress: informal. No reservations. No credit cards.*

Royal Canton. This large, attractively decorated Cantonese restaurant is very popular with locals and visiting groups, who use it for family parties and celebrations, as well as for breakfast and morning dim sum. The menu is very extensive and the service friendly and efficient. *Royal Hotel, tel. 552–22. Dress: informal. Reservations not necessary. AE, DC, MC, V.*

Lodging

A decade ago Macau's accommodations were, at best, merely adequate. But in recent years, the situation has changed dramatically with the opening of several hotels that are of high international standards. These can be booked worldwide through offices overseas or in Hong Kong. Macau's hotels depend on occupancy by Hong Kong residents, who often make plans to visit at the last moment, so business fluctuates with weather conditions and holidays. This means that sizeable discounts are usually available for midweek stays. These are best obtained through Hong Kong travel agents or at the hotel itself.

Macau also has two Portuguese *pousadas* (inns), modeled after the national inns of Portugal, with distinctive Macanese elements incorporated.

In general, hotels listed as *Expensive* are of the highest international standard, with swimming pools and health clubs, meeting rooms for conferences and parties, fine restaurants, public areas that are design showcases, business centers, and guest rooms with all the modern comforts and conveniences. Those in the *Moderate* category are efficient, clean, and comfortable, with air-conditioning, color TV (with English and Chinese programs from Hong Kong as well as the local channel), room service, and restaurants. They cater primarily to gamblers, regular Hong Kong visitors, and budget tour groups. *Inexpensive* hotels tend to be old and run-down.

The most highly recommended hotels are indicated with a star ★.

At press time there were 7.8 patacas to the U.S. dollar.

Category	Cost*
Expensive	over 500 patacas
Moderate	250–500 patacas
Inexpensive	under 250 patacas

*per room; add 10% service and 5% tax

The following credit card abbreviations are used: AE, American Express; CB, Carte Blanche; DC, Diners Club; MC, MasterCard; V, Visa.

Expensive

★ **Hyatt Regency and Taipa Island Resort.** Opened in early 1983, the Hyatt is the first in Asia to have guest rooms that were fully prefabricated (in the United States) and shipped as modules. They conform to Hyatt Regency's high standards, with all the modern conveniences and attractive furnishings. The public areas were built in Macau to designs by Dale Keller, and they combine the best of Iberian architecture and Chinese decor. The foyer is a spacious lounge with white arches, masses of potted plants, and fabulous Chinese lacquer panels. Beyond is the coffee shop, an aptly named Greenhouse salon, and Afonso's Portuguese restaurant. A small casino is located off the lobby.

The Taipa Resort, which adjoins the hotel, has a complete
health spa, with different baths, massage and beauty treat-
ments; facilities for tennis, squash, and ball games; a large pool
and botanical garden; a jogging track; and the marvelous Flamingo Macanese veranda restaurant. The hotel is close to the
race track, and operates a shuttle-bus service to the wharf and
Lisboa. The hotel is very popular with Hong Kong families.
*Taipa Island, tel. 2/7000, in Hong Kong 5/463–773, elsewhere
Hyatt Hotels Reservations. 365 rooms with bath. Facilities:
restaurants, bars, casino, health spa, outdoor pool, 2 squash
courts, 4 tennis courts, sauna, whirlpool, gym, massage,
beauty parlor/barber, baby-sitting, car rental, tours, shuttle
bus service to wharf. AE, DC, MC, V.*

Mandarin Oriental. Built on the site of the old Pan Am seaplane
terminal, with marvelous views of the Pearl River and islands,
this is a beautifully designed and furnished hotel. Its lobby features reproductions of Portuguese art and antiques, the Grill
Room has a wood ceiling inlaid with small oil paintings, and the
Cafe Girassol could have been transported from the Algarve.
The Bar da Guia is probably the most elegant drinking spot in
town, and the casino is certainly the most exclusive. Recreation
facilities consist of two pools, tennis and squash courts, and a
health club, all overlooking the outer harbor. The guest rooms
have marble bathrooms and teak furniture. *Avenida da
Amizade, tel. 567–888, in Hong Kong 5/487–676, elsewhere
Mandarin Oriental reservation offices. 438 rooms with bath.
Facilities: restaurants, bars, casino, 2 outdoor pools, 2 tennis
courts, 2 squash courts, gym, sauna, massage, beauty parlor,
car rental, tours, shuttle bus to wharf. AE, DC, MC, V.*

★ **Pousada de Sao Tiago.** This is as much a leading tourist attraction as a place to stay. It is a traditional Portuguese inn that
was built, with enormous imagination and dedication, into the
ruins of a 17th-century fortress. For instance, the ancient trees
that had taken over the fort were not cut down but incorporated
into the design, and the position of their roots dictated the
shape of the coffee shop and terrace. A classic European fountain plays over the site of the old but still operative water
cistern, and the small restored chapel of *S. Tiago* (St. James)
can be hired for weddings. Furnishings, made to order in Portugal, include mahogany period furniture, blue-and-white-tile
walls, and crystal lamps, plus terra-cotta floor tiles from China
and carpets woven in Hong Kong. The entrance is the original
entry to the fort, and natural springs have been trained to flow
down the rocky wall in tile channels on either side of the staircase. There is also a swimming pool, sun terrace, meeting
room, and superb restaurant. Each of the rooms, complete
with four-poster beds and marble bathrooms, has a balcony for
great views with breakfast or cocktails. Rooms for weekends
have to be booked well in advance. *Avenida da Republica, tel.
781–11, in Hong Kong 5/810–8332. 23 rooms with bath. Facilities: restaurant, bar, terrace, outdoor pool, chapel, car rental.
AE, DC, MC, V.*

Royal. The Royal has an excellent location, with fine views of
Guia, the city, and Inner Harbour. It has a marble-clad lobby
with a marble fountain and lounge, plus some excellent shops.
In the basement are the health club, squash court, sauna
rooms, and a sing-along bar. Upstairs is the glass-roof swimming pool and four restaurants: the Royal Canton for Chinese
food, the Japanese Ginza, the Portuguese-Continental Vasco
da Gama, and the coffee shop. The hotel has shuttle bus service

to the wharf and casinos. *2 Estrada da Vitoria, tel. 552–22, in Hong Kong 5/422–033, elsewhere Dai-Ichi Hotels reservation offices. 380 rooms with bath. Facilities: restaurants, bar, lounge, indoor pool, squash court, sauna, gym, shuttle bus to wharf and casino. AE, DC, MC, V.*

Moderate

Estoril. In the residential district, this hotel caters primarily to Hong Kong Chinese and patrons of the Paris Nightclub on the ground floor. It has a good Chinese restaurant and elaborate sauna. *Avenida Sidonio Pais, tel. 572–081. 89 rooms with bath. Facilities: restaurant, sauna, nightclub. DC, MC, V.*

Lisboa. Rising above a two-story casino, with walls of mustard-color tiles, frilly white window frames, and a roof shaped like a giant roulette wheel, the main tower of the Lisboa has, for better or worse, become one of the popular symbols of Macau and is an inescapable landmark. A new wing houses the Crazy Paris Show, the superb A Galera restaurant, a disco, billiards hall, and raucus children's game room, plus an ostentatious collection of late Ching Dynasty art objects and a small, lobby-level exhibition area. The original tower has restaurants serving some of Macau's best cuisine of Chiu Chow province of China, Japan, and Shanghai. Also contained in the complex are a video arcade, a four-lane bowling center, a nonstop coffee shop, some very good shops, a sauna, and a sometimes operative pool terrace. *Avenida da Amizade, tel. 776-66, in Hong Kong 5/591–028. 750 rooms with bath. Facilities: restaurants, bars, casino, game rooms, disco, theater, bowling center, sauna, outdoor pool, tours, shuttle bus to wharf. AE, DC, MC, V.*

Metropole. This centrally located hotel is managed by the China Travel Service, and it contains an office where bookings can easily be made for trips to China. It has pleasant, comfortable rooms and an excellent Portuguese-Macanese restaurant. The hotel is popular with business travelers and China-bound groups. *63 Rua da Praia Grande, tel. 881–66, in Hong Kong 5/406–333. 109 rooms with bath. Facilities: restaurant, China tour arrangements. MC, V.*

Pousada de Coloane. This *pousada* is a small, delightful resort inn. Among the delights are the huge terrace overlooking a good sandy beach, a pool, and a superb restaurant serving excellent Macanese and Portuguese food. The Sunday buffets (when weather permits) are renowned and, at 65 patacas per person, a great bargain. The rooms have good-size balconies and stocked refrigerators. This is a place for lazy vacations and, during the summer, is usually packed with families from Hong Kong. There is a shuttle bus to and from the wharf. *Praia de Cheoc Van, Coloane Island, tel. 2/8144, in Hong Kong 3/696–922. 22 rooms with bath. Facilities: restaurant, bar, terrace, outdoor pool. MC, V.*

Presidente. The Presidente has an excellent location and is very popular with Hong Kong visitors. It offers an agreeable lobby lounge, European and Chinese restaurants, the best Korean food in town, a sauna, and a great disco with a skylight roof. *Avenida da Amizade, tel. 5/553–888, in Hong Kong 5/266–873, elsewhere Utell International reservations offices. 340 rooms with bath. Facilities: restaurants, sauna, nightclub/disco. AE, DC, MC, V.*

Sintra. A sister hotel of the Lisboa, the Sintra is, in contrast, quiet, with few diversions apart from a sauna and European restaurant and bar. It is ideally located, overlooking the Praia Grande bay and within easy walking distance of the Lisboa and downtown. *Avenida Dom Joao 1V, tel. 851–11, in Hong Kong 5/408–028. 236 rooms with bath. Facilities: restaurant, bar, tours, shuttle bus to casino. AE, DC, MC, V.*

Inexpensive

Bela Vista. At the time of writing there were plans afoot to turn this century-old colonial landmark into a luxury pousada. On the other hand, many people have tried and failed to change the hotel over the years, so you may well find it as old-fashioned, run-down, and delightful as ever. One of Macau's great delights is to sit on the spacious balcony of the Bela Vista and have tea or cocktails while enjoying the marvelous panoramic view. The rooms are big and usually in need of redecoration, the food quality varies from excellent to awful, and service can be very slow, no one will deny the appeal of the atmosphere here. *8 Rua Comendador Kou Ho Neng, tel. 573–821, in Hong Kong 5/408–180. 25 rooms with bath. Facilities: restaurant, bar, terrace. AE, DC, MC, V.*

Central. In the very heart of town, this was once the home of Macau's only legal casino and best brothel. Now it is a budget hotel with clean but basic rooms and an excellent Chinese restaurant. *Avenida Almeida Ribeiro, tel. 777–00. 160 rooms with bath. Facilities: restaurant. AE, MC, V.*

In addition, there are some small, old hotels and boarding houses called villas. They usually cater to Chinese visitors, so the staff generally speaks little English. However, they are clean and inexpensive, sometimes with private bath and TV. The Department of Tourism and Macau Tourist Information Board (MTIB) can provide details.

Nightlife

According to old movies and novels about the China coast, Macau was a city of opium dens, wild gambling, international spies, and slinky ladies of the night. It might come as a letdown to some visitors to find the city fairly somnolent after sunset. Most people spend their evenings at the casinos or over long dinners. There is, however, some action.

Lisboa Theater. Apart from a few concerts by visiting performers or shows by local artists, theater in Macau means the Crazy Paris Show at the Lisboa. This was first staged in the late 1970s and has become a popular fixture. The stripper-dancers come from Europe, Australia, and the Americas, while the choreographer and director are Parisian professionals. The show is very sophisticated and cleverly staged. By the end of most acts, the performers have shed their clothes, but there's nothing lewd about the show. In fact, half the audience is likely to be made up of female tourists. The acts are changed completely every few months, and are a tribute to the imagination of the director's team, with superb use of lights and music as well as the athletic prowess of the artists. One show-stopping act has become a regular. It features a woman, with apparently magical breath control, who does Esther Williams-type routines in a huge tank of water on stage—but, unlike the movie star, she wears no clothes. *Lisboa Hotel, 2nd floor, new wing, daily shows at 8:30 and 10 PM, with additional shows on weekends and public holidays at 11:30 PM. Admission: HK$90 weekdays, HK$100 weekends and holidays. Tickets available at hotel desks, Hong Kong and Macau ferry terminals, and the theater.*

Discos

Macau's first disco was the **Green Parrot** in the Hyatt Regency. It was created by Hong Kong's Manhattan Discotheques and is both elegant and fun, with a good selection of music and a professional disc jockey. *Hyatt Regency Hotel, tel. 2/7000. Admission: 40 patacas weekdays, 70 patacas weekends and holidays; includes one drink. Open 9 PM–4 AM.*

The **Skylight** is a disco and nightclub, with floorshows by English strip-tease artists. *Presidente Hotel, Ave. da Amizade, tel. 553–88. Admission: 48 patacas; includes one drink. Open 9 PM–4 AM.*

The Lisboa's **Mikado** disco is a bright, brassy place with high-tech lighting and a lively crowd. *Lisboa Hotel, new wing, tel. 776–66. Admission: 50 patacas; includes one drink. Open 9 PM–4 AM.*

The **Paris Nightclub** is the most popular in Macau among locals and Hong Kong visitors. Like other clubs in the city, it has Thai and Filipina hostesses and reasonably good music. Photos of the women, with numbers, are displayed at the entrance so that customers can choose a hostess in advance. The Paris has an attractive decor, good dance floor, and excellent band. *Estoril Hotel, Ave. Sidonio Pais, tel. 572–081. The minimum charge is 33 patacas weekdays, 45 patacas weekends and holidays. Hostesses cost 15 patacas for 15 minutes, 60 patacas to*

take out (other services are negotiated separately). DC, MC, V.
Open 9:30 PM–4 AM.

For those who want to dance and maybe have a meal without strobe lights and deafening music, there is the **Portos do Sol** in the Lisboa. It is an attractive room with a live band 8 PM–midnight, later on weekends. The minimum charge is 35 patacas on weekdays, 45 patacas on weekends. There is occasionally a floor show. The food is good Continental fare.

Casinos

The glamorous images summoned up by the word "casino" should be checked at the door with cameras before entering the Macau variety. Here you'll find no opulent floor shows, no free drinks, no jet-setters in evening dress, and no suave croupiers. What you do find is no-frills, no-holds-barred, no-questions-asked gambling. Open 24 hours a day, most of the rooms are noisy, smoky, shabby, and in constant use. The gamblers, mostly Hong Kong Chinese, are businesspeople, housewives, servants, factory workers, and students, united in their passion—and what a passion it is! There is almost certainly more money wagered, won, and lost in Macau's casinos than in any others in the world. The total amount is unknown except to Sociedade de Turismo e Diversoes de Macau (STDM), the syndicate which has the gambling franchise. In return for the franchise, STDM is paying the government a premium of HK$1.3 billion (about US$162.5 million) over a 10-year period, plus 26% to 30% of gross income, plus money to build homes for 2,000 families, provide new passenger ferries, and keep the harbor dredged. The syndicate does not complain, so judge the profits for yourself.

There are six casinos in Macau, but for Westerners only five count: those in the *Lisboa, Mandarin Oriental,* and *Hyatt Regency* hotels, the *Jai Alai Stadium,* and the *Palacio de Macau,* usually known as the floating casino. The busiest is the two-story operation in the Lisboa, where the games are roulette, boule, Blackjack, Baccarat, Keno, and the Chinese games *fan tan* and "big and small." There are also hundreds of slot machines, which the Chinese call "hungry tigers."

There are few limitations to gambling in Macau. No one under 18 is allowed in, although identity cards are not checked. Although there are posted betting limits, high rollers are not discouraged by such things. There are 24-hour money exchanges, but most gamblers use Hong Kong dollars.

The solid mass of punters in the casinos might look rather unsophisticated, but they are as knowledgeable as any gamblers in the world. They are also more single-minded than most, eschewing alcohol and all but essential nourishment when at the tables. (Small bottles of chicken essence are much in evidence!) And they are superstitious. All of which adds up to certain "Macau Rules" and customs, which any serious visiting gambler should learn. The rules are printed out and available at the casinos, and there are two good books on the subject: *Gamblers Guide to Macau,* by Bert Okuley and Frederick King-Poole, and the *Macau Gambling Handbook,* by A-O-A publishers, both available in Hong Kong.

Baccarat has, in recent years, become a big status game for well-heeled gamblers from Hong Kong, who brag about losing a million as much as winning one. An admiring, envying crowd usually surrounds the baccarat tables, which occupy their own special corners. Minimum bets are HK$100 or HK$500, and the official maximum is HK$60,000. In Macau the player cannot take the bank, and the fixed rules on drawing and standing are complex, making it completely a game of chance.

Big and Small is a traditional game in which you bet on combinations of numbers for big or small totals determined by rolled dice.

Blackjack is enormously popular in Macau and there are frequently dozens of people crowded around the players, often placing side bets. An uninitiated player might feel flattered to have others bet on his skill or luck—until he learns that by Macau rules anyone betting more than the player can call the hand. Otherwise the rules are based on American ones. The dealers, all women, must draw on 16 or less and stand on 17 or more. Minimum bets are HK$10 or HK$100, depending on the table. Many of the dealers are rude, surly, and greedy. In the Lisboa they take a cut of any winnings automatically, as a tip, and it's a battle to get it back. Punters do, however, have a chance for revenge. No matter how bad a run of luck a dealer is having, she has to sit out her hour's stint.

Fan Tan is an ancient Chinese game which has, surprisingly, survived Western competition—surprising because it is so boringly simple. A pile of porcelain buttons is placed on the table and the croupier removes four at a time until one, two, three, or four are left. Players wager on the result, and some are so experienced that they know the answer long before the game ends.

Keno lost favor among local gamblers some years ago, but its new popularity in Australia and the United States has encouraged STDM to buy a U.S.$1-million computerized keno system and install it in the Lisboa. Tickets are on sale at various restaurant outlets in the building. Thanks to the new system, games, which used to take half an hour, will now last about 10 minutes.

Roulette is based on the European system, with a single zero, but with some American touches. Players buy different-colored chips at an American-shaped table, and bets are collected, rather than frozen, when the zero appears. The minimum bet is HK$10.

Slot Machines line the walls of all five Western casinos, and seem in constant use. The newest attraction is a "mega-bucks" system with computer links to all casinos and million dollar pay-out possibilities.

The casino scene has been changing recently, with the opening of more elegant and exclusive rooms in the Mandarin Oriental and Hyatt Regency. Another change is the rejuvenation of the casino in the Jai Alai Stadium. It attracted few customers when located on the second floor; it has been spruced up and moved to a larger area on the ground floor where it is doing excellent business, especially with visitors who have time to spare before leaving for Hong Kong. Meanwhile, the floating casino is looking rather the worse for wear and there are plans to rebuild it on land.

There are also plans to upgrade the Kam Pek casino, which currently offers only Chinese games. Plans are to increase its capacity and add a baccarat table.

Index

A Galera
(restaurant), *194*
A-Ma Temple, *180,
186*
Aberdeen, *64, 77–80,
91, 164*
restaurants 1n, *100,
133*
Adriatico
(restaurant), *139*
Afonso's (restaurant),
194–195
Air travel, *16–17, 54*
from Britain, *17*
with children, *13*
insurance for, *11–12*
Alcohol, law on, *160*
Amah Rock, *87*
Ambassador (hotel),
152
American Chamber
of Commerce, *26,
30, 31*
American Express,
7–8, 56
Amigo (restaurant),
137
Amusement parks,
*59–60, 64, 80, 91,
100*
Anglican Church, *71,
90*
Antiques, shopping
for, *68–70, 103, 108,
110–112*
in Macau, *187–188*
Aplichau Island, *80*
Aquarium, *91, 100*
Art
framing of, *111*
shopping for, *70, 103,
107, 108, 111, 112*
Art museums, *65, 73,
77, 86, 93, 94*
in Macau, *177, 180*
Arts, the, *157–160*
Arts Centre, *73, 112,
157*
Ashoka (restaurant),
135
Asian Delights
(restaurant), *154*
Au Trou Normand
(restaurant), *138*
Avenida Almeida

Ribiero, *174–176,
187*
Avenida da
Republica, *180*
Aviaries, *59, 71, 83,
91, 100*
in Macau, *183*
Aw Boon Haw
Gardens, *76–77, 91,
99*

Ballet, *160*
Bangkok Royal
(hotel), *153*
Banks, *7, 20, 23–24,
29, 65, 90*
Barbers, street, *69,
80, 92*
Bargaining, *50–51*
Baron's Table
(restaurant), *137*
Barra Point, *180*
Basic Law, *21, 37, 38*
Batik, shopping for,
118
Battery Street, *92*
Beaches, *64, 88,
96–99, 125*
of Macau, *182*
Bela Vista Hotel,
180, 202
Bella Donna
(restaurant),
139–140
Belvedere, The
(restaurant), *150*
Benkay (restaurant),
135
Beverly Hills Deli,
32, 138
Bicycles, in Macau,
172
Big Wave Bay, *64,
96, 97*
Bird cages, shopping
for, *106*
in Macau, *177, 188*
Bird Market, *84, 92*
"Bird's nest," *46*
Bishop's Palace, *180*
Blackwood furniture,
shopping for, *114,
115*
Blake Pier, *64*
Bloom, The

(restaurant), *132*
Boating Centre, *125*
Bocarinos Grill
(restaurant), *148*
Bonham Strand East
and West, *68, 69,
103*
Bookshops, *83, 92*
Booth Lodge
(Salvation Army
guest house), *153*
Border Gate
(Macau–China), *179,
184–185*
Borneo Mountain
ponies, *100*
Bottania Cafe
(restaurant), *154*
Boutiques, *50, 103,
106–108, 121–122*
Bowling, *107*
Brasserie
(restaurant), *152*
Bric-a-brac, shopping
for, *91, 103*
British Army, *65*
British Chamber of
Commerce, *30*
British Council, *160*
British travelers, *3–4*
travel from U.K. by,
17
Brothels, in Macau,
176
Buddha
birthday of, *6*
statue of, *88*
Buddhism, *77, 85–88*
in Macau, *179, 181,
185*
Buses, *27, 57*
in Macau, *172*
Business
information, *29–30*
for Macau, *171*
Buttons and bows,
shopping for, *103,
106*

Cabarets, *161*
Café de Paris
(restaurant), *139*
Cafe Rendezvous
(coffee shop), *150*
Cafe Serena

(restaurant), *151*
California
(restaurant and
disco), *139, 165*
Caliph Room
(restaurant), *152*
Calligraphy,
shopping for
materials for, *70, 72*
Cameras, shopping
for, *106, 112*
Cammino
(restaurant), *147*
Camões Grotto and
Garden, *177–178*
Camões Museum, *177*
Camper's beach, *98*
Camphorwood chests,
shopping for, *114*
in Macau, *177*
Canidrome, *179*
Canton Road, *84*
Cantonese opera,
157, 159
Car racing, *6, 191*
Car rental, *12, 27–28*
in Macau, *172*
Caravelle (hotel), *148*
Caritas Bianchi
Lodge (hotel), *153*
Carpets, shopping
for, *108, 111, 112*
Carvings, shopping
for, *69, 110*
Casa Mexicana
(restaurant), *139*
Casa Ricci, *180*
Casinos, *176, 199,
200, 204–206*
Cat Street, *70, 90*
Causeway Bay, *44,
45, 63, 73, 91, 100*
hotels in, *143,
147–148*
restaurants in,
133–135, 137, 139
shopping in, *106, 109,
118*
Causeway Centre, *72*
Cemeteries, *77–80*
in Macau, *178, 181*
Cenotaph monument,
65
Central Building,
103, 107

Central District, *25, 63*

exploring, *64–70, 90–91*

hotels in, *142, 147–148*

restaurants in, *45, 132–133, 135, 138–140*

shopping in, *103, 107–109*

Central Hotel, *176, 202*

Ceramics, shopping for, *112–113*

Chai Wan (Chaiwan), *64, 81*

Chambers of commerce, *30*

Chapel of St. Francis Xavier, *182–183*

Chater Garden, *68*

Chesa (restaurant), *137, 149*

Cheung Chau Island, *6, 58, 89, 154*

Cheung Chau Warwick Hotel, *89*

Cheung Sha, *58, 88, 98*

Children

shopping for clothes for, *107, 113*

traveling with, *13*

what to see and do with, *99–100*

Children's Library, *94*

Chili Club (restaurant), *136*

China

1844 treaty between USA and, *179, 185*

express trains to, *58*

gate from Macau to, *179, 184–185*

Hong Kong trade with, *21*

refugees from, *xxi, 23, 34*

repossession of Hong Kong by, *xvii, xxii, 20–22, 34–35, 38*

repossession of Macau by, *169*

shopping for goods from, *109*

China Coast Pub (restaurant), *152*

China Trader's

Centre, *25, 26, 152*

Chinese Arts & Crafts (stores), *83, 103, 107, 108, 112, 117–119*

Chinese Garden, *83*

Chinese language, *10, 26*

Chinese opera, *84, 158, 159*

Chinese orchestra, *159*

Chinese University, *86, 94*

Ching Chung Koon Taoist Temple, *85–86*

Chiu Chow Garden (restaurant), *133*

Chiu Chow people, *43*

Chocolates, shopping for, *32*

Chops, shopping for, *69, 103, 118*

Christianity, *xvii, 71, 88*

Chuk Lam Sim monastery, *85*

Chung Hom Kok, *97*

Chung King Mansions (hotel), *146*

Chung Yeung Festival, *6*

Chung Ying Theatre Company, *160*

City Contemporary Dance Company, *160*

City Hall, *64–65, 157*

City Hall Libraries, *94*

Clearwater Bay Golf & Country Club, *60, 100, 124*

Climate, *4–5*

Clocks, shopping for, in Macau, *176*

Cloisonné, shopping for, *108*

Cloth Alley, *68, 103, 109*

Clothes

to bring, *6–7, 26*

factory outlets for, *114*

shopping for, *68, 76, 90, 91, 103, 106–110, 118, 121–122, 188*

tailor-made, *106, 107,*

120

Clubs, *28–29, 41, 160*

Cocktail bars, *161–162*

Coffee Mill (restaurant), *151*

Coffee Shop, The (restaurant), *151*

Coloane Island, *182–183*

Colony Cruises, *125*

Comedy, *161*

Commissions, *55*

Computers, shopping for, *107, 113–114*

Confucius, birthday of, *6*

Connaught Centre, *64, 107, 162*

Consulates, *55*

Cosmetics, shopping for, *119*

Cost of trip, *8–9*

Crafts. *See* Handicrafts

Credit cards, *7, 188*

Cricket fighting, *126*

Cross-Harbour Tunnel, *54, 62*

Cruises, *59, 60, 125*

Cultural Revolution, *xxi*

Curios, shopping for, *106, 108, 111, 115*

Currency, *8, 24*

Customs and duties

British, *3*

Hong Kong, *10*

ivory in, *116*

D'Aguilar Street, *103, 165*

Dance, *159–160*

Dancescope, *159*

Deep Water Bay, *64, 80, 96, 124*

Delicatessen, *32, 138*

Democracy, *22, 35, 37–40*

Department stores, *103, 108–109, 118*

Japanese, *50, 76, 106, 107, 109*

Des Voeux Road, *68*

Des Voeux Road West, *69*

Designer fashions, shopping for, *122*

Diamonds, shopping for, *116*

Dining. *See* Food; Restaurants

Disabled travelers, *13–14*

Discos, *163–164*

in Macau, *203–204*

Discounts, *50–51*

Discovery Bay Golf Club, *124*

Diving equipment, shopping for, *120*

Dog racing, *179, 190*

Dolls, shopping for, *110, 115*

Dom Pedro V Theater, *180, 185*

Dragon boat racing, *190*

Dry cleaning, *33*

Dynasty (restaurant), *148*

Dynasty Room (restaurant), *152*

Eagle's Nest (restaurant), *132, 147, 161*

East Garden (restaurant), *197*

Economy of Hong Kong, *22–23*

Eggs, shopping for, *68*

Elderhostel, *14*

Electronics, shopping for, *76, 106, 109, 110, 112, 114, 115–116, 121*

Embroidery, shopping for, *69, 103, 118*

Emerald (hotel), *148*

Emergencies, *55*

Emigration from Hong Kong, *35–37, 40*

Empress (hotel), *152*

English language, *10, 26, 50*

policemen speaking, *55*

Estoril (hotel), *201*

Excelsior (hotel), *29, 73, 106, 147–148, 162*

Exchange Square, *64*

Expatriates, *40–41*

Exports from Hong Kong, *22*

Factory outlets, *114*
Fanling, *86*
Fat Siu Lau (restaurant), *195*
Fenwick Street, *164*
Ferries, *27*, *58*, *87–89*
Macau, *171*
Festivals, *5–6*, *158*
guided tours for, *3*
Filipinos, *65*
Films. *See* Movies; Photography
First (hotel), *153–154*
Fish markets, *86*, *92*, *101*
"Fishball stalls," *164*
Fishing supplies, shopping for, *120*
Five Continents (restaurant), *152*
Flagstaff House, *70–71*, *93*
Flamingo (restaurant), *195*
Flea market, *70*
Florists, *32*
Flower Lounge (restaurant), *152*
Flying clippers, *174*
Food, *43–48*. *See also* Restaurants
central market for, *68*
cost of, *8–9*
hotel "home delivery" of, *32*
visitor's guide to, *46*
Food Street, *76*, *91*
Fortaleza (restaurant), *194*
Fortuna (restaurant), *152–153*
Four Five Six (restaurant), *197*
Free activities, *99*, *158*
Funerals, Chinese, *69*, *84*
Funerary objects, Han, *94*
Fung Ping Shan Museum, *77*, *93*
Furama Inter-Continental (hotel), *29*, *103*, *148*
Furniture shopping for, *106*, *108–110*, *114–115*
in Macau, *188*
Furs, shopping for,

115
Futures Exchange, *24*

Gaddi's (restaurant), *137*, *149*
Galo (restaurant), *195*
Gambling, *126*, *160*
in Macau, *168*
Gardena (restaurant), *153*
Gardens. *See* Parks and gardens
Genji (restaurant), *147*
Gifts, shopping for, *118–119*
Ginza (restaurant), *197*
Godown (bar-restaurant), *163*, *164*
Gold markets, *25*
Golden Bull (restaurant), *135–136*
"Golden Mile," *106*
Golden Pagoda, *100*
Golf, *6*, *81*, *86*, *124*, *190*
Government House (Hong Kong), *71*
Government House (Macau), *186*
Government Palace (Palacio, Macau), *180*, *185*
Graffiti (restaurant), *139*
Grand (hotel), *153*
Grand Tower (hotel), *153*
Granville Road, *106*
Great George Street, *76*
Great Shanghai (restaurant), *134–135*
Greyhound racing, *179*, *190*
Guangdong (hotel), *154*
Guia Fort and Lighthouse, *184*
Guia Hill, *174*
Guided tours, *2–3*, *59–60*
in Macau, *172–173*

Hac Sa beach, *182*
Hakka language, *xvii*
Han Dynasty, *xix*, *6*, *94*, *101*
Han Suyin, *23*, *63*
Handbags, shopping for, *68*, *106*, *107*, *110*, *118*
Handicapped travelers, *13–14*
Handicrafts, shopping for, *68–70*, *106–108*, *115*
in Macau, *188*
Hankerchiefs, shopping for, *118*
Hap Mun, *98*
Happy Hours, *161*
Happy Valley
hotel in, *148*
restaurant in, *137*
shopping in, *106*, *119*
Happy Valley Race Course, *60*, *64*, *91*, *126*
Harbour (hotel), *148*
Harbour City, *45*, *92*, *107*, *108*
hotels in, *143*
restaurant in, *139*
Harbour Road Indoor Games Hall, *124*
Harbour View International House (hotel), *146*, *148–149*
Hats, women's, shopping for, *122*
Health, *11*
Hennessy Road, *72*, *106*, *115*
Henri's Gallery (restaurant), *195–196*
Hi-fis, shopping for, *106*, *107*, *115–116*
High Island, *95*
Hiking, *95*
Hilton (hotel), *29*, *60*, *65*, *70*, *107*, *132*, *147*, *161*, *166*
Historical museums, *72–73*, *83–84*, *93*
in Macau, *177*
History of Hong Kong, *xix–xxii*, *34*, *63*, *69*
History of Macau, *168–169*, *174*, *183*, *184–185*
Hoi Mei, *97*

Holiday Inns (hotels), *29*, *137*, *139*, *150*, *161*
Hollywood Road, *69*, *90*, *103*, *111*, *116*
Hong Kong
flora and fauna of, *95*
1997 changeover of, *xvii*, *xxii*, *20–22*, *34–35*, *38*
statistics on, *xx–xxi*, *39*, *86*
Hongkong, The (hotel), *150*
Hong Kong Academy for Performing Arts, *73*, *157*
Hongkong and Shanghai Bank, *65*, *90*
Hong Kong and Yaumati ferries (HYF), *58*, *88*
Hong Kong Arts Centre, *73*, *112*, *157*
Hong Kong Arts Festival, *5*, *158*
Hong Kong Ballet, *160*
Hong Kong Chinese Orchestra, *159*
Hong Kong Clipper, *174*
Hong Kong Club, *29*, *41*, *65*
Hong Kong Coliseum, *157*
Hong Kong Computer Centre, *114*
Hong Kong Convention and Exhibition Centre, *28*, *73*, *143*
Hong Kong Country Club, *29*
Hong Kong Cricket Club, *29*, *68*
Hong Kong Dance Company, *159*
Hong Kong dollar, *8*, *21*, *24*, *36*
Hong Kong Football Club, *29*
Hong Kong Fringe Club, *157*, *158*, *160*, *165*
Hong Kong Hotel, *107*, *108*

Hong Kong
International
Airport. *See* Kai Tak
Airport
Hong Kong Island
beaches of, *96–97*
exploring, *63–81,
90–91*
guided tour of, *59*
hotels in, *147–149*
libraries of, *94*
museums on, *93*
parks and gardens of,
95–96
performance halls of,
157
shopping in, *103–106,
107*
Hong Kong-Macau
Work Committee
(HMWC), *39*
Hong Kong Museum
of Art, *65, 93, 112*
Hong Kong Museum
of History, *83–84,
93, 99*
Hong Kong
Philharmonic
Orchestra, *159*
Hong Kong Running
Clinic, *124*
Hong Kong Space
Museum. *See* Space
Museum
Hong Kong Tourist
Association (HKTA),
*2, 30, 44, 50, 54, 99,
142, 158, 160*
Hong Kong Trade
Development
Council, *29, 31*
Hong Kong
University, *64, 77,
91, 93*
Hong Kong
Zoological and
Botanical Gardens,
71, 91, 95–96, 99
Hong Lok Street, *92*
Hopewell Centre, *72*
Horse racing, *60, 87,
125–126*
in Macau, *182,
190–191*
Horseback riding, *88,
100*
Hospitals, *55*
Hostess clubs, *165*
in Macau, *203–204*
Hotels, *81, 142–155.*
See also specific

hotels
business centers of,
25–26
business guests at, *29*
cost of, *8*
in Macau, *199–202*
as meeting places, *28*
reservation service
for, *54*
Hours of business,
29, 49
House museum
(Macau), *181*
Houseboats, *77*
Hover-ferries, *58, 171*
Hugo's (restaurant),
138, 151
Hung Hom, *58, 107,
118*
Hung Shing Temple,
72, 93
Hung Shing Yeh, *98*
Hurricanes
(typhoons), *4–5, 62,
184*
Hyatt Regency and
Taipa Island Resort
(hotel), *199–200,
204, 205*
Hyatt-Regency Hong
Kong (hotel), *29,
138, 150–151, 166*
Hydrofoils, *170–171*
HYF (Hong Kong
and Yaumati
ferries), *58, 88*

Ice skating, *107, 124*
Imperial (hotel), *153*
Imports into Hong
Kong, *22–23*
Inagiku (restaurant),
149
Indian Curry Club
(restaurant), *136*
Institute of Chinese
Studies, *86*
Insurance, *11–12*
for British travelers,
3–4
International (hotel),
153
Islam, *83*
Islamic Food
(restaurant), *134*
Ivory, shopping for,
116

Jade, shopping for,
84, 92, 109, 117
Jade Lotus

Restaurant, *147*
Jaffe Road, *106*
Jai alai, *191*
Jai Alai Stadium,
174, 204, 205
Jamal Masjid and
Islamic Centre, *83*
Japanese Christians
in Macau, *183*
Japanese department
stores, *50, 76, 106,
107, 109*
Japanese invasion of
Hong Kong, *xxi, 80,
139, 180*
Jardines Crescent,
76
Jazz clubs, *163*
Jetfoils, *170*
Jewelry, shopping
for, *68, 103,
106–108, 110,
116–117*
in Macau, *176,
188–189*
Jogging, *124*
Johnston Road, *72,
106*
Joint Liaison Group,
22
Jones Street, *76*
Joss sticks, *72*
Jubilee Sports
Centre, *87*
Jubilee Street, *68*
Judo, *6*
Jumbo (restaurant),
45, 60, 133
Junk Bay, *6, 86*
Junks, *80, 84, 125*

Kadoorie beach, *97*
Kai Hing Wai, *93*
Kai Tak Airport, *xvi,
27, 30, 54*
Macau information
desk at, *171*
Kam Tin Walled
Villages, *86, 93*
Kei Ling Ha, *95*
Kent Windsurfing
Centre, *97, 98*
King's (hotel), *154*
King's Road, *106*
Kiu Tsui, *98*
Kowloon, *xvii, 25*
exploring, *81–84,
92–93*
guided tour of, *59*
hotels in, *143,
149–155*

museums in, *93–94*
performance halls of,
157
restaurants in,
132–140
shopping in, *106–110*
Kowloon–Canton
Railway, *27, 58, 81,
82, 85*
Kowloon City
Market, *109, 113*
Kowloon Club, *29*
Kowloon Cricket
Club, *29*
Kowloon Park, *83*
Kowloon Shangri-La
(hotel), *13, 149, 162*
Kun Iam Temple,
179, 185
Kung-fu supplies,
shopping for, *117*
Kwan Ti Temple, *91*
Kwong Fat Cheung
Ivory and Mahjong
Factory, *116*
Kwun Yum Wan, *99*

La Brasserie
(restaurant), *151*
La Restaurant de
France, *138*
La Ronda
(restaurant), *148*
La Rose Noire
(restaurant), *140*
Lacquerware,
shopping for, *110,
114*
in Macau, *188*
Ladder Street, *70, 90,
103*
Ladies Walking
Group, *124*
Lai Chi Kok, *xx, 84*
Lai Ching Heen
(restaurant), *132,
150*
Laichikok
Amusement Park,
100
Lalique (restaurant),
152
Lamma Island, *44,
58, 77, 88–89*
beaches on, *98*
Lan Kwai Fong, *139,
162, 165*
Landau's
(restaurant), *139*
Lantau Island, *58,
88, 124, 154*

beaches on, *98–99*
Lantau Tea Gardens,
100
Lau Fau Shan, *86*
Leal Senado (Loyal
Senate), *176,
183–184*
Leather goods,
shopping for, *107,
117–118*
Lee Gardens (hotel),
133, 148, 161
Lee Theatre, *157*
**Legal system of
Hong Kong,** *20–21*
**Lei Cheng Uk
Museum,** *xix, 94,
101*
Lei Yue Mun, *77, 92,
101*
Leighton Centre, *106*
Leighton Road, *106*
Les Celebrites
(restaurant), *151*
**Li Yuen streets East
and West,** *68, 90,
103, 110, 118*
Libraries, *94*
of Macau, *176,
178–179*
Lido beach, *97*
**Lighthouse, in
Macau,** *174, 184*
Limousines, *54, 58*
Lin Fung Miu, *179,
185*
Linens, shopping for,
*103, 106, 108, 110,
118*
**Lingerie, shopping
for,** *109, 118, 122*
Lisboa (hotel), *201,
204*
Lisboa Theater, *203*
Lo So Sing, *98*
Lo Wu, *85*
Lockhart Road, *72,
106*
Lodging, *142–155.
See also* Hotels
Lok Kok teahouse,
177
Lok Ma Chau, *86*
Long Ke, *95*
Long Kei
(restaurant), *197*
**Lou Lim Ieoc
Garden,** *179*
Luard Road, *72*
Luggage
in air travel, *16, 54*

shopping for, *68*
Luk Kwok Hotel, *72*
Luk Yu Teahouse
(restaurant), *44, 128,
133*
Lyemun, *44*

**Ma On Shan
Mountain,** *95*
Macau, *168–206*
climate of, *5*
currency in, *8*
exploring, *174–186*
historic sites of,
183–186
history of, *168–169,
174, 183, 184–185*
languages in, *10*
1999 changeover of,
39, 169
population and size
of, *169*
tourist information
on, *2*
travel from Hong
Kong to, *169–171*
**Macau Ferry
Terminal,** *107*
Macau Forum, *174*
Macau Grand Prix,
6, 191
MacLehose Trail, *95*
Mail, *55–56*
Man Mo Temple,
69–70, 90
Man Wa Lane, *68,
103, 118*
Man Wah
(restaurant), *147*
Man Yue Street, *107*
Mandarin Oriental
(hotel in Hong
Kong), *29, 58, 68,
90, 103, 138, 147*
Mandarin Oriental
(hotel in Macau),
200, 204, 205
Maps, shopping for,
111
Marathons, *5, 191*
**Marco Polo Hong
Kong, The** (hotel),
151
Marco Polo Pizza, *32*
Margaux
(restaurant), *149*
**Marine mammal
theater** (Ocean
Theatre), *80, 91, 100*
Maritime Museum,
180–181

Markets
financial, *24–25*
fish, *86, 92, 101*
night, *103, 110*
shopping, *109–110*
street, *99*
Maxicabs, *57*
Mayfair Coffee Shop
(restaurant), *152*
Medical assistance,
11
**Memorial Home of
Dr. Sun Yat-Sen,**
179
Messengers, *32–33*
Metropole (hotel),
201
Middle Bay, *96*
Mid-Levels area, *64,
71, 91*
Mien laps, **shopping
for,** *118*
**Min Fat Buddhist
Monastery,** *86*
Minibuses, *27, 57*
Miramar (hotel), *151*
Mistral (restaurant),
139, 150
Mody Road, *106–107*
Mokes, *172*
Monasteries, *xx, 6,
85, 88*
lodging in, *146*
Money, *7–8*
Monte Fort, *183*
Monte Hill, *177*
Mosque, *83*
Motor racing, *191*
Mozart Stub'n
(restaurant), *140*
**MTR (Mass Transit
Railway),** *27, 56, 62*
Mui Wo, *88*
**Museum of Chinese
Historical Relics,**
72–73, 93
**Museum of Tea
Ware,** *70–71, 93, 99*
Museums, *93–94, 99.
See also specific
museums*
Music, *68, 159*

Nathan (hotel), *153*
Nathan's
(restaurant), *151,
166*
Nathan Road, *83–84,
92, 106–107,
108–109, 112*
hotels on, *143,*

150–154
**Nature trail, in
Macau,** *183*
NCNA. *See* Xinhua
News Agency
Nestorial crosses,
exhibit of, *93*
New Cafeteria beach,
97
New Harbour (hotel),
149
New Territories, *xvii,
25*
beaches of, *97–98*
exploring, *85–87, 93*
guided tour of, *59, 85*
hotels in, *146, 154*
museum in, *94*
parks in, *95*
performance halls of,
158
restaurants in, *154*
New Town Plaza, *87*
New towns, *86*
New World (hotel),
151
Newspapers, *31*
Ngong Ping, *58, 88*
Nightclubs, *161*
Nightlife, *41–42,
160–166*
in Macau, *203–206*
tour of, *60*
Nikko Hong Kong
(hotel), *151*
Nineteen '97
(restaurant), *165*
Ning Po Street, *84*
Nishimura
(restaurant), *152*
Noonday Gun, *73, 91*
North Point, *58, 77,
106*
restaurant in, *139*

Ocean Centre, *81, 92,
107, 108, 161*
**Ocean City
Restaurant & Night
Club,** *161*
**Ocean Palace
Restaurant & Night
Club,** *161*
Ocean Park
(amusement park),
59–60, 64, 80, 91, 100
Ocean Terminal, *81,
92, 107, 108, 158*
Ocean Theatre
(marine mammal
theater), *80, 91, 100*

Old Citadel (Macau), 177–178
Old Protestant Cemetery (Macau), 178
Older travelers, 14–15
Omar Khayyam (restaurant), 140
On Lan Street, 103
Opera, Chinese, 84, 158, 159
Opium Wars, xx, 34, 63
Optical goods, shopping for, 107, 112, 119
Our Lady of Carmel, church of, 181
Outer Harbor (Macau), 174
Outer Islands, 87–89. See also specific islands
beaches of, 98–99
hotels in, 89, 154–155, 146
Outlying Islands Pier, 58

Package tours, 3
Padang Restaurant, 137
Paintings, shopping for, 69
Pak Sha Chau, 98
Pak Sha Wan, 98
Pak Tam Au, 95
Pak Tam Chung, 95
Palacio de Macau (floating casino), 204–206
Panorama (restaurant), 151
Paper goods, shopping for, 92
Park (hotel), 153
Park 27 (restaurant), 148
Park Lane (hotel), 148, 164
Parks and gardens, 76–77, 83, 86, 91, 94–96
in Macau, 177–178, 179
Passports, 3, 9
Patisserie, The (restaurant), 151
Pavilion (dinner-dance restaurant), 161
Peak Tower Building, 60, 71
Peak Tram, 27, 57–58, 71, 90
Pearls, shopping for, 116–117
Pedicabs, 171–172
Peking opera, 157, 159
Peng Chau Island, 58, 88, 89
Penha Hill, 180, 186
Peninsula, The (hotel), 58, 81, 83, 92, 132, 137, 149–150, 162
Performance halls, 157–158
Performing arts, 73, 158–159
Perfume, shopping for, 119
Philharmonic orchestra, 159
Photography, 10, 60, 84
Physicians, 11, 55
Pickpockets, 110
Pierrot (restaurant), 147
Pink Giraffe (supper club), 152, 161
Pinocchio's (restaurant), 196
Pizzeria, 140
Planetarium, 83, 92, 94
Plume, The (restaurant), 138, 150
Po Lin Monastery, xx, 6, 146
Po Toi Island, xix
Pok Fu Lam, 77, 100
Police, 55, 83, 160
Porcelain, shopping for, 69, 91, 106, 109, 110, 112–113
in Macau, 187, 188
Portas do Cerco, 179
Portugues (restaurant), 196
Portuguese language, 169
Post Office (Hong Kong), 64
Post Office (Macau), 176
Pottinger Street, 103
Pou Tai Un Temple, 181
Pousada de Coloane (hotel), 182, 201
Pousada de Coloane (restaurant), 196
Pousada de São Tiago (hotel), 180, 200
Praia Grande, 180
Praya Promenade, 89
Precious Lotus Monastery, 88
Prescription drugs, 11
Presidente (hotel), 201
Prices, sample, 9
Prince (hotel), 151
Prince's Building, 103, 107
Prints and engravings, shopping for, 111
Public Square Street, 92
Publications
on Hong Kong, 15, 31
on travel with children, 13
Pubs, 162
Pui O, 98

Quarry Bay, 64, 77, 106, 107
Queen Elizabeth Stadium, 157
Queen's Road Central, 68, 70
Queen's Road East, 72, 106
Queen's Road West, 69
Quilted jackets, shopping for, 110

Rainbow Room (restaurant), 133, 148
Ramada Inn Hong Kong (hotel), 149
Rangoon (restaurant), 136–137
Rattan, shopping for, 91, 114
Reclamation Street, 92
Red Pepper (restaurant), 135
Refugees, xxi, 23, 34, 42, 188
Regal Airport (hotel), 25, 151–152
Regal Meridien (hotel), 152, 163
Regal Riverside (hotel), 154
Regal Seafood (restaurant), 152, 154
Regent, The (hotel), 83, 108, 138, 150, 162
Repulse Bay, 64, 80, 96, 106, 136
Repulse Bay Verandah Restaurant and Bamboo Bar, 80, 139
Reservoir, 95
Restaurant de France, 152
Restaurants, 43–48, 76, 89, 128–140
in Macau, 193–198
tipping in, 9
Restoration Row (Macau), 178–179
Rib Room, The (restaurant), 151
Rickshaws, 58, 64
Riquexo (restaurant), 197
Ritz (hotel), 154
Rock carvings, 89
Roller skating, 107, 124
Rotisserie (restaurant), 148
Rowboating, 96
Royal (hotel), 200–201
Royal Canton (restaurant), 197–198
Royal Garden (hotel), 152
Royal Hong Kong Golf Club, 6, 29, 86, 124
Royal Hong Kong Jockey Club, 29, 41, 73, 80, 100, 126
Royal Hong Kong Yacht Club, 29, 101
Royal Navy, 65
Royal Thai Restaurant, 136
Rua Cinco do Outubro, 176–177
Rua da Felicidade,

176
Rugby, *6*
Rugs. *See* Carpets

Sagano (restaurant), *151*
Sai Kung Peninsula, *87, 95, 97, 155*
St. Augustine church, *180, 185*
St. John's Cathedral, *71, 90*
St. Joseph's Seminary, *180, 185*
St. Lawrence church, *180*
St. Paul's church (Macau), *177, 183*
St. Stephen's beach, *97*
Salesian Institute, *180*
Salisbury Road, *83*
Sampans, *76, 80, 84, 87, 89, 98*
San Francisco Steak House, *139*
Sanmalo, *174–176, 187*
Santa Casa da Misericordia, *176, 184*
São Domingos (St. Dominic's) church, *176, 184*
SAR (Special Administrative Region), *37*
Scuba diving, *125*
Sealink, *171*
Seasonal events, *5–6*
Sekkong Airstrip, *58*
Senate Square, *176, 183–184*
Senior citizens, *14–15*
Sewing, shops selling items for, *103*
Sha Ha, *98, 125, 155*
Shamrock (hotel), *154*
Shang Palace Chinese restaurant, *149*
Shanghai Street, *84, 92, 159*
Shatin, *87, 154, 158*
Shatin Racecourse, *60, 87, 126*
Shaukiwan, *64, 77,*

106
Shek-O, *64, 81, 97–98*
Shenzhen River, *86*
Shenzhen Special Economic Zone, *21*
Sheraton Hong Kong Hotel & Towers, *29, 107, 135, 152, 161, 162*
Shing Mun Reservoir, *95*
Ship travel to Hong Kong, *17*
Shirts, shopping for, *120*
Shoes and boots, shopping for, *68, 106, 108, 109, 119*
Shopping, *9, 49–52, 68, 72, 73, 83–84, 103–122*
complaints in regard to, *50*
guided tour for, *2*
in Macau, *187–189*
map of, *104–105*
Shopping centers, *107–108*
for computers, *114*
free entertainment at, *99*
Shui Tau, *93*
Sichuan Garden (restaurant), *135*
Sidewalk Cafe (restaurant), *152*
Silks, shopping for, *103, 108, 109, 118*
Silvermine Bay, *88, 98*
Silvermine Beach Hotel, *154*
Silverstrand, *97–98*
Silverware, shopping for, *111*
Singles, meeting places for, *165–166*
Sintra (hotel), *201–202*
Snakes, shops selling, *69*
Social clubs, *28–29*
Sok Kwu Wan, *89*
Solmar (restaurant), *196–197*
Someplace Else, The (restaurant), *152*
South Bay, *97*
South China Sea Race, *76*
Southern

Playground, *72*
Spa on the Square (health club), *29*
Space Museum, *83, 92, 94, 100*
Specialty stores, *110–122*
Spice Market (restaurant), *150*
Spices (restaurant), *136*
Sporting goods, shopping for, *119–120*
Sports, *124–126*
in Macau, *190–192*
Sports centers, *73, 87*
Sports tour, *3, 60, 100*
Sportswear, shopping for, *106, 109, 110, 188*
Spring Deer (restaurant), *134*
Spring Garden Lane, *106*
Spring Moon (restaurant), *132*
Squash, *124, 191*
Stanley Market, *106, 110, 115*
Stanley Village and Beach, *64, 80–81, 91, 97, 100, 125*
Stanley's French Restaurant, *140*
Star Ferry, *25, 27, 58, 63, 64, 81–83, 90, 99*
photographic cruise of, *60*
Star House, *83*
Stationery, shopping for, *108*
Statue Square, *65*
Stereos, shopping for, *115–116*
Stock Exchange, *24, 31, 40, 64*
String quartets, *92*
Stripper-dancer shows, *203*
Student travel, *12–13*
Subway, *27, 56, 65*
Sun Yat-Sen, *179*
Sung Dynasty, *xix–xx, 81, 88*
Sung Dynasty Village, *xx, 59, 84, 93, 94, 100*
Surf Hotel, *98, 155*

Surfing, *97*
Sutherland Street, *69*
Suzie Wong Hotel, *72*
Swatow, *43*
Swatow cuisine, restaurant with, *153*
Swimming, *125. See also* Beaches
Swimsuits, shopping for, *122*
Swire House, *103, 107, 162*
Sze Chuen Lau (restaurant), *135*
Szechuen Lau (restaurant), *135*

Tablecloths, shopping for, *118*
Tai Au Mun, *98*
T'ai chi ch'uan, *71, 177*
Tai Koo Shing, *77*
Tai Mo Shan, *87*
Tai O, *88*
Tai Pan Grill (restaurant), *150*
Tai Ping Shan, *71. See also* Victoria Peak
Tai Tam Country Park, *95*
Tai Tau Chau, *81*
Taikoktsui ferry pier, *171*
Tailors, *106, 107, 120*
Taipa House Museum, *181*
Taipa Island, *169, 181–182*
Taipo, *86*
Tam Kong Temple, *182*
Tamar, HMS, *65*
Tan Kok (restaurant), *153*
Tang Dynasty, *xix*
Tanka language, *xvii*
Taoism, *xvii, 77, 85–86*
in Macau, *181, 185*
Tattoos, *103–106*
Taxes, *9, 31, 40*
Taxis, *12, 27, 50, 56–57*
in Macau, *172*
Tea and tea equipment, shopping for, *110, 119, 120–121*

Tea plantation, *88*
Tea Ware, Museum of, *70–71, 93, 99*
Telegraphing money, *8*
Telephone, *32, 54, 55*
emergency, *55*
Telex, *32*
Telford Gardens, *124*
Temple Street, *84, 110*
Temples, *69–70, 72, 76, 80, 84, 87, 89–92, 99*
in Macau, *179–182, 185, 186*
Ten Thousand Buddhas, Temple of, *87*
Tennis, *124–125, 191*
Theater, *160*
in Macau, *185, 203*
Tien Heung Lau (restaurant), *134*
Tiger Balm Gardens, *76–77, 91*
Tin Han Temple, *76*
Tin Hau
birthday of, *6*
temples of, *6, 80, 84, 91, 92, 96, 186*
Tipping, *9, 48*
Toh Lee (restaurant), *151*
Tolo Harbour, *87, 125*
Topless bars, *164*
Tote, the, *64*
Tourist information, *2, 30, 54–55*
for British travelers, *3*
for Macau, *171*
Tourist newspapers, *99*
Tours
for British travelers, *4*
package, *3*
Toys, shopping for, *106–108*
Trade information, *29–30*
Trail, *95*
Trams, *27, 57, 60, 99*
Tramways Depot, *100*
Translations of documents, *26*
Transportation, *27–28, 56–59*

in Macau, *171–172*
Trappist Monastery, *88, 89, 146*
Travel information. *See* Tourist information
Traveler's checks, *7*
Treetops (restaurant), *153*
Tshimshatsui, *81, 92*
Tsimshatsui
hotels in, *143, 150–153*
nightlife in, *164*
restaurants in, *45, 134–140*
shopping in, *106–109, 112*
Tsimshatsui East, *83, 92, 107, 108*
hotels in, *143, 149, 151*
restaurants in, *134, 135, 138*
Tsuen Wan, *58, 86, 158*
Tsui Hang Village (restaurant), *150*
Tuen Mun, *85–86*
Tun Wan Beach, *125*
Tung Chung, *88*
Tung Wan, *89, 98–99*
Turtle Cove, *97*
Typhoons, *4–5, 62, 76, 84, 184*

Umbrellas, shopping for, *119*
United Chinese Cemetery, *181*
United States Information Service Library, *94*
University of East Asia, *169, 181*
Unkai (restaurant), *135, 152*
Upper Lascar Row, *70*
Upper Wyndham Street, *112*
Urban Council, *xix, 157, 159*
USIA Library, *94*

Vasco da Gama (restaurant), *200*
Verandah (restaurant), *80, 139*

Victoria Centre, *139*
Victoria City, *xvii, 63*
Victoria Clock Tower, *83*
Victoria Hotel, *148*
Victoria Park, *76, 91, 96, 124*
Victoria Peak, *57, 60, 64, 71, 87, 90, 91*
Vietnamese boat people, *xxi, 42*
in Macau, *183*
Viking (restaurant), *153*
Visas
for China, *3*
for Macau, *169–170*

Wan Fu (brigantine), *60*
Wan Lai (teahouse), *120*
Wanchai, *35, 63*
exploring, *71–73, 91*
hotels in, *142–143, 149*
nightlife in, *164*
restaurants in, *45, 134, 136, 139–140*
shopping in, *103–106, 108*
Wanchai Post Office, *72, 91*
Wanchai Road, *72, 106*
Wanchai Sports Grounds, *73*
Warwick (hotel), *98, 154*
Watches, shopping for, *106, 108, 110, 121*
in Macau, *176*
Water, *11, 128*
Water sports, *125*
Water World (amusement park), *64, 80, 91, 100*
Waterskiing, *125*
Wax museum, *94*
Weather, *4–5*
Wellington Street, *103, 116*
Western District, *59, 63, 91*
hotel in, *148*
shopping in, *103*
White Paper, *22, 37*

Why Fu Estate, *77*
Windjammer Restaurant, *162*
Windsor House, *109*
Windsurfing, *97, 98, 100, 125, 154, 155*
Wine, Portuguese, *193*
Wine bars, *162–163*
Wing Lok Street, *68, 103*
Wing Lung Wai, *93*
Wing On Lane, *118*
Wing On Plaza, *108*
Wing On Street, *68, 90, 103, 109*
Wing Sing Street, *68*
Wong Chuk Hang, *64*
Wong Nai Chung Road, *106, 119*
Woodlands (restaurant), *137*
Woolens, shopping for, *68*
World of Whimsy, *99*
Wyndham Street, *103, 116*

Xavier, Chapel of St. Francis, *182–183*
Xu Jiatun, *39*

Yacht Club, *73–76*
Yacht clubs, *29, 101, 125*
Yaumatei, *92, 108*
YMCAs, *83, 146, 148–149*
Youth travel, *12–13*
Yucca de Lac Restaurant, *87*
Yuen Long, *86*
Yung Kee (restaurant), *133*
Yung Shue Wan, *89, 98*
YWCA, *146*

Zoo, amusement-park, *100*
Zoological and Botanical Gardens, *71, 91, 95–96, 99*
Zuni Icosehedron, *160*

Personal Itinerary

Departure *Date*

Time

Transportation

Arrival *Date* *Time*

Departure *Date* *Time*

Transportation

Accommodations

Arrival *Date* *Time*

Departure *Date* *Time*

Transportation

Accommodations

Arrival *Date* *Time*

Departure *Date* *Time*

Transportation

Accommodations

Personal Itinerary

Arrival *Date*   *Time*

Departure *Date*   *Time*

Transportation

Accommodations

Arrival *Date*   *Time*

Departure *Date*   *Time*

Transportation

Accommodations

Arrival *Date*   *Time*

Departure *Date*   *Time*

Transportation

Accommodations

Arrival *Date*   *Time*

Departure *Date*   *Time*

Transportation

Accommodations

Addresses

Name	Name
Address	Address
Telephone	Telephone
Name	Name
Address	Address
Telephone	Telephone
Name	Name
Address	Address
Telephone	Telephone
Name	Name
Address	Address
Telephone	Telephone
Name	Name
Address	Address
Telephone	Telephone
Name	Name
Address	Address
Telephone	Telephone
Name	Name
Address	Address
Telephone	Telephone

Fodor's Travel Guides

U.S. Guides

Alaska
American Cities
The American South
Arizona
Atlantic City & the
  New Jersey Shore
Boston
California
Cape Cod
Carolinas & the
  Georgia Coast
Chesapeake
Chicago
Colorado
Dallas & Fort Worth
Disney World & the
  Orlando Area

The Far West
Florida
Greater Miami,
  Fort Lauderdale,
  Palm Beach
Hawaii
Hawaii (Great Travel
  Values)
Houston & Galveston
I-10: California to
  Florida
I-55: Chicago to New
  Orleans
I-75: Michigan to
  Florida
I-80: San Francisco to
  New York

I-95: Maine to Miami
Las Vegas
Los Angeles, Orange
  County, Palm Springs
Maui
New England
New Mexico
New Orleans
New Orleans (Pocket
  Guide)
New York City
New York City (Pocket
  Guide)
New York State
Pacific North Coast
Philadelphia
Puerto Rico (Fun in)

Rockies
San Diego
San Francisco
San Francisco (Pocket
  Guide)
Texas
United States of
  America
Virgin Islands
  (U.S. & British)
Virginia
Waikiki
Washington, DC
Williamsburg,
  Jamestown &
  Yorktown

Foreign Guides

Acapulco
Amsterdam
Australia, New Zealand
  & the South Pacific
Austria
The Bahamas
The Bahamas (Pocket
  Guide)
Barbados (Fun in)
Beijing, Guangzhou &
  Shanghai
Belgium & Luxembourg
Bermuda
Brazil
Britain (Great Travel
  Values)
Canada
Canada (Great Travel
  Values)
Canada's Maritime
  Provinces
Cancún, Cozumel,
  Mérida, The
  Yucatán
Caribbean
Caribbean (Great
  Travel Values)

Central America
Copenhagen,
  Stockholm, Oslo,
  Helsinki, Reykjavik
Eastern Europe
Egypt
Europe
Europe (Budget)
Florence & Venice
France
France (Great Travel
  Values)
Germany
Germany (Great Travel
  Values)
Great Britain
Greece
Holland
Hong Kong & Macau
Hungary
India
Ireland
Israel
Italy
Italy (Great Travel
  Values)
Jamaica (Fun in)

Japan
Japan (Great Travel
  Values)
Jordan & the Holy Land
Kenya
Korea
Lisbon
Loire Valley
London
London (Pocket Guide)
London (Great Travel
  Values)
Madrid
Mexico
Mexico (Great Travel
  Values)
Mexico City & Acapulco
Mexico's Baja & Puerto
  Vallarta, Mazatlán,
  Manzanillo, Copper
  Canyon
Montreal
Munich
New Zealand
North Africa
Paris
Paris (Pocket Guide)

People's Republic of
  China
Portugal
Province of Quebec
Rio de Janeiro
The Riviera (Fun on)
Rome
St. Martin / St. Maarten
Scandinavia
Scotland
Singapore
South America
South Pacific
Southeast Asia
Soviet Union
Spain
Spain (Great Travel
  Values)
Sweden
Switzerland
Sydney
Tokyo
Toronto
Turkey
Vienna
Yugoslavia

Special-Interest Guides

Bed & Breakfast
  Guide: North America
1936...On the
  Continent

Royalty Watching
Selected Hotels of
  Europe

Selected Resorts
  and Hotels of the U.S.
Ski Resorts of North
  America

Views to Dine by
  around the World

Join us in updating the next edition of your Fodor's guide

Title of Guide:

1 Hotel ☐ Restaurant ☐ *(check one)*

Name

Number/Street

City/State/Country

Comments

2 Hotel ☐ Restaurant ☐ *(check one)*

Name

Number/Street

City/State/Country

Comments

3 Hotel ☐ Restaurant ☐ *(check one)*

Name

Number/Street

City/State/Country

Comments

Your Name *(optional)*

Address

General Comments

Business Reply Mail

First Class   *Permit Nº 7775*   New York, NY

Postage will be paid by addressee

Fodor's Travel Publications

201 East 50th Street
New York, NY 10022